MW01251377

This book is a gift

To:

From:

Date:

Message:

366 devotions for a closer walk with God

Words of Jesus for daily living

"I tell you the truth, whoever hears My word and believes Him who sent Me has eternal life." John 5:24

Jan de Wet

CHRISTIAN ART PUBLISHERS

Originally published by Christian Publishing Company
under the title *Jesus se woorde vir elke dag*

CHRISTIAN ART PUBLISHERS
PO Box 1599, Vereeniging, 1930

First edition 2004

Translated by Lynette Douglas

Cover designed by Christian Art Publishers

Set in 11 on 14 pt Palatino by Christian Art Publishers

Printed in China

ISBN 1-86920-236-8

04 05 06 07 08 09 10 11 12 13 – 10 9 8 7 6 5 4 3 2 1

Preface

This devotional focuses on the words of Jesus as recorded in God's Word.

Maybe today, more than ever, we need to be sensitive to His voice and listen with renewed understanding to the words He spoke when He came to dwell on earth. Perhaps then we will find answers to the many questions that people around us ask about Jesus each day. May we begin to gain new insight and fresh understanding of who Jesus really is.

It was an immense privilege for me to meditate on His words and to write down my thoughts and reflections. My deepest prayer is that the words that I have written will not detract from His words.

May *Words of Jesus for Daily Living* help us to get to know Him better, to love Him more deeply, and follow Him more faithfully.

January

January 1

Water for those who thirst

"Whoever drinks the water I give him will never thirst. Indeed, the water I give him will become in him a spring of water welling up to eternal life."

ꕤ JOHN 4:14 ꕤ

In the hot afternoon sun she walked toward the well. A few children, half-brothers and half-sisters of each other, were running around her. The clay jar rested on her shoulder. When she saw Him, He was taking a nap while His disciples had gone to buy food. Half nonchalantly, half cautiously, she drew closer to the well. She had, after all, had enough of men. Her heart had been broken so many times by men that mistrust had become part of her life. Five broken relationships lay behind her. Each one had left her more cynical. She had no confidence left in men or in love. The disillusionment had been too great. Suddenly He spoke to her. *"Will you give me a drink?"* (v. 7). With a cynical twist to her mouth, somewhat surprised when she noticed that He was a Jew, the Samaritan woman said to Him, *"You are a Jew and I am a Samaritan woman. How can you ask me for a drink?"* (v. 9).

And then the Source of Living Water began, piece by piece, to put her broken heart back together again. With deep compassion He helped her to acknowledge the truth of her dry and empty life, and then He spoke to her about water. A different kind of water. The water of peace, of salvation, of forgiveness. He offered her the Living Water – water that would spring up like a fountain and give her eternal life. Oh, how she longed for that water. And Jesus drew it for her with the words of His mouth.

Later on in John 4 we read that her life changed completely. Hurts in her heart had been healed. New hope and peace filled her soul. The Living Water quenched her thirsty spirit.

You, too, can drink of this Living Water today.

The Father

"Our Father in heaven."

∞ Matthew 6:9 ∞

Jesus came to show us the Father. Never before in the history of humankind had the Father so clearly been presented and explained to all people. In the Old Testament the Israelites focused on God's power, omniscience and distinctness from man when they worshiped Him. Jesus, too, focused on these attributes of God, but He also emphasized the Fatherly aspects of God's nature.

When Philip asked Jesus to show them the Father, He answered, *"Anyone who has seen me has seen the Father. How can you say, 'Show us the Father'?"* (Jn. 14:9). Jesus reveals the Father-heart of God to us. He proclaimed that everything He did, He did in the name of the Father (Jn. 10:25), that the Father was the One who drew His followers to Him (Jn. 10:29), that He did the works of His Father (Jn. 10:37), that in His Father's house there are many mansions (Jn. 14:2), that He was going to His Father (Jn. 14:12) and that those who love Him would also love His Father (Jn. 14:21, 23).

Therefore, when Jesus teaches us to pray, His first point is that we must first know the Father. Remember that we are children of the heavenly Father who not only created us, but who understands all there is to know about us. He gave all those who believe in Him the right to be called the children of God (Jn. 1:12).

Paul clarifies this further in Romans 8:15. He says that children of God who have received the Holy Spirit no longer need to be afraid of God because *"you did not receive a spirit that makes you a slave again to fear, but you received the Spirit of sonship. And by him we cry, 'Abba, Father.'"*

Because we are His children, our relationship with God is not based on fear. We have the freedom to be ourselves in the presence of a loving Father who understands us and wants to share every moment of our lives with us.

January 3

His Name

"Hallowed be your name."

⅏ Luke 11:2 ⅏

When Jesus gave us this model prayer, the first thing He mentioned was that we should glorify the name of the Father. It was something that was close to the heart of Jesus Christ: God the Father should be worshiped and known in His glorious splendor by His children.

It is not really possible to separate a person's identity from his name. Mention the name of a famous person, and various images of that person begin to form in your mind. These images will be positive or negative depending on the perception that you have formed of that person.

When Jesus spoke to His disciples about His Father, He declared that His name must be glorified. God is holy, different, set apart, perfect in all He says and does, and must be worshiped wholeheartedly for who He is.

The Old Testament worshipers did not even allow the name of God to cross their lips. He was too awesome in His being. They were afraid that they might take His name lightly and thereby dishonor Him. Perhaps we could learn from them. We should think twice before we casually mention the name of the Lord. That does not mean that we cannot speak freely to our heavenly Father. But when we do, we should approach Him with respect and awe. People today tend to use the name of the Lord too lightly. Think of the thousands of times the name of our Lord is casually misused on TV or in movies.

As Christians, we should honor the name of the Lord. His name is precious to us. He is the Lord of our life. Our purpose is to glorify Him and to tell others of His marvelous deeds and to bring Him the glory and honor due to Him in everything we do. Let us glorify His holy name today.

Your kingdom

"Your kingdom come."

ꝏ Luke 11:2 ꝏ

Jesus taught us to be passionate about the kingdom of God. Our God is a monistic God. That means that He alone is God. Every knee shall bow before Him and every tongue will confess that Jesus is Lord. Bow or tremble! He is King.

As King, He rules over His kingdom. God is in control of this broken world, and He causes the events of history to move in the direction He has ordained. Many things that happen cannot be attributed to His direct actions, because there is no sin or darkness in Him. But God will never be caught off guard by any dark deed that is the result of sin. He is in control. His kingdom of light is being established in this dark world.

We, as children of the Light, yearn to see His kingdom come. There is a burning desire in our hearts to declare that God is King in every aspect of our lives. We want to establish the kingdom of God in our workplace, on the sports field, in the world of commerce, in our marriages and families, in the way in which we relax and enjoy ourselves. God must reign as King in everything that we do.

Where God reigns there is always light and truth, and life is worth living. His kingship is never tyrannical, it is always glorious. The well-known hymn expresses this with passion: "O worship the King, all glorious above; O gratefully sing His power and His love."

May God rule over everything we do and everything we are. May His kingdom come through us.

January 5

Daily bread

"Give us each day our daily bread."

ꕥ Luke 11:3 ꕥ

We expend a lot of energy just to be able to place bread on our tables. From early morning to late at night, sometimes all through the night, we work so that we can provide in the basic needs of our families. We lie awake at night worrying that we might not have enough, and if we're not careful, this fear can cause us to harm other people. Think about how many people are driven to burglary or embezzlement because of their lack.

The wonder of being a child of God is that we depend on our heavenly Father for everything in our lives and we know that God can and will provide for us. Jesus taught us to freely ask the Father for everything we need – for our daily bread. What peace! It's wonderful to know that God knows our needs and that He will provide.

Sometimes we think that God is not aware of our emergencies, but He, through the prophet Isaiah, tells us that He does not ignore the righteous, and He sees all that we do. We can confidently trust in the Lord for our daily bread.

Pour out your heart before Him and tell Him what you need. James reminds us that we should not approach God with our selfish desires, but if we truly seek His kingdom and His righteousness then He will give us everything that we need. You can trust Him for your needs today.

When God provides for you out of the riches of His glory, you too should allow Him to use you to put bread on someone else's table. There are so many needy people around us. The Lord blesses us so that we can be a blessing to others.

Forgive us

"Forgive us our sins."

ꕥ LUKE 11:4 ꕥ

See the woman at the well in Sychar, drawing water on her own, ashamed to be with other people because they condemn and rebuke her because of her ugly and sinful life. Listen as Peter bitterly weeps when the rooster crows and he realizes how deeply he has disappointed Jesus. Observe Judas as he hangs from the tree because the guilt of betraying the Savior of the world became too much for him.

We all live with guilt for our sins. There is not one who is righteous, the Bible tells us. There is not one person who walks consistently in the paths of righteousness. We all make mistakes and we all break the law of our God. There is no person on earth who does not blush when he thinks back on his sins and trespasses.

We all know the feeling of shame. That is why we rejoice in the wonderful, glad news of the gospel of Jesus Christ that provides the only way of escape for us.

There is forgiveness for our sins. Jesus made it possible for us to be forgiven. He paid the price on Golgotha for our guilt.

The heart of the gospel message is found in 1 John 1:9, *"If we confess our sins, he is faithful and just and will forgive us our sins and purify us from all unrighteousness."* And this is what Jesus teaches us with the words " forgive us." Confess your sins right now, and you will be set free from the burden of guilt.

January 7

Let go

"For we forgive everyone who sins against us."

Luke 11:4

There are thousands of people locked up in the prison of condemnation. I am not referring to those who have done wrong, but to those who have pronounced judgment. When you judge someone else because he wounded your pride, or acted against you, or did something that just wasn't to your liking, then you are treading on dangerous ground.

The opposite of condemnation is one of the most wonderful things we can experience: a forgiving word that sets us free. Freedom comes not only from hearing it from someone else, but also from being the one who forgives another. Let go of your bitterness, forget about judging others, put aside your arrogant way of looking at and speaking to others. It just isn't worthwhile to live life this way.

When we respond out of our self-righteousness, we preside as judge over other people and their situations. Of course there will be many occasions when people will hurt you, and you, because of your normal human reactions, will feel indignant because their actions were unnecessary. Our first reaction is usually to want revenge. But the Bible tells us that vengeance belongs to the Lord. Rather exonerate others and you will set yourself free from the feeling of condemnation in your heart.

Jesus taught us to forgive all those who trespass against us. Think about these words of Jesus: *"If you do not forgive men their sins, your Father will not forgive your sins"* (Mt. 6:15).

Make that call today. Absolve others. Forgive. Remove that grudge against someone else from your heart. Let go, and be set free.

Keep your eyes open

"Forgive us our sins, for we also forgive everyone who sins against us. And lead us not into temptation."

ꟹ Luke 11:4 ꟹ

Fools rush in where angels fear to tread. For people who act so impulsively, the consequences are usually disastrous.

Jesus teaches us to pray that we won't end up in places where we will be tempted. We need to ask God to help us to make decisions that will keep us from being exposed to things that we don't have the strength to withstand. Jesus is not teaching us to isolate ourselves from everything. We do not need to spend our lives in a monastery in order to be protected from difficult situations. Instead, we need to have the wisdom to make the right choices so that we can live our lives meaningfully in the reality of the world around us.

Praying that God will keep us from temptation does not take away our own responsibility to make the right decisions. It is not God's responsibility to prevent evil from coming near us. We are responsible for keeping ourselves away from evil situations. He will support and help us as we make a stand for what is right. We have God's Word as a light for our path and a lamp to our feet and we have the Holy Spirit who will lead us into all truth. We need to take God's Word to heart and allow the Holy Spirit to lead us. And if we do this we should never find ourselves trapped in a foolhardy situation.

This prayer should be prayed with an inner desire to want to follow God's way and not our own. And if we do find ourselves being tempted, Paul reminds us that, *"No temptation has seized you except what is common to man. And God is faithful; he will not let you be tempted beyond what you can bear. But when you are tempted, he will also provide a way out so that you can stand up under it"* (1 Cor. 10:13).

January 9

Ask, seek, knock

"So I say to you: Ask and it will be given to you; seek and you will find; knock and the door will be opened to you."

Luke 11:9

It's late at night and there's a knock on your door. Imagine your surprise when you open the door and see a family you know well standing on the doorstep, wanting a place to sleep for the night. Your immediate response is one of joy because you haven't seen them for a very long time. And you want to be as hospitable to them as possible. So you invite them in, carry their luggage from the car, and think of everything you can do to make them feel at home.

You quickly realize that they're very hungry after their long journey. But horror of horrors, you realize that there's no bread or any other food in the house. Your grocery cupboard is empty. All the supermarkets are closed for the night, and it's so late that even the corner store has closed its doors. But you think of a plan. You phone a good friend of yours. He is already in bed and his attitude is, "Don't bother me with your problem!" And yet when you explain that guests have arrived and you have nothing to give them, he offers to give you everything you need.

This is pretty much the parable that Jesus told to encourage us to keep our telephone line to heaven open. He began the parable with these words, "*Suppose one of you has a friend …* " (v. 5). We do indeed have a phenomenal Friend in our heavenly Father. He asks us to ask, so that we will receive; to seek, so that we can find; to knock so that the door will be opened for us.

Never think that God is fast asleep or in any way not ready to help you. Take the liberty of contacting Him about your special needs right now.

Do not mourn!

When the Lord saw her, his heart went out to her and he said, "Don't cry."

ꕥ LUKE 7:13 ꕥ

When Jesus saw the woman, He was filled with compassion. Perhaps it was because of her tears. Perhaps it was the lines that sorrow had etched in the corners of her mouth. Of course, He knew immediately what had happened. The wailing and weeping of the mourners pierced the air. The large crowd milled around the corpse of the dead man in the open coffin. It was the woman's only son who lay there.

If anyone could understand what it felt like to lose an only son, it was God. That is why Jesus told the woman, "Don't cry." And then He turned and looked at the body of her son. The words of Jesus resounded through the realm of the dead and echoed deep within the tiniest dead cell in the young man's body. *"Young man, I say to you, get up!"* (v. 14).

The next thing people heard was the voice of the dead boy as Jesus gave him back to his mother. Oh, what a wonder!

Don't ever doubt Jesus' empathy with your distress, your grief, and your heartache. Perhaps the outcome will differ from that in this story, but be assured that Jesus stands beside you today, fully aware of what you are going through. And He assures you of His support and resurrection power.

January 11

Like Him

"A student is not above his teacher, but everyone who is fully trained will be like his teacher."

℘ LUKE 6:40 ☙

The apple doesn't fall far from the tree. This saying expresses the sentiment of the above verse. What you are taught usually determines the way you live. People will know what we are and what we have learned because our lives reflect what we have been taught.

People are great imitators. If someone or something impresses us, then it's almost as if a magnetic force draws us to that person's way of doing things. You identify yourself with him or her, and before you know what's what, something of that person has rubbed off on you.

Children often act just like their parents, and it's a funny thing, but after many years of being together marriage partners even start looking like each other!

Christians are to be imitators of God. We should be influenced by His character. What Jesus said and did is so important to Christians that after a while they cannot help but portray something of Jesus in their lives.

As Jesus says, a student who has learned his lessons well will become like his teacher. Let us, therefore, become like Him. Let us do what He asks us to do. Let us look deep into His eyes and listen carefully to the words of His mouth and become like Him. He is, after all, the perfect teacher.

X-ray vision

Jesus knew their thoughts.

ᘓ Luke 11:17 ᘐ

I am often amused and interested when I realize that we sometimes think that the Lord has no idea what we are thinking about. Thousands of thoughts flash through our minds regularly, and often we're not even aware of what we are thinking. We have all experienced the situation of talking to someone, only to find that our thoughts were not on the conversation.

Or perhaps when someone else has been talking, you've been busy thinking of what you'd like to say. But you're actually a little afraid to say what you think in case your words offend that person. So you keep quiet, but your thoughts have already been heard. Perhaps you have caught yourself thinking, "If you only knew what's going on in my head … "

God's thoughts are not our thoughts, but our thoughts are not unknown to Him. Jesus knew what was going on in the hearts of people long before they said a single word. We cannot deceive Him with secret, hidden thoughts. He knows everything about us and tests our deepest motives.

This would be a stressful thought if we did not also know that He understands us and loves us unconditionally. He knows our weaknesses and our sin. He also knows the struggle we have to keep our thoughts pure. The more honestly we share our thoughts with God, the better our spiritual life will become. Share everything you think with Him today.

January 13

Divide and conquer

Jesus knew their thoughts and said to them: "Any kingdom divided against itself will be ruined, and a house divided against itself will fall."

LUKE 11:17

One of the devil's strategies is to cause division among Christians so that he can rule over us. When people stand together and attempt to understand one another, and walk together in harmony, the results are overwhelmingly positive. But when there is continuous strife among people and they do not try to understand one another, when they don't try to work together in one team, then discord occurs and they begin to work against each other.

There are congregations that fall apart and there are families that divide. We even see division caused by disagreements between kingdoms and nations.

In today's Scripture verse, Jesus underlines the fact that He was doing the Father's work, and so could not be serving the forces of evil at the same time. He lives in harmony with His Father and does only what the Father asks of Him.

Oh, what a lesson this is for us as Christians. The Bible says that we must pursue those things that lead to peace and that will build others up (cf. Rom. 14:19). Let us make an effort to do this in our families, in our churches, and with all our fellowmen. Pursue peace and do not allow differing opinions to cause discord.

The strong man

"When a strong man, fully armed, guards his own house, his possessions are safe. But when someone stronger attacks and overpowers him, he takes away the armor in which the man trusted and divides up the spoils."

LUKE 11:21-22

A strong and powerful man lives in a house with a battalion of bodyguards to protect him and his possessions. The house is so well fortified that no one can break in. But the problem is that this man is a villain and a threat to society.

But there is another man who, with his team, is much stronger than the villain. He also has a much better strategy. With strategic planning and better weapons he attacks the first man's house, takes him and his cronies captive, and confiscates all the weapons the villain has left behind.

This is a paraphrase of the parable Jesus told to convey a very important spiritual truth to us. The first strong man is the devil. He has much strength and a legion of helpers to support him in his evil deeds. He possesses far more than just material objects. The lives of people are often in his clutches.

The second and stronger man is the One to whom all authority has been given. It is Jesus Himself, together with the Father and the Holy Spirit, and the millions of angels who fight on the side of light. As reborn Christians, you and I also have the privilege of being part of His kingdom. In the name of Jesus we too can take the evil man's possessions away from him.

January 15

Make a decision

"He who is not with me is against me, and he who does not gather with me, scatters."

℘ LUKE 11:23 ℘

It is not possible to remain neutral regarding the kingdom of God. Either you choose the light or you support the darkness. Your choice is between the truth and a lie. You are either spiritually alive, or spiritually dead. Either you choose Jesus, or you choose yourself, and perhaps, without knowing it, evil itself.

Jesus invites you to join His side, but this means that you need to make the decision to follow Him. If we are on His side then we need to do what He asks of us and support His kingdom. If we are not on His side then we are opposed to Him. Then, like Peter, we will hear from His mouth that we are a stumbling block in His way. A wolf in sheep's clothing, a thief and a robber instead of a shepherd. Not someone who gathers the sheep together, but one who scatters them.

Let us examine our motives and actions before God. May the decisions you make today show that you are on God's side. How sad it would be if, when we came to give account of our actions before God, we realize that some of the decisions we made for His church were actually decisions against Him. Ask yourself regularly whether your choices are for Him or against Him.

Fill your house

"When an evil spirit comes out of a man, it goes through arid places seeking rest and does not find it. Then it says, 'I will return to the house I left.' When it arrives, it finds the house swept clean and put in order."

༄ LUKE 11:24-25 ༄

Jesus cast many demons out of people when He was on earth. As the Son of God, Jesus was in direct opposition with the devil. John puts it very clearly, *"The reason the Son of God appeared was to destroy the devil's work"* (1 Jn. 3:8). And Jesus Himself said that He cast out evil spirits by the finger of God (cf. Lk. 11:20).

Jesus used a short parable to explain that when an unclean spirit leaves a person, it wanders through arid places looking for a place to rest. If the evil spirit does not find such a place, then he decides to return to the house out of which he was cast. Imagine his surprise when he finds the house neat and clean and everything in order! So he goes and finds seven friends, each bigger and more evil than himself, and they all move in and take up residence in the beautiful, clean house.

Jesus seems to be saying that a house should not only be kept clean but it also needs to be filled with someone who has authority. That is why you need to keep the evil ones out.

Fill your house with the glory of the presence of God. When the Holy Spirit fills your heart there will be no place for evil to creep in, and it will remain pure.

January 17

Idolatry vs. the Word

He replied, "Blessed rather are those who hear the word of God and obey it."

LUKE 11:28

There was a certain woman who had been following Jesus for a quite a while. Like many others, she was in awe about this young Rabbi from Nazareth. Each morning she got up early and hurried to wherever He would be teaching about the Kingdom of God that day. Like many others, she deeply admired this Man who spoke so sincerely and with so much authority. She hung on His every word. She was attracted to Him like metal filings to a magnet.

Even though Jesus was busy preaching, she couldn't stop herself from calling out. Her heart was so full and her emotions so intense that, before she realized what she was doing, she shouted out loudly. It was a cry of admiration. But her exclamation revealed that she was a little jealous not to be personally involved with this Man, Jesus. If only she could have been His mother. She said, *"Blessed is the mother who gave you birth and nursed you"* (v. 27).

Jesus was always aware of the motives of people. And He would not accept the admiration of people for Himself. Pride and thinking too highly of oneself are extremely dangerous when it comes to spiritual work. Jesus knew what lay hidden behind this woman's words. She was focused on a person. The words she spoke were words of honor, but they drew attention away from God the Father and the focus away from the Kingdom of God. That is why Jesus said, *"Blessed rather are those who hear the word of God and obey it"* (v. 28).

Jesus found a way out of the trap of personal tribute by referring to the Word of God. He said that we are blessed and privileged if we hear God's Word and do what He asks of us. Take your eyes off human spiritual leaders – who are after all, only instruments that God uses – and focus on God.

Jesus' baptism

Jesus replied, "Let it be so now; it is proper for us to do this to fulfill all righteousness." Then John consented.

℘ Matthew 3:15 ℘

John the Baptist could usually be found in the desert region somewhere outside Jerusalem, standing in the waters of the Jordan River. Dressed in camelhair clothes, he appeared different, unusual, strange, and a fire burned in his eyes. The fire of God. He was compelled to preach by the inner calling of God on his life.

John urged people to repent, and to begin to serve God with all their hearts. And those who responded to his call, he baptized. John was yet again at the Jordan when suddenly he saw Jesus walking toward him. And the Holy Spirit called through John as he pointed a trembling finger to the approaching Jesus, *"Look, the Lamb of God, who takes away the sin of the world! ... [the reason] I came baptizing with water was that he might be revealed to Israel"* (Jn. 1:29, 31).

Jesus explained to John why He had come to the river. He wanted to be baptized. But John tried to prevent Him, saying *"I need to be baptized by you, and do you come to me?"* (Mt. 3:14). Jesus, however, replied, *"Let it be so now; it is proper for us to do this to fulfill all righteousness"* (v. 15).

Yes, even the Son of God, the one without sin or blemish, had to be baptized. He wanted to do everything according to God's will, and that was what set Him apart from the rest of the world. And so He obeyed and was baptized.

And as He rose up out of the waters of baptism, the heavens above Him split open and He saw the Holy Spirit descending like a dove, and coming to rest on Him. And a voice was heard from heaven, saying, *"This is my Son, whom I love; with him I am well pleased"* (v. 17).

Let you and I, too, do all things that God asks of us and so live according to His will.

January 19

Repent

From that time on Jesus began to preach, "Repent, for the kingdom of heaven is near."

ꟷ Matthew 4:17

Jesus was deeply upset when He heard that Herod had imprisoned John. John had prepared the way for Him to minister to the Jewish people, but more than this, they were cousins. When Jesus heard this sad news, He withdrew to Galilee.

And it was there, by the beautiful shores of the Sea of Galilee that He let His light shine before men. And so the words of the Prophet Isaiah were fulfilled, *"The people living in darkness have seen a great light; on those living in the land of the shadow of death a light has dawned"* (v. 16). There Jesus began to preach. Matthew tells us that this was His first public sermon. What were the first words that He spoke?

"Repent, for the kingdom of heaven is near" (v. 17). He asked the people listening to Him to look around and take note of the new thing that was happening in their midst. A new kingdom has been established. If they turned away from their previous way of life, they would simply be able to walk into this new kingdom. What were they to turn away from? From their own human kingdoms, from their own choices and self-interest, from sin and foolishness.

Jesus stands before us today, and His words ring just as true as when He delivered His first sermon. He calls us, too, to turn from our own ways and from an alien, worldly kingdom to the kingdom of heaven. It is only as we turn to Him in true repentance that we will find that the kingdom of heaven is very near.

Perhaps you are living with your back to God, looking at a different kingdom. You live for yourself only, make decisions that benefit you, and serve your own interests. There is a better option: turn around, repent, because the kingdom of heaven has come to you. Jesus is opening the door for you.

Touch the Lord

"Who touched me?" Jesus asked. When they all denied it, Peter said, "Master, the people are crowding and pressing against you."

ꕤ LUKE 8:45 ꕤ

She was desperate. There was nothing left to hope for. She had lost count of the number of doctors she had seen and the medical costs had tapped her resources dry. No one could help her. The prognosis was hopeless, and the loss of blood had drained her of any physical strength. But there was one last glimmer of hope. Jesus.

People pressed and milled around Jesus. They all wanted to be near Him. She almost couldn't find the strength to push through the crowd, but she pressed forward with faith in her heart and hope in her soul. Perhaps He could help her. With a final resolute effort, she reached out her hand and, through the people thronging around, clasped the seam of His robe. As her hand grabbed hold of His clothes, a heavenly exchange occurred. A miracle flowed from God Himself into her bloodstream. Suddenly the hemorrhaging ceased. She knew it, and Jesus knew it, too.

And so He asked, *"Who touched me?"* (v. 45). The crowd surrounding Jesus became still, not quite sure what was happening. One by one they quickly demurred – they hadn't touched Jesus, and Peter was quick to point out that people were surging around his Master, and constantly bumping into Him, brushing against Him. But Jesus insisted, *"Someone touched me; I know that power has gone out from me"* (v. 46).

The woman realized He was talking about her. She trembled in fear as she knelt before Him. Then, laughing and crying, she told everyone why she had touched Him, and that when she had, she had immediately been healed. Her faith had saved her.

Perhaps you and I should once again strive to reach out to Him in faith.

Fishermen

"Come, follow me," Jesus said, "and I will make you fishers of men."

ꕥ Matthew 4:19 ꕥ

The Sea of Galilee is a fisherman's paradise. This large inland sea teems with freshwater fish. Fishing is a lucrative business in the area, and the competition is fierce. Each day, scores of fishing boats can be seen on its waters.

Jesus walked along the shore of Galilee. His eyes looked over the blue waters, but His heart saw much more than the sea. The calling of God burned like a fire within His heart. He saw what was invisible to others. The time was right to invite people to become involved in His kingdom. People who could learn of a new reality from Him, and who would be able to effectively communicate the good news of salvation and new life to others.

He noticed two brothers, Simon, a well-known fisherman in the area, and his brother Andrew. Tanned from hours in the sun, they were casting a net into the sea. They were focused on the job at hand because they needed to bring the catch in. People were waiting to buy their fish. But the words of Jesus carried across the water to them, *"Come, follow me"* (v. 19).

It must have been the authority of the Holy Spirit that compelled Peter and Andrew to do exactly that. Especially when we consider Peter, who, the Bible shows us, was a man who had a strong self-will. Jesus asked them to follow Him and to become fishers of men. It is astounding to consider that they immediately left their nets and followed Him. Something happened within their hearts. Somehow they realized that they could not let such an opportunity pass them by. Even if they didn't quite understand it.

God is still calling people to be part of His plan for building His kingdom today. He is calling you by name, won't you follow Him?

To pray

He said to them, "When you pray, say: 'Father, hallowed be your name, your kingdom come.'"

☙ Luke 11:2 ❧

Jesus' disciples had the immense privilege of seeing their Master praying often. Prayer was part of His lifestyle. Sometimes He prayed through the night, and sometimes He became so deeply engrossed in His conversations with His Father that He seemed to be lost to His surroundings. This way of praying must have fascinated His disciples. That is why they asked Jesus to teach them to pray.

Jesus answered their request with a model prayer that we call The Lord's Prayer. The question that naturally arises is if we should use only this model in our prayers. The answer, of course, is no. Prayer is, after all, conversation with God. In prayer, we can pour out our hearts to our heavenly Father. Everything that worries us can be brought before the throne of God in prayer. Of course, God already knows what we feel and think. Long before we pray God knows what we want to share with Him. It is not for His sake but for ours that we need to open our hearts before Him. In prayer we show how much we depend on Him. In prayer we turn our backs on our self-reliance. In prayer we move from depending on ourselves to depending on God. At its most basic, prayer is an act of faith.

A prayer of faith is a prayer of expectation. James tells us that if we do not believe when we pray, then we will not receive what we pray for. Prayer is holding fast to the promises of God.

Perhaps the secret of effective prayer is to pray according to the will of God. To discover what God's will is, we need to spend time with Him and listen carefully to His voice. When we develop this sensitivity in our relationship with God, we will communicate more effectively with Him in prayer. We just have to keep praying.

January 23

Dependence

"Blessed are the poor in spirit, for theirs is the kingdom of heaven."

ꕤ MATTHEW 5:3 ꕤ

In a radio interview, James Dobson of *Focus on the Family*, was asked this question, "Dr. Dobson, what, in your opinion, is the definition of spiritual maturity?" His answer was surprising. We might have expected him to say that spiritual maturity is when a person spends hours in fervent prayer, or when he reads the Bible through in a year. Or perhaps, that a spiritually mature person is a committed and involved member of a church. But no, Dr. Dobson's answer was, "The extent to which you understand and live in dependence on God, that is the extent to which you are spiritually mature." This comment hit me like a bomb! Not independence, but dependence.

We are taught, from a young age that we need to be independent. To stand on our own feet. To make our own decisions in life. The less dependent we are on others, the better. The more self-sufficient we are, the more we are admired. But God's kingdom works differently from the kingdoms of men. Of course, we do need to be adults who are not dependent on other people for everything. But when we carry this independence through to our relationship with God, we show little understanding of how things really work in His kingdom.

Jesus, in the Sermon on the Mount, clearly explained that those who are dependent on God will be blessed. The Lord likes it when we express our needs to Him, and live in submission to Him. We should ultimately strive to be like Paul who said that we have nothing that we have not received from God. Our abilities come from God. Each day we should bow before Him and acknowledge our dependence on Him. Then He can carry us, teach us, and provide for us. So stop trying to be self-sufficient and acknowledge God in every aspect of your life. Depend on Him for everything. Listen for His voice and follow Him.

Soft hearts

"Blessed are the meek, for they will inherit the earth."

ꕥ MATTHEW 5:5 ꕥ

After a man has made some mistakes in his marriage, he is kicked out of the house by his wife. He then goes for counseling, is truly repentant and decides that he wants to make a fresh start. But there's one problem. His wife no longer believes him. He keeps going back to her – knocks on the door, phones her, pages her. He even asks his counselor to phone. But her heart has become hard. The door is closed and she no longer wants to let him in.

The Lord Jesus specializes in hard hearts. Quite often past hurts can harden our hearts, but sin is more often the cause of a hardened heart. And then the Heart Specialist from Nazareth comes to offer us His help.

Jesus reminds us of the prophet Ezekiel, who outlined God's plan for His people, *"I will give them an undivided heart and put a new spirit in them; I will remove from them their heart of stone and give them a heart of flesh"* (Ezek. 11:19). God wants to break open our hard hearts. The Holy Spirit, over time, influences our hearts and we are changed into people of gentleness and sensitivity.

Allow God to massage your hard heart until it becomes soft. Then you will be one of those who will inherit the new earth. You will be known as a child of God. Be understanding of the weaknesses of others, and forgive them. Let Jesus Himself heal the hurts of the past that caused your heart to become hard, and then everything you do will be governed by sensitivity and peace.

January 25

A different message

"Blessed are you when people insult you, persecute you and falsely say all kinds of evil against you because of me."

Matthew 5:11

You find yourself in a situation where you need to make an important decision. Someone has asked you for a favor, but in your heart you know that it would mean doing something that goes against the Word of God. It would be easy to refuse to do it if it had no direct impact on your relationship with that person or on your future. But what if it were, for example, your boss, the organization for which you work, perhaps even the pastor, or someone you really want to impress? It wouldn't be so easy, would it?

And yet, as a child of God, you know that if you comply with such a request, you will lose the peace you have from the Lord. There is a growing conviction inside you that you are unable to do something that opposes God's will, even though you have been asked to do it. And so you make your decision – you choose to follow God. You choose the truth and you do the unpopular thing of going against expectations. As a result, you experience what so many other Christians go through: abuse, criticism, rejection, misunderstandings, uneasy relationships. Suddenly you find out that people are talking about you behind your back. You might even be falsely accused.

But into the midst of all this, Jesus comes with a surprising command. He tells you to be glad and jump up and down for joy when such things happen. Yes, you heard right. Turn your hurt into something positive. Put a smile on your face, close your bedroom door, and marvel joyously with these words, *"Rejoice and be glad, because great is your reward in heaven, for in the same way they persecuted the prophets who were before you"* (v. 12).

This is not an act of self-delusion, but the result of pure joy in Jesus because you chose the truth.

Too high a price

A certain ruler asked him, "Good teacher, what must I do to inherit eternal life?"

ↀ Luke 18:18 ↀ

The rich young ruler had good intentions when he contacted Jesus. He was, after all, a man who had good connections. His money saw to that. Money is power, and he was able to influence situations so that they would turn out the way he wanted them to. And he decided that connecting with Jesus would be beneficial. Something about Jesus fascinated him intensely. He had heard Him preach a few times and each time his heart had been stirred by what he had heard. It's true that he lived a comfortable life, but there was a great emptiness in his heart. His earthly life was pleasant, but he longed for eternal life.

That is why, when he stood face to face with Jesus and looked deep into His eyes, he asked, *"Good teacher, what must I do to inherit eternal life?"* (v. 18). And Jesus looked through his eyes and into his heart. And there He saw a young man who was so bound by his possessions, so fond of the luxury and power that his wealth granted him that he was not able to give it all up. For him to choose eternal life would cost too much. The young man explained that he had kept all the commandments from a young age. He hoped that that would be sufficient to earn him eternal life.

But Jesus had bad news for him. Jesus understood how attached he was to his possessions and knew that he had to be set free. That is why He told him to sell all he had, give the proceeds to the poor, and then follow Him. This was too difficult for him. Sadly, the young man turned away.

Serve God with your possessions. Money and property become a problem if they lure you away from your decision to follow Jesus.

January 27

Know what the Word says

Jesus answered, "It is written: 'Man does not live on bread alone, but on every word that comes from the mouth of God.'"

℘ MATTHEW 4:4 ℘

Imagine the drama that must have played itself out in the wilderness. Jesus had just been baptized, the Holy Spirit had filled Him with power, and then, the Word of God tells us, *"Jesus was led by the Spirit into the desert to be tempted by the devil"* (Mt. 4:1). Once Jesus had been endued with the power of the Holy Spirit, He was ready to tackle the devil. The Holy Spirit is more than capable of putting evil spirits in their place! And so He led Jesus into a confrontation with evil.

Then followed forty days and forty nights when Jesus ate nothing, and after some time He began to feel hungry. He might have been fasting, or He might have been so involved in conversation with His Father and overwhelmed by the knowledge of the task ahead of Him that He didn't have time to think of food. What we do know is that He began to feel hungry. And that was when the devil appeared before Him. When you and I are at our most vulnerable, that is when the devil is at his most active.

He offered bread to Jesus, but not as you and I would expect. He challenged Christ to use His power as the Son of God to turn stones into bread. The devil would not have suggested such a thing if it were not possible for Jesus to do it. But Jesus answered, *"It is written ... "* and the devil got his answer from the Word of God.

Because the Word is powerful and more effective than a double-edged sword, according to the writer of Hebrews, it keeps the devil in his place. When the devil confronts you with his temptations, make sure that you don't only have intellectual knowledge of the Word. It needs to be in your heart.

The Bread of Life

Jesus answered, "It is written: 'Man does not live on bread alone, but on every word that comes from the mouth of God.'"

so MATTHEW 4:4 cs

A friend of mine who sustained head injuries in a car crash, temporarily lost his sense of taste. He loves to tell people how that was one of the most difficult experiences of his life. Eating was simply a mechanical action – he ate because he was hungry – but he was not able to enjoy the delicious meals that people prepared for him. He couldn't taste a thing. He was overjoyed when the Lord touched him supernaturally and restored his sense of taste. He is once again able to enjoy all the wonderful flavors of food.

Eating is a very big part of our lives. Think of all the great restaurants that prepare the most incredible dishes. People are prepared to spend exorbitant sums of money simply so that they can enjoy exotic meals.

The Lord even taught us to pray for our daily bread, because the Father knows that we need food.

Even though food is so important, Jesus reminded Himself, and the devil, that we do not live by bread alone. It is simply not enough. It might be sufficient for our physical survival, but what does it do for our souls? And our spirits?

The Lord offers us His heavenly bread: the Word of God. And we only truly begin to live when we savor every word that comes from the mouth of God. Taste His Word. Enjoy it.

January 29

To see the Lord

"Blessed are the pure in heart, for they will see God."

☙ MATTHEW 5:8 ❧

In Exodus 33 we read that Moses was overwhelmed by the glory of the Lord. He was alone with God on top of the mountain and caught a glimmer of His glory. It was such an amazing experience that, as soon as he could, he asked the Lord to show him His glory yet again. But God explained that no one can see His face and live. And yet God honored Moses' desire. He hid him in the cleft of a rock, covered it with His hand, and walked past Moses. He saw the back of the Lord as He passed by.

There are people who have had near-death experiences, and who tell about the wonder of God's glory that they experienced in His presence. It was so marvelous that they were reluctant to leave it to return to earth. It's incredible to think that you and I will see the Lord in the fullness of His glory the moment we exchange this temporal life for our eternal home.

But there is a condition. Jesus said that those who are holy will see the Lord. That means that we need to be washed clean before we can appear before God. That can only be done by the blood of Jesus, shed when He died on the cross. Let us keep ourselves pure and holy so that we will be ready to enjoy the presence of God in all His glory.

Peacemakers

"Blessed are the peacemakers, for they will be called sons of God."

Matthew 5:9

There are many troublemakers in the world. We're subjected to one violent scene after another on our TV screens. Different countries are at war with each other, and so are families, towns, and cultures. Everywhere we look we see conflict and fighting. And that's not even taking into consideration the normal bad relations between people who once were good friends, but who are now hostile toward each other.

When God forgives our sins, we establish a relationship of peace with Him. And we learn to live at peace with ourselves. This peace then spills over into our relationships with other people. That does not mean that we won't ever have misunderstandings. And our perceptions will sometimes cause conflict in our relationships. But Christians have a deep, powerful drive to establish peace. We are not comfortable with conflict and hostility. At heart, Christians are peacemakers.

If you are in conflict with someone, try your best to go and make peace. Then you will be called a child of God.

January 31

Bow in worship

Jesus said to him, "Away from me, Satan! For it is written: 'Worship the Lord your God, and serve him only.'"

MATTHEW 4:10

Toward the beginning of last century, the heir-apparent to the throne of Great Britain (Edward VIII) lost his heart to a woman. The man who should have ascended to the throne of one of the most important nations in the world bowed his knee before the beauty of a woman, and so had to abdicate.

And that's just what the devil wanted to make Jesus do. Christ, the Son of God, the One who would receive a name above any other name ever given, was asked to bow His knee before another power. The ruler of this world, the devil, was originally an angel of exceptional beauty and power. Through his disobedience to God he caused the whole world to fall in sin. He is the father of lies, and one of his biggest lies is that people can find life apart from God, and that such a life can be meaningful. The trump card that he uses to convince us of this lie is the possession of material goods. He makes us believe that the more we own, the happier we will be.

When he showed Jesus all the kingdoms of the world in their glory, he said, "*All this I will give you, if you will bow down and worship me*" (v. 9). But Jesus saw right through Satan's lie and ordered him to depart, "*Worship the Lord your God, and serve him only*" (v. 10).

Because of the Fall there is a sense of loss in each person's life. God promises to help us satisfy our needs, but when we cross the line and we develop an avaricious desire for everything that is shinier, bigger, and better, then we are heading for spiritual trouble. Then we are bowing before the ruler of this world and are governed by our desires. The Bible teaches us that we should worship God first, and then He will provide all that we need, all that we desire.

February

February 1

Faith in a storm

"Where is your faith?" he asked his disciples. In fear and amazement they asked one another, "Who is this? He commands even the winds and the water, and they obey him."

℘ Luke 8:25 ☙

It was a beautiful day when they got into the boat and set out for the other side of the lake. The water lay still and blue and the distant green hills of Galilee shimmered in the midday sun. The wind filled the sail and the water beat rhythmically against the side of the boat, and Jesus slept.

Suddenly a violent stormy wind broke across the lake and the little boat began to rock violently from side to side. Water washed over the sides and the boat began to fill rapidly. The disciples thought that they would die in the vicious storm. But Jesus still slept. So they shook Him awake shouting, "We're going to drown!" Jesus got up, rebuked the wind, and admonished the waves. Suddenly everything became still, the waves subsided, the wind dropped and peace and quiet reigned. Perhaps Jesus was so tired that He didn't even wake up when the storm broke. Or perhaps His inner peace and calm allowed Him to sleep in the midst of the storm.

And then Jesus asked them, "Where is your faith?" Here we find the key. If you know who you are, to whom you belong, and who holds you firm in His hand, then the worst storm will simply be a test of your faith. Do we become fearful and unsure in the turbulance of life, and cling desperately to the sides of our lifeboat? Remember, that just as we think we will not get through the storm, we once again hear the voice of Jesus saying, "Where is your faith?" Then we fall to our knees, look into His loving eyes, and confess our unbelief. After all, He promised that He is in control and He holds us in His hands.

What people think

Once when Jesus was praying in private and his disciples were with him, he asked them, "Who do the crowds say I am?"

ꟹ LUKE 9:18 ꟹ

Jesus had withdrawn a little way away from the disciples. He wanted to spend some time praying privately. His disciples drew near to Him, because they wanted to be in His glorious presence. Perhaps He smiled as He started to talk to them. The question He asked was an important one, *"Who do the crowds say I am?"* (v. 18).

It could be that while Jesus had been talking to His Father, emphasis had once again been placed on His purpose to show people the way to the heart of the Father. Perhaps He wondered if He had been truly effective in His preaching. Did people really understand what He was trying to tell them?

Jesus was not concerned with the opinions of people. He did not have a burning desire to be accepted. He never tried to get the number one spot on the "most popular" lists. His words were too direct and pointed for that, and He spent too much time with ordinary people on the streets for Him to be considered one of the elite, therefore the question He asked was aimed at testing the hearts of His disciples. After they had given Him various answers to His question – some said that He was John the Baptist, others that He was Elijah and some that He was an old-time prophet – He asked them a more personal question. *"But what about you? Who do you say I am?"* (v. 20) And He waited expectantly for their answer.

Perhaps the answer He heard surprised Him. It was Peter who declared, *"The Christ of God."* (v. 20) They had grasped the truth.

There are many modern human opinions about who Jesus is. In this era of unbelief and increasing skepticism about who Christ really is, let our answer ring out loud and clear, "You are the Christ!"

February 3

Follow Him

Then he said to them all: "If anyone would come after me, he must deny himself and take up his cross daily and follow me."

ꕥ Luke 9:23 ꕥ

Jesus invited people to follow Him, to become His disciples. During His time of ministry on earth – His last three years on earth – He often stood before people, looked deep into their eyes, and said, "Follow Me!" Some responded to His invitation but others did not. Some followed Him for a while, listening to what He had to say and finding out all they could about this teacher from Nazareth. Some accepted His words, but others rejected them. Some enjoyed hearing what He had to say, but when His words became too direct and challenging, they no longer wanted to listen to Him.

The call of Jesus still resounds today, inviting all who hear it to follow Him. Those who respond positively to His call become His disciples. They walk with Him and seek His presence, and enjoy being near Him – they listen to His words and respond to what He says. That is the crux of being a Christian: becoming a disciple of Jesus Christ.

The irony is that many so-called disciples of Jesus actually want to run ahead of Him. They want to lead, not follow. They make decisions, and do so in the name of Jesus, but do not submit to Him as true disciples should. They take the lead. But Christians should wait for the Lord to move before they begin to move. If you are a follower then that means that there is someone who goes ahead of you. You hear His voice and you respond by moving in the direction that He points out to you.

Do you want to walk with Jesus? Then you will need to follow Him. That is the only way to be spiritually successful. Make a decision that, from today, you will truly follow Him.

Deny yourself?

Then he said to them all: "If anyone would come after me, he must deny himself and take up his cross daily and follow me."

LUKE 9:23

One of the most unpopular statements that Jesus ever made was that if we want to be His disciples, we have to deny ourselves. This goes against the grain of everything that human nature desires. Each of us has an inner need to be considered worthwhile. Usually we are taught to stand up for ourselves against everything and everyone who opposes us. In the corporate world it's considered completely acceptable to stand on the heads of others as you climb the ladder of success – the only thing that matters is that you come out ahead.

People expect you to take revenge if someone harms you in some way. But the kingdom of God works differently. The Lord teaches us not to take revenge – instead we should forgive those who persecute us. We should not justify ourselves – but sacrifice ourselves. We should not seek to be served by others, but to serve them. The Bible calls this self-denial. Self-denial does not mean that you consider yourself a worm that has no personal significance. Self-denial does not mean that you develop a pathetic attitude that allows everyone or everything to walk all over you. Rather, self-denial means that actions motivated by a heart of pride and arrogance give way to actions that treat others as more important than you. At heart, self-denial for a Christian means laying your life down and allowing Christ to take over the reins. Self-interest is replaced by God's interest. Self-righteousness is replaced with God's righteousness. Your own ideas give way before God's ideas. Your life is set aside for a better life – a life of and in Jesus Christ.

Christ calls us today to do what is seen as completely foolish in the eyes of the world, that is to lay down our lives and follow Him.

February 5

Doubt vs. faith

"Blessed is the man who does not fall away on account of me."

∞ MATTHEW 11:6 ∞

John the Baptist was called to prepare the way for Jesus, the Savior of the world and the Lamb of God. For quite a few years he preached his message of redemption with passion and conviction. Many people wanted to be baptized by him and to recommit themselves to God. But then John was thrown in prison and, in that forlorn prison cell, John began to doubt his own message and to wonder if Jesus was truly the anointed Savior.

That is why John sent his disciples to Jesus with a message. He wanted to know if He was the One who was promised, the Messiah, or if there was someone else they should look for.

Jesus answered, *"Go back and report to John what you hear and see: The blind receive sight, the lame walk, those who have leprosy are cured, the deaf hear, the dead are raised, and the good news is preached to the poor"* (vv. 4-5). Jesus drew John's attention to the miracles that were taking place and the good news that He was preaching to all who needed to hear it.

God still works miracles among us today. There are dozens of people who have been changed through the gospel of Jesus Christ, who have developed new insights through the power of the Holy Spirit, who have been miraculously healed, and so much more. But all these miracles are often overshadowed by all the bad news we hear – the stories of brokenness and hurt all around us. If we do not look carefully at all that God is doing we might too begin to doubt, as John the Baptist did. But remember the words of Jesus, *"Blessed is the man who does not fall away on account of me"* (v. 6).

Miracles and salvation

"Woe to you, Korazin! Woe to you, Bethsaida! If the miracles that were performed in you had been performed in Tyre and Sidon, they would have repented long ago in sackcloth and ashes."

Matthew 11:21

Wherever Jesus went, He performed miracles. It was clear that God was with Him. Some people recognized this and praised God. They then turned to Him for salvation. But most did not. It's strange that we can see miracles right in front of our eyes and yet still look for reasons not to believe. People are constantly seeking things that will convince them of the truth about God, but when the sign is placed right in front of them, their preconceived ideas blind them so that they don't believe what they see.

Matthew tells us that Jesus began to condemn the towns in which He had performed most of His miracles because they didn't come to repentance. He spoke out strongly against Korazin and Bethsaida. Even the devout Jewish inhabitants in these villages did not believe in Him.

Jesus could not help but think that the inhabitants of Tyre and Sidon, and even of Sodom, would have been more accepting of His message, and more moved by the miracles He performed. That is why He said that it would be more bearable for Sodom on the day of judgment than for Capernaum, situated along the shores of the Galilee, where He had done so many miracles.

The miracles that God does in our midst these days should also encourage us to believe in Him and repent. When we hear of the miraculous way that God works in the lives of others, we should not become skeptical, but rather praise and honor God and recommit ourselves to Him.

Come and rest

"Come to me, all you who are weary and burdened, and I will give you rest."

ꟷ MATTHEW 11:28 ꟷ

One thing that has definitely become scarce in our day is rest. I don't mean sleep or vacations. Many people sleep each night but wake up still tired in the morning. And think of how many people come back from vacations tired and stressed.

Rest is more than sleep or relaxation. It is a spiritual condition. In a time of stress, anxiety, and haste, it has become necessary to rediscover exactly what true rest means. Rest is that special kind of peace that God puts into our hearts in spite of, and in the midst of, our circumstances. It is this kind of rest that gave Jesus the serenity to sleep through the storm. It is what helped Paul and Silas to sing in prison. It means to stand in faith when chaos erupts around you. This kind of peace is available to all who turn to God in faith.

That is why Jesus invites us, *"Come to me, all you who are weary and burdened, and I will give you rest"* (v. 28). Something wonderful and supernatural occurs when we turn to God in faith. A peace that passes all understanding begins to fill our hearts, and God, through His Holy Spirit, will keep us in peace in the middle of the most difficult circumstances.

The writer of Hebrews says that we must strive to enter the rest of God, and to stay there (cf. Heb. 4:11). We must come to Jesus, and abide with Him. That is where we will find rest.

Not just for the clever

At that time Jesus said, "I praise you, Father, Lord of heaven and earth, because you have hidden these things from the wise and learned, and revealed them to little children."

ꟷ MATTHEW 11:25 ꟷ

Some preachers and theologians present the gospel in such a way that they create the illusion that only highly intellectual people can understand it. Nothing could be further from the truth. The good news of Jesus Christ is not complicated. Jesus Himself said that we need to become like little children if we want to see the kingdom of God. And in 1 Corinthians 1:26, Paul says, *"Not many of you were wise by human standards; not many were influential; not many were of noble birth"*. The gospel is not just for intellectuals.

Jesus praised the Father because the secrets of the kingdom have been hidden from the clever and learned and have been revealed to those who receive it with simplicity. The Father's mercy and grace were meant to be understood by all. With that, Jesus confirmed that the gospel is available to the ordinary man or woman on the street. It is not reserved for those who are brilliant by the world's standards. It is for ordinary people of average intelligence.

The wonder of the gospel is that even those who are below average can rejoice in the message of Jesus. Experience shows that it is more often those with simple understanding who are the ones who most readily accept the message of the gospel with enthusiasm and make it their own.

There is no excuse for not believing. The simplicity of the gospel can be understood by anyone.

February 9

An easy yoke

"Take my yoke upon you and learn from me, for I am gentle and humble in heart, and you will find rest for your souls."

MATTHEW 11:29

The message of the gospel is easy to understand and Jesus invites everyone to come to Him and learn of Him. Like oxen that have been yoked together to pull a plow, like people who throw their weight behind a new project, we need to be willing to walk a new road with Christ, and learn from Him.

Jesus tells us that His yoke, or work, is easy. It is not hard to follow Jesus. We no longer have to strive to keep the old commandments of the old covenant. He writes new laws on our heart through His Holy Spirit and He, through His love, compels us to be able to love. That is why His yoke is easy.

Eventually we find that the burden He talks of is not a burden at all – it is pure joy. The joy that comes from knowing Him and following Him and serving Him. He who leads us is humble and gentle of heart. He understands our hearts and has patience with our weaknesses. He encourages us to find His path and to walk in it. He is indeed humble of heart.

Even though He is King of kings and the Son of God, He is still humble and gentle in His dealings with us. Come, let us learn from Him.

A precious person

"If any of you has a sheep and it falls into a pit on the Sabbath, will you not take hold of it and lift it out? How much more valuable is a man than a sheep! Therefore it is lawful to do good on the Sabbath."

꧁ MATTHEW 12:11-12 ꧂

The man with the shriveled hand was a marked man. His friends had mocked him about his ugly, withered, dysfunctional hand since childhood. He soon learned to take hold of things in different ways and to compensate for his crippled hand. It was not pleasant. Along with the defects of the hand, there were whispers, silly jokes, the uncertainty when people greeted him, the pain of being abnormal.

But he believed in God. That was why he could be found in the synagogue every Sabbath. Over the years he had made peace with God about his disability. But then on that particular day Jesus was also in the synagogue.

A group of Pharisees was also there. Like wolves, they circled voraciously around Jesus. They weighed His every word and action. They had decided it was time to put an end to His influence on people and to His message that undermined them. That is why they tried to trap Him by asking Him to answer their question, *"Is it lawful to heal on the Sabbath?"* (v. 10). Jesus pointed them to the Old Testament law that stated that if a sheep fell in a ditch on the Sabbath day, it could be taken out immediately. He went on to say that people are more valuable than sheep. And then He asked the man to stretch out his withered hand. Jesus touched it and it was healed.

People are more important than laws and theological debates.

February 11

Set free from evil

"If I drive out demons by the Spirit of God, then the kingdom of God has come upon you."

ꕤ MATTHEW 12:28 ꕤ

Helen Keller was blind, deaf and mute. Through the love of someone who was dedicated to helping her, she was able to learn to communicate effectively. She was later able to explain that she thanked God for her disabilities because through them she was able to find herself, her calling, and her God.

Another man, who, for other reasons was also blind and mute, was brought to Jesus by compassionate friends. Can you imagine what it must be like to wander around in total darkness and not be able to say one word? This man's condition was the result of the work of a demonic spirit. He was completely helpless, lost and confused when he was brought to Jesus, and Jesus healed him. Suddenly he could see and speak. The Pharisees scornfully suggested that this miracle was only possible with the help of Beelzebub, the chief of the evil spirits. Jesus replied that He cast out demons by the Spirit of God, because He came to bring the Kingdom of God to people.

We often do not know the cause of a problem or sickness. We need the ability to discern when someone is under the power of evil spirits. One thing we do know for certain is that we can come to Jesus for help. He is still the Healer.

Count your words

"But I tell you that men will have to give account on the day of judgment for every careless word they have spoken."

ꟾ Matthew 12:36 ꟾ

Words carry weight. Every syllable uttered is laden with meaning. Without effective communication of words and concepts, the world would collapse into chaos, which is what happened at the tower of Babel.

Jesus cautions us not to use words lightly. God will weigh each word that we speak in the light of our intention and meaning. The Lord knows and tests our hearts, and listens to our words. In this passage, Jesus was addressing the Pharisees who were inclined to say things that sounded good, but whose disposition was bad. He told them that on judgment day they would have to give account of every word that was casually spoken. Then He said, *"For by your words you will be acquitted, and by your words you will be condemned"* (v. 37).

We too should think carefully about the words we speak. Do we say things too quickly? We would do well to take note of the old adage that reminds us that we have two ears and one mouth and so we should listen twice as much as we speak. We should be very careful of the words we speak.

Paul says that we should ensure that every word we speak builds others up, and does not break them down. We should be speaking God's thoughts. We should speak to others with His words of love. Remember, we will be judged for every word we say.

February 13

The peach orchard

"Make a tree good and its fruit will be good, or make a tree bad and its fruit will be bad, for a tree is recognized by its fruit."

ℵ MATTHEW 12:33 ℵ

When last did you wander through a peach orchard and look at the wonderful, juicy, red-cheeked peaches hanging from the trees? I doubt that any peach tastes as delicious as one that has been picked straight from the tree. But imagine biting into a juicy luscious-looking peach and finding it tasteless and riddled with worms. It looked better on the outside than it actually was on the inside.

Jesus reminds us that a tree can be known by its fruit. Of course we know that a peach tree doesn't bear figs. In the same way someone with a good heart and who is in a right relationship with God through Jesus Christ his Savior is expected to produce fruit in keeping with repentance.

The fruit of the Holy Spirit should be evident in our lives. We cannot say one thing and do another. Such fruit is not in keeping with the tree from which we have grown. The fruit we produce should bear the evidence of the decision we have made to follow Jesus; we should bear good spiritual fruit. Only God can bring this about in our lives, which is why we need to stay attached to the Vine (cf. Jn. 15).

Our fruit should also be of the best quality. We must bring forth an abundant harvest, according to the fullness of the measure of Christ, so that others can see the work that God is doing in us.

Show me your heart

"The good man brings good things out of the good stored up in him, and the evil man brings evil things out of the evil stored up in him."

MATTHEW 12:35

In verse 34, Jesus calls the Pharisees a brood of vipers. Have you ever thought that this description might have been a bit extreme? One hardly expects Jesus, the One who is so holy and loving, to say something that is so harsh and critical. And yet He did say it, because as the Son of God He declares what He knows is the truth. They really were like snakes, and they were like wolves in sheep's clothing. They were supposed to show people the way to God but instead they set up barriers, confused people and caused them to wander from the truth. In fact, they did the same work as the serpent in the Garden of Eden, which is why they were so threatened by God and His Kingdom.

Jesus put His finger directly on their problem. Because their hearts were not right He could not expect them to say anything that was good. Out of the overflow of the heart the mouth speaks forth. If there are good things in your heart then they will come out in what you say. Evil people cannot help but reveal the bad things in their heart by the words that they speak.

God offers to heal our hearts. He wants to wash them clean by the blood of Jesus. Then He wants to fill our hearts with good things so that everything that we say will bear witness to the new life that we have received from Jesus. Let us rededicate our hearts to Him today and let Him fill us with good things. If our hearts are filled with His presence then our mouths will speak of Him and we will be a shining light to those around us.

February 15

Afraid of the glory

But Jesus came and touched them. "Get up," he said. "Don't be afraid."

Matthew 17:7

Jesus took Peter, James, and John with Him to a high mountain where they were all alone. Suddenly, as the three disciples watched, a miracle took place before their eyes. They had read how the face of Moses had begun to shine with the glory of the Lord when he spent time in His presence on Mount Sinai. And now Jesus' face also began to shine like the sun and His clothes became as white as the light around them. Then suddenly they noticed something more: Moses and Elijah appeared and began to talk to Jesus.

This glorious and extraordinary situation proved too much for Peter. In trying to gain control of the situation, he made a foolish, fleshly suggestion. He wanted to build three shrines – one for Jesus, one for Moses, and one for Elijah.

The glory of God is something beyond our human experience and expectations. When we at times experience His glory we, like Peter, might also begin to feel a little out of our depth. We try to make sense of it with our human understanding, or we try to find an explanation for it.

While Peter was still speaking a cloud of bright light covered them and a voice thundered from within the cloud, *"This is my Son, whom I love; with him I am well pleased. Listen to him!"* (v. 5). When the disciples saw the cloud and heard the voice they were terrified and fell facedown to the ground. Then Jesus came to them, and touched them. *"Get up," he said. "Don't be afraid"* (v. 7). When they looked around them, they saw only Jesus standing there.

When we encounter Christ in an unusual way, it is best to wait in quiet anticipation and in an attitude of worship before the Lord.

Comfort not guaranteed

Jesus replied, "Foxes have holes and birds of the air have nests, but the Son of Man has no place to lay his head."

ꕥ LUKE 9:58 ꕥ

One day while Jesus was walking with a group of travelers, one man was thrilled and excited about what he heard. He walked close to Jesus, not wanting to miss anything. After a while he called out, *"I will follow you wherever you go"* (v. 57). Wow! Talk about commitment. Or perhaps he thought it would be glamorous to follow Jesus. He would see so many places, meet hundreds of different people, a visit here, a chat there ... What an adventure!

The words Jesus used to answer him were intended to bring him back to earth with a bump. *"Foxes have holes and birds of the air have nests, but the Son of Man has no place to lay his head"* (v. 58). One can't help but wonder just how far this man actually traveled with Jesus in the months that lay ahead.

Serving God in ministry is definitely an adventure, but your comfort cannot be guaranteed. It requires commitment to follow Jesus. He could call you to go to places where you might experience discomfort. Think of all the missionaries who are called to distant countries and strange cultures to preach the gospel. A friend of mine regularly goes to the Far East on mission work. He is ill most of the time that he's there and finds the living conditions extremely uncomfortable. But still he continues to go because he believes that God has sent him to preach the gospel there, even though it isn't always very comfortable.

Gospel singers are frequently told that they have a wonderful job – singing for the Lord and for people. It looks so easy and so fantastic. But just spend a bit of time touring with some of them, lug the sound equipment around and catch a few hours of fitful sleep at night while traveling thousands of miles to the next venue, and the gloss will quickly rub off. It is plain hard work. You need to be called to do such work otherwise you will not last long.

February 17

Looking back is not an option

Jesus replied, "No one who puts his hand to the plow and looks back is fit for service in the kingdom of God."

℘ LUKE 9:62 ℘

Many companies focus on encouraging their employees to work purposefully and productively. Their aim is to motivate people to such an extent that they will do more than what is required of them.

But often it seems that integrity in the workplace no longer exists. Staff seem to be lazy or to have no real interest in what they are doing. A director of a large organization admitted that his greatest concern is that his workers do not deliver the quality of service that he expects of them. They want to do as little as possible with the least amount of effort, for the most amount of money.

Jesus invited two men to follow Him but both had excuses for not being ready to follow immediately. The one first wanted to arrange his father's funeral. The other first wanted to settle things with his family. Two valid reasons, we would say.

But Jesus saw things differently. Those who follow Him need to have such a burning commitment to Him and His kingdom that they will give up anything to follow Him. And that includes the sentimental attachment to parents and family. This sounds a bit harsh to us, but behind Jesus' answers we hear the beat of His heart – just as He was prepared to leave His heavenly Father and the glories of heaven for a broken world, He expects us to commit ourselves to His service. He wants an active decision from us. All or nothing. Follow or go back. No dallying or procrastinating. Listen as Jesus says, *"Let the dead bury their own dead, but you go and proclaim the kingdom of God"* (v. 60).

Come, let us follow Him with commitment, with enthusiasm, without excuses. Full steam ahead.

The greatest joy

"However, do not rejoice that the spirits submit to you, but rejoice that your names are written in heaven."

LUKE 10:20

Jesus sent seventy-two messengers ahead of him into the towns and places He was about to visit. They went in pairs with only the bare essentials, but with fiery determination in their hearts to share His message with everyone.

But they only really began to understand everything that they had experienced when they reported to Jesus after they returned from their "mission trip". The Bible tells us that they came back rejoicing and praising God for all that had happened. If you, in obedience to God, share His Word and give yourself unselfishly to the service of God and people, you will find a deep, inner sense of fulfillment that quite simply makes you glad. You discover that it is indeed more blessed to give than to receive.

Their shining faces told the story that seemed almost too good to be true. Of course they had seen Jesus in action. But He was, after all, a powerful teacher sent by God. But them? They couldn't even begin to do what He did. And yet now they had. *"Lord, even the demons submit to us in your name"* (v. 17). Hallelujah! They had seen God's mighty hand in action through their obedience. It was amazing.

Jesus confirmed that He has power over the works of the evil one and that He had imparted that power to them. As their teacher, He used the opportunity to bring an even greater truth home to them. He said, *"However, do not rejoice that the spirits submit to you, but rejoice that your names are written in heaven"* (v. 20).

The greatest miracle is that we, through Jesus, can be reconciled to God and that we belong to Him and that our names are written in heaven. Is your name there? Let's praise Him for His salvation.

February 19

A bolt of lightning

He replied, "I saw Satan fall like lightning from heaven."

ꟷ Luke 10:18 ꟷ

In one of the conversations Jesus had with His disciples about evil, He made the following statement, "I saw Satan fall like lightning from heaven."

Could this be a reference to the words of Isaiah 14? This passage is widely accepted to be a biblical, prophetic account of Satan's fall from heaven. Jesus, as the Son of God, would have been there when he fell and He would have seen exactly what happened.

> *How you have fallen from heaven, O morning star, son of the dawn! You have been cast down to the earth, you who once laid low the nations! You said in your heart, "I will ascend to heaven; I will raise my throne above the stars of God; I will sit enthroned on the mount of assembly, on the utmost heights of the sacred mountain. I will ascend above the tops of the clouds; I will make myself like the Most High." But you are brought down to the grave, to the depths of the pit* (Is. 14:12-15).

It could be that Jesus, in His times of quiet meditation in the presence of His Father, had been reminded that Satan had been thrown out of heaven and that his power is now limited – although still deadly. That is why Jesus taught His disciples that, in His name, they could wreak havoc against the prince of darkness. *"I have given you authority to trample on snakes and scorpions and to overcome all the power of the enemy; nothing will harm you"* (Lk. 10:19).

Beloved, be assured that, in Jesus' name, you can stand firm against the attacks of the evil one. Don't ever try to take on the devil in your own strength, but stay standing right where you have been placed, fully equipped with the complete armor of God (see Eph. 6:10-18) and resist him with the name of Jesus constantly on your lips.

A tasty morsel!

"You are the salt of the earth. But if the salt loses its saltiness, how can it be made salty again? It is no longer good for anything, except to be thrown out and trampled by men."

ꟹ MATTHEW 5:13 ꟹ

Food that has not been properly seasoned is generally bland and definitely not good to eat. Even though taste differs from one person to the next, we all agree that at least a pinch of salt is needed to bring out the full flavor of a dish.

Therefore, when Jesus makes this short, pithy observation, it is easy for us to understand what He was getting at. *"You are the salt of the earth."* It's about taste, it's about making a difference, it's about being effective. In Jesus' time, salt was used to preserve food from bacteria and decay, and we are to preserve the goodness and morality of the community in which we live. It was also used in medicinal treatments.

We bring out the goodness in people as we live out the goodness of God where we are. We ensure that sin does not destroy everything around us. And sometimes we are the salt in the wounds of the world, when we bring the healing gospel to those who hurt.

But Jesus warns us that salt that loses its strength is useless. Christian, make sure that your strength in Christ does not lose its flavor! Each day be sure that you are refreshed and refilled and renewed by the Holy Spirit and then you will not lose your godly strength. There are too many Christians who are weak, and ineffectual, and powerless. They have the appearance of godliness, says Paul, but the strength of it has dissipated (2 Tim. 3:5).

And finally – remember that salt that stays in the salt cellar has no effect. Venture out of your cozy Christian circle and into the world among the broken people who need to be restored. Be God's salt in the world and you too will make a difference.

February 21

Do you write your own rules?

> *"Anyone who breaks one of the least of these commandments and teaches others to do the same will be called least in the kingdom of heaven, but whoever practices and teaches these commands will be called great in the kingdom of heaven."*
>
> ꕤ MATTHEW 5:19 ꕤ

The spiritual leaders of Jesus' day thought that He was doing away with all the laws that had been passed down from one generation to another, and on which the Jews based their whole lives.

But Jesus assured those who listened to Him that He did not come to nullify the law. He explained that His ultimate intention was to bring out the full meaning of the law and the prophets.

Jesus went on to say that anyone who undermines the commandments of God, or teaches anyone else to do so, will be the least respected in the Kingdom of Heaven. It is therefore important to understand the new dimension that Jesus brought to the laws. We have the New Testament to help us with this, and, even more wonderful, we also have the person of the Holy Spirit to lead us into the fullness of truth.

Jesus ends this discourse by saying that we need better spiritual understanding and insight into righteousness than the scribes and Pharisees had. They were so focused on the letter of the law that they no longer heard the heart of God. He declared, *"For I tell you that unless your righteousness surpasses that of the Pharisees and the teachers of the law, you will certainly not enter the kingdom of heaven"* (v. 20).

Beloved, guard against two things. Do not be so legalistic that you do not grasp Jesus' new approach to the law. And secondly, do not be so unaware of God's law that you begin to formulate your own laws, rules, and regulations.

Looking back will mess things up

Jesus replied, "No one who puts his hand to the plow and looks back is fit for service in the kingdom of God."

Luke 9:62

The Bible does not paint a very flattering picture of the citizens of Sodom. They were pleasure seekers and completely committed to extravagance. Sodomy was the order of the day at their hedonistic parties. And then God decided that enough was enough. He could not find even ten righteous people in the city! He sent two angels to destroy the city, and they warned Lot and his family to leave Sodom. Lot's sons-in-law did not heed the warning, and finally the angels even had to grab Lot, his wife and their two daughters by the hand and drag them out of Sodom. But as God began to rain down sulfur over Sodom, Mrs. Lot turned around and there she still stands today – outside the kingdom of God.

When Jesus calls us He expects us to set our faces firmly toward His kingdom. He says, *"No one who puts his hand to the plow and looks back is fit for service in the kingdom of God"* (Lk. 9:62). Working for the Kingdom of God is a lot like plowing. Furrows must be dug in preparation for the seed that needs to be sown, and that requires focus. Your eyes should be looking ahead, and you need to move forward, in as straight a line as possible, with your eyes fixed on a set landmark. If you look back, all your good work will come to nothing – your plowing will be crooked and the field will be messed up.

My friend, what is it that you want to see behind you? Disappointments? Sin? Passions? Hurt? Missed chances? Stop looking behind you. Bring all the issues of your past to Jesus right now, and have done with them once and for all. And then look ahead of you. There is work for you to do. Do it well, with your eyes fixed on Jesus.

February 23

At His Word

Simon answered, "Master, we've worked hard all night and haven't caught anything. But because you say so, I will let down the nets."

ꕥ LUKE 5:5 ꕥ

"Fishing is in my blood, in my veins. It has always been my life, that is ... until today when Jesus turned everything in a completely new direction.

"Jesus of Nazareth came to the shores of the sea today and preached to the crowds from a boat. When Jesus had finished talking, He told us to let down our nets for a catch. I told Him it wouldn't be worth our while. We had labored hard all the previous night and still we had caught nothing.

"Because he asked us to, we threw our nets into the blue-green waters of the Galilee, and slowly began to pull them in. I could hardly believe my eyes. There were so many fish in the nets, and they were so heavy that it felt as if both the nets and my muscles wouldn't hold out! We even had to call the other boat to come and help us.

"Suddenly it was all too much for me. Something inside me broke. I looked into the eyes of this man from Nazareth and knew that I had seen a miracle. And when He looked at me I felt as though He could see right into the depths of my heart. Before I knew what I was doing, I, Simon, was kneeling in front of Him. My voice was thick and my throat dry as I said, *"Go away from me, Lord; I am a sinful man!"* (v. 8). Deep down in my heart I knew that He was indeed the Lord. And then He said to me, *"Don't be afraid; from now on you will catch men"* (v 10). As soon as we had pulled the boats ashore, I left everything and followed Him."

Perhaps Peter would have liked to say, too, that when Jesus speaks, we must listen carefully and then do everything that He says and trust and wait. At His Word things can change and miracles can happen because His Word will never return void.

Sent

But he said, "I must preach the good news of the kingdom of God to the other towns also, because that is why I was sent."

℘ Luke 4:43 ℘

Early in the morning, as the sun rose slowly over the hills surrounding the Sea of Galilee and the fishing boats rocked gently on the still waters, Jesus withdrew to a quiet place to pray.

While Jesus was away praying, people were looking for Him. He had become so well-known by this time, and was in such demand that people went to a lot of trouble to get close to Him. When they tracked Him down, they begged Him to stay with them, and not to go to another area.

It would probably have been very easy for Jesus to stay in the beautiful province of Galilee. There were so many people there who wanted to hear what He had to say, and their needs were great. He could easily have spent a year or more working purposefully among them. But He said to them, *"I must preach the good news of the kingdom of God to the other towns also, because that is why I was sent."*

For Jesus it was about much more than simply keeping busy and continuing to serve. A passion burned in Him to reach as many people as He could with the good news of the Kingdom of God. There were distant, forsaken, unromantic places filled with lost, spiritually starving, sick, bound and needy people who also needed to hear the gospel.

Jesus knew His calling. He had received His mission from God, His Father. That is why the despair that He saw in the people in Galilee could not keep Him there. He had to go. He was sent to other towns and to other people.

What calling has God placed on your life? Do you know why you were born? What instructions has your heavenly Father given you today? And what is holding you back?

February 25

Jesus in His hometown

"Today this scripture is fulfilled in your hearing."

ꕥ LUKE 4:21 ꕥ

After Jesus had been in the desert for forty days, where He had been tempted by the devil, He went into the province of Galilee, full of the power of the Holy Spirit. He taught people in the synagogues and everyone spoke very highly of Him. And then He decided to visit His hometown, Nazareth.

On the Sabbath He went to the synagogue, as was His custom. When He stood up to read from the Scriptures, He was handed the book of Isaiah. When He opened it, He began to read, *"The Spirit of the Lord is on me, … to preach good news to the poor … to proclaim freedom for the prisoners … to proclaim the year of the Lord's favor"* (v. 18-19). Then He turned and addressed the people, saying, *"Today this scripture is fulfilled in your hearing"* (v. 21).

When the people heard this they were furious. "Who does He think He is, trying to come here and teach us?" "We've known Him since He was a toddler. He grew up right under our noses, just across the street in Joseph's house." "One of the tables He made is in our kitchen!" And so Jesus' words that *"no prophet is accepted in his hometown"* (v. 24) came to pass. They rejected Him. The child from Nazareth. The Bible tells us that they were so angry that they wanted to throw Him off a cliff. But He simply turned and walked through the mob … and left. It was not yet time for Him to die.

Be careful that your familiarity with the gospel message or with certain preachers does not keep you from receiving the blessing of God. After all, it isn't about the messenger, but the message.

Come and see!

"Nazareth! Can anything good come from there?" Nathanael asked. "Come and see," said Philip.

JOHN 1:46

Jesus called Philip to follow Him and Philip immediately ran to tell his friend Nathanael the amazing thing that had happened to him. He did not want to keep it to himself

He said to Nathanael, *"We have found the one Moses wrote about in the Law, and about whom the prophets also wrote – Jesus of Nazareth, the son of Joseph"* (v. 45). We can't be quite sure whether Nathanael was kidding around, or if he was just plain skeptical. But he exclaimed, *"Nazareth! Can anything good come from there?"* (v. 46). And Philip simply replied, "Come and see." Seeing is believing. So come and see for yourself, and then you will know.

As Philip and Nathanael walked toward Jesus, He described Nathanael as a true Israelite, a man with no guile and who had no deceit in him. Nathanael wanted to know how Jesus knew about him. So Jesus said, *"I saw you while you were still under the fig tree before Philip called you"* (v. 48).

Nathanael knew this was impossible in human terms and he shouted out, "Rabbi, you are the Son of God; you are the King of Israel!'"(v. 49). Wow! What an expression of faith! Nathanael had discovered the truth, and he followed Jesus for the rest of his life.

Philip was the one who brought Nathanael to Jesus. He wanted to share what he had found with his friend. And I'm sure you already know what I am going to ask: how many people have you invited to "Come and see!" what you have found in Jesus? Won't you come and meet Jesus today?

February 27

Born again

In reply Jesus declared, "I tell you the truth, no one can see the kingdom of God unless he is born again."

ꕥ JOHN 3:3 ꕥ

Nicodemus was a member of the Pharisees, the largest and most powerful religious-political force in Israel. It wasn't easy becoming a member of the party. It required commitment and party loyalty. But the privileges made it all worth while. As a Pharisee, he had authority, and a voice. Of course, the Pharisees didn't really tolerate other voices. Power was maintained through manipulation.

He needed to be careful that his fellow-Pharisees didn't know what he was planning so he decided to go to Jesus in the dark of night. He really wanted to speak to this new Rabbi. He had heard Him preach a few times, and although he had been skeptical at first, he couldn't deny that he had been deeply moved by some of the things this Rabbi had said. And the miracles He performed!

Nicodemus declared, *"Rabbi, we know you are a teacher who has come from God. For no one could perform the miraculous signs you are doing if God were not with him"* (v. 2). In reply Jesus said, *"I tell you the truth, no one can see the kingdom of God unless he is born again"* (v. 3).

What could He mean when He said that he had to be born again? He was an old man. How could he be born a second time? Oh, Nicodemus! This is a new birth that the Holy Spirit brings about in your spirit. And the birth waters are living water, from the hand of God. And the water bears witness when you are baptized. The words of Jesus continue to resound across the centuries. Even if you know the Scriptures, the law and the Prophets; no matter how religious you are, you can only see and enter the Kingdom of God if you are born again.

Let your light shine

"You are the light of the world. A city on a hill cannot be hidden."

Matthew 5:14

God is Light and He lives in unapproachable light. There is no darkness in Him at all. In His light, we too can see light. And He sent His light into this world – for the world lay in the grip of the forces of darkness. John tells us, *"The true light that gives light to every man was coming into the world"* (Jn. 1:9) and *"The light shines in the darkness, but the darkness has not understood it"*(v. 5).

Just as the light of God is a reality, so too are the forces of darkness. Every place where the light of God does not shine is dominated by the darkness. And how terrible that darkness is! There is political darkness (which we see in wars and the battle for domination among people groups); social darkness (seen in murders, rape, child abuse, AIDS, abortions, and so much more); there is even theological darkness (in which men and women make statements about God that are contradictory to what the Bible says.)

And yet Jesus tells us, *"You are the light of the world … let your light shine before men, that they may see your good deeds and praise your Father in heaven"* (vv. 14, 16). The key that unlocks the light of God through our lives are the good deeds that we do in His name. And the good deeds that we do come out of a new heart and spirit that line up with the will of God and the words of Jesus.

So what should we do? James says, *show me your deeds and then I will see what you believe. Faith without works is dead*. As one man said to another, "It doesn't help that you keep telling me about Jesus. The wrong things that you do shout so loudly, that I can't hear the words you say."

What a shame it is when we Christians do not let the light of the Lord shine brightly through our good deeds.

February 29

What have you been called to do?

"I have brought you glory on earth by completing the work you gave me to do."

JOHN 17:4

We can become really stressed with everything we have to get through. Sometimes there are just too many things on our to-do lists for each day or each week. So often the routine actions of our daily lives keep us busy with things that rob our lives of meaning. We become involved in things that we have not been called to do. We are, of course, all called to love others and help them where we can, but we have not all been called to look after needy people on a full-time basis.

We can so quickly feel guilty if we think that we should be doing more for others. Jesus could so easily have felt the same way. And yet He seemed to know exactly what He needed to do, and what to leave alone. Think about how many times He withdrew from people so that He could spend time alone praying to His Father. Was this selfish of Him? Not at all. He knew that there was a time to minister and a time to be ministered to by His Father. He knew when to give out and when to be filled.

We read that He said, *"I have brought you glory on earth by completing the work you gave me to do"*(v. 4). In other words, He completed God's work on earth. This hardly sounds possible! What did He actually mean? What of the millions who still haven't heard of Him? What of the thousands who have not been set free from slavery?

"The work you gave me to do ..." That was what He had finished. The need is not the calling, the calling is the need. What work has the Father given you to do? Just do it. Let go of your false guilt about all that you cannot do, and all those you cannot reach. Do what you have been called to do.

March

March 1

An eye for an eye

"You have heard that it was said, 'Eye for eye, and tooth for tooth.'"

∞ Matthew 5:38 ∞

An eye for an eye and a tooth for a tooth. This was the Old Testament law for public defense. It was meant to ensure that people did not take revenge on those who had wronged them. If someone gouged your eye out because he was angry with you then you had the right to take out his eye (cf. Lev. 24:20 and Ex. 21: 24-25). The Pharisees upheld this law strictly, particularly when it suited their desire to take revenge. They did not take the original motivation of the law into account. It was supposed to prevent people from taking revenge but they used the law to justify their vengeful actions against others.

But here Jesus says that we should not even resist an evil person. He does not mean that we should allow ourselves to become punching bags, but He underlines the fact that we should always try to act in love. The spirit and attitude in which we act must bear witness against the lack of love in other people's lives, and against hatred and vengefulness.

Rather walk a while with the person who has wronged you. If someone forces you to carry his things, take it further than what he thought you would. If someone asks you to give him something, give him a little something extra. And if someone wants to borrow something from you, don't send him away empty-handed. And when Jesus says that we should turn the other cheek, then that is exactly what He is saying. We should not harbor a grudge against others and we should not desire to pay back a person who has wronged us.

Rather than becoming bitter and vengeful toward someone who has wronged you, rather show that person the love of Jesus Christ. The Bible is full of examples of people who did just this. This command is difficult to obey but it is possible to do in the strength of the Holy Spirit.

Bad company

"I tell you that in the same way there will be more rejoicing in heaven over one sinner who repents than over ninety-nine righteous persons who do not need to repent."

℘ LUKE 15:7 ℘

One thing that particularly irritated the Pharisees about Jesus was the way He befriended the ordinary sinners and tax collectors who came to listen to Him preach. They could still understand that He moved among the tax collectors and sinful people, but the fact that He ate with them was something that they found incomprehensible and shocking. From their legalistic standpoint, it was unthinkable and horrific for a rabbi to mix with overtly sinful people.

It is interesting to see how often the prostitutes, tax collectors, and sinners invited Jesus to their homes. It is even more interesting that He accepted their invitations. But it isn't that strange when we remember that He left behind His heavenly glory to come to the ash heap of the earth (cf. Phil. 2:6-7). Why would He remain aloof from the very people He had come to be with? This was why He could so often be found surrounded by sinners. He had come to offer them salvation and redemption. He wanted to show them the heart of God. He came to set them free from sinful bonds and from eternal judgment. Jesus' love compelled and motivated Him to move among these people. He saw how desperately they needed help and salvation, and He came to offer it to them. He wanted to help them find God. Quite simply, He loved them.

Many churchgoers these days look down their noses at so-called bad people and sinners. They would not even dream of mixing with "bad" company. They think that it is impossible to be friends with the homeless, alcoholics, and prostitutes. But this was not how Jesus responded to such people. We must also choose to mix with those who need God. We do not sin with them, but bring them the hope of salvation.

March 3

He rejoices over his sheep

"And when he finds it, he joyfully puts it on his shoulders and goes home."

LUKE 15:5

Jesus told the parable of the lost sheep in answer to the Pharisees when they criticized Him for spending time with ordinary, sinful people.

Jesus told the story of a man who had 100 sheep. One of them wandered away and got lost. Because he loved his sheep and cared about what happend to them, he left the ninety-nine in a safe place and went to look for the one that was lost. He kept searching until he finally found it. He was so glad when he did, that he lifted it onto his shoulders and carried it home with a song in his heart. When he got home he called all his friends and neighbors together and invited them to celebrate with him because he had found his lost sheep. And then Jesus said, *"I tell you that in the same way there will be more rejoicing in heaven over one sinner who repents than over ninety-nine righteous persons who do not need to repent"* (v. 7).

Jesus was not saying that He does not love the ninety-nine good sheep. Who are these ninety-nine? Perhaps He wasn't talking about righteous people, but about self-righteous ones. People who were good in their own eyes. People like the Pharisees. People who think that they are right with God simply because they are extremely religious. But they refuse to cooperate with the will of God. Jesus would rather go and look for the one sheep that had a real need to be saved. Such as the ordinary sinners who acknowledge their sin and really want to get rid of it.

Jesus wants us to know that He loves us very much. He cares so much about us that He will do everything He can to make sure that we do not get lost. That is why He became Immanuel – God with us. The Lord wants to come and sit beside you – an ordinary person with ordinary needs – and pick you up in His arms. He wants to be your Good Shepherd today (cf. Ps. 23, Ezek. 34:15-16).

The money disappeared

"And when she finds it, she calls her friends and neighbors together and says, 'Rejoice with me; I have found my lost coin.'"

Luke 15:9

A woman had ten silver coins. Each one was approximately equivalent to a day's wages for a laborer. It was probable that this woman carried these ten silver coins in a pouch around her neck. The material might have worn thin and she lost one of the coins. So, in order to find it, the woman lit a lamp and began to sweep her house. Houses in those days had very small rooms and they were quite dark. Because of the intense heat of the sun in that part of the world, the windows were very small and gave very little light to the rooms.

The woman swept and swept until she found the coin she had lost. She was so excited that she invited her friends to come and share in her joy. They rejoiced with her because she had not suffered any loss.

Once again, the meaning of this parable is quite simple. The love of God compelled Him to send His only Son to earth so that we will not be lost but can receive eternal life. This gift cost Jesus His very life. He set aside His glory and became a person. He walked the dusty roads of this earth to seek and to find people who were lost. Like the woman in the story, He did everything He could to find those who were lost. Yes, the One who had been worshiped by the angels in heaven came to earth to seek sinners. And He rejoices over each one that repents and turns to God.

All of heaven celebrates with great joy each time one sinner repents and is born again. Like the woman and her friends, the angels hold a feast every time someone turns away from a life of sin to walk with Jesus on the path of truth. We should never be untouched or unmoved when people come to know their savior. Let us celebrate with them and with the angels.

March 5

Back home!

"'For this son of mine was dead and is alive again; he was lost and is found.' So they began to celebrate."

ꕤ LUKE 15:24 ꕤ

The son wanted new adventures. He took his share of the estate and traveled far and wide. The money burned a hole in his pocket and he spent it carelessly. Much of it went on drinking, gambling, and prostitutes. And before he knew what was what he was bankrupt. He found a job feeding pigs and was so hungry he wished he could eat the pods the pigs were eating. But even that was denied him. He became depressed and began to think that life was not worth living. His father had tried to warn him, but he hadn't wanted to hear what he had to say. He had wanted adventure and this was where he had ended up.

But a glimmer of hope began to shine. He thought of his father's house, and decided it was worth taking the risk. He would get up and go back to his father and to his home. He would tell him that he was sorry about everything that he had done and ask if he could just be a laborer in his father's fields. He began the long journey home, and when he finally drew near to the house, his father saw him. And suddenly his father began to run toward him, calling his name and when he got to him, he threw his arms around his son and hugged him tight against his heart. Oh, what a relief! His father did not even think of rejecting him, nor did he question him about all that he had done. He was simply glad to see him.

This parable reminds us that Father God unconditionally welcomes back those people who are remorseful and who repent of their sins. The Lord wants to embrace you today. He does not question you about the bad things you have done, but He welcomes you just as you are.

He was angry

"The older brother became angry and refused to go in. So his father went out and pleaded with him."

ꟷ Luke 15:28 ꟷ

The elder son labored in the hot sun every day, and he was out in the fields when his younger brother returned home. He had harbored anger in his heart because his brother had left him alone to carry the load of work on the farm, while he went off to have a good time.

When he arrived home, tired out from his hard day, he heard music and the sound of people singing. So he called one of the servants and asked what was going on. The servant told him that his younger brother had returned home and that their father had arranged a party to welcome him back. He was livid, and he stubbornly refused to go into the house. A little later his father went out to find him. He tried to talk to his son, but for once the son told his dad exactly what he felt. He pointed out that he had slaved away on the farm for years and done everything that his father had asked, and yet his father had never held a party for him. And now there was a celebration for his good-for-nothing brother, who had wasted his father's money on prostitutes.

The elder brother's attitude reeked of selfishness and self-righteousness. He said he had worked like a slave. He was justified in his own eyes and felt that he deserved something for having obeyed his father. But his father said, *"My son, you are always with me, and everything I have is yours"* (v. 31).

The elder son's heart was hard and his judgment was harsh. This attitude is prevalent among some church members today. They have no sympathy for those who have messed up their lives. They point out how good *they* are and have no time for the weaknesses of others. But that is not how God treats us. Let us rid ourselves of the attitude of the elder brother.

March 7

Sometimes they are better

"The master commended the dishonest manager because he had acted shrewdly. For the people of this world are more shrewd in dealing with their own kind than are the people of the light."

ꟾ LUKE 16:8 ꟾ

Jesus made a startling statement. We would not really expect Him to say something like this and it would be quite easy to misinterpret what He was saying. What could He have meant by saying that sometimes the people of this world act in more intelligent ways than the people of His Kingdom?

Of course, Jesus does not want us to imitate the sly connivings of the world. The way the world acts, without the Word of God, is not the standard we should take for our behavior. And yet often the people who do not serve God show more wisdom and a better understanding than the children of God. To our shame, we must acknowledge that this is true. Someone once said that there is more love, understanding and sympathy in a bar than in a church. When drinking buddies cry on each other's shoulders, there is often a sense of real camaraderie that the church often shies away from. The world often shows more patience toward sin because they are surrounded by it all day long!

And the world is often more careful and diligent than the body of Christ when it comes to business. Christians often begin a project "in faith" and then make a mess of things because they didn't take the time to plan carefully and to act with discernment.

When Jesus says that sometimes people of the world act with more intelligence and insight than the children of the light, He is really pointing out the irony that we, who have received the Holy Spirit and can be led by God along the right paths in life, should have more wisdom than unbelievers. God wants to show us what we should do in every situation and so we should be showing the world what to do.

The clever scoundrel

"The master commended the dishonest manager because he had acted shrewdly. For the people of this world are more shrewd in dealing with their own kind than are the people of the light."

LUKE 16:8

This man came up with a clever plan. He was the manager of a rich man's property, but the rich man accused him of having cheated him of some of his money. He was actually a poor manager. The rich man called him in to give account, and said that he needed to submit a report of the way he had been managing the business.

The manager was in trouble. He had squandered money, and he was probably going to be fired. What could he do now? He came up with a clever plan. He went and negotiated with people who owed his boss money. One owed a hundred barrels of olive oil and he reduced the debt to fifty. Another owed a hundred bags of corn and he said he need only pay back eighty. Of course, the debtors were delighted with the new arrangements. They went around telling everyone how wonderful the rich man was – and what a good manager he had employed! Everyone in the community soon heard about the rich man's kindness.

When the owner of the property heard the way other people were talking of him and his manager, he realized he could not go back on the promises the manager had made. At least he got something of what was owed him and he was held in high regard. He had to make the best of a bad situation because his reputation was on the line. And he had to admit to himself that his manager was actually a clever scoundrel. And so the rich landlord ended up praising the manager because he had been so clever, sharp, and cunning. And in this way the manager secured his future.

Once again, Jesus is not saying that we should be sly and devious, but that we should plan carefully and strategize so that we can be successful in the tasks that He has given us to do.

March 9

Use mammon

"I tell you, use worldly wealth to gain friends for yourselves, so that when it is gone, you will be welcomed into eternal dwellings."

☙ Luke 16:9 ❧

The word Mammon is used only twice in the Bible, once in Matthew 6:24 and then here in Luke 16. It is the transliteration of an Aramaic word, *Mamona*. It quite simply means abundance or profit, but Jesus saw more behind it than that. He saw that it is an egocentric compulsion for gaining more and more possessions that rules a person's heart and so alienates him from God. When Mammon is your master, you do not possess riches, but they possess you.

Mammon can also be seen as possessions and luxuries that are available to people. It refers to the worldly desire for owning things. John describes it as, "*Everything in the world – the cravings of sinful man, the lust of his eyes and the boasting of what he has and does – comes not from the Father but from the world*" (1 Jn. 2:16).

Mammon, luxury, money, possessions are all things that are part of our lives. But Jesus says that we should be intelligent enough to use worldly wealth for the furtherance of His kingdom.

Be diligent in earning money, but do not make it the god of your life. It is a means through which you can serve the Lord. God gives you money and possessions so that you can use them to *"gain friends for yourselves, so that when it is gone, you will be welcomed into eternal dwellings."*

Let's make sure that we are not slaves to money but let us use what we have intelligently to build the kingdom of God and so store up eternal treasures for ourselves in heaven. Money is not something dirty, or bad, but provides an opportunity for us to serve God.

Trustworthy?

"Whoever can be trusted with very little can also be trusted with much, and whoever is dishonest with very little will also be dishonest with much."

ꕤ LUKE 16:10 ꕤ

In Luke 16 Jesus teaches about money and possessions and how we can use them to build His kingdom. We can learn much from unsaved people about handling our money with diligence and intelligence. He does not, however, want us to be devious, but to be trustworthy.

You and I have been appointed as stewards of God's money. He gives us certain things and expects us to manage them for Him with the wisdom that He gives us. Remember – they are not *your* trusts, not *your* shares, not *your* savings account, not *your* annuity. All of these belong to God, and you simply manage them. And the way you manage your money will show what kind of a steward you are.

Jesus says that if we are faithful in the little things, then we will be trustworthy with bigger things. But if we are dishonest about the little things, then we will also be dishonest in bigger things. Sometimes we try to separate spiritual and earthly things. We go to church and we dedicate ourselves to God, but on Monday in the office and in the world of business we apply a different set of standards. We don't think that we need to behave in a "spiritual" way there. But Jesus says that if we are not faithful to do the small things God's way then we will also fail in the big things.

Can you be trusted with the little things? When no one sees you and you are busy with your own thoughts, are you still loyal to God? If you and I can be faithful to God in the little moments of our lives, if we consistently act according to the Word, then God might use us for bigger things. Jesus says, *"So if you have not been trustworthy in handling worldly wealth, who will trust you with true riches?"* (v. 11). Let's be faithful in the little things.

March 11

Either, or

"No servant can serve two masters. Either he will hate the one and love the other, or he will be devoted to the one and despise the other. You cannot serve both God and Money."

೫ LUKE 16:13 ೞ

Jesus called on people to make a choice. There is no place for fence-sitters in His kingdom. Day by day we are called on to make the right choice in all things. We will either choose for Christ and His kingdom or for our own interests and ourselves.

Jesus says that no servant can work for two masters at the same time. If you have to work for two bosses at the same time, you will begin to neglect the things one of them asks you to do. And that is why Jesus says, *"You cannot serve both God and Money."*

Mammon represents the world's focus on owning things. It is all about having more, about the desire to gather more and more for yourself, often at the cost of other people. It is the unquenchable drive to accumulate more and bigger and better of everything.

There is a fine line between diligence and greed. We all need things just to survive from day to day, but when you step over the line to greed, Mammon becomes your master. Then your possessions own you. Then you serve the world and all that it consists of. As Christians we know that we can never be happy if we choose to live for material things.

Jesus teaches us to put God first and to live for Him. Make the choice today. Choose God and His kingdom or choose Mammon and the pursuit of things. What is your choice?

They mocked Him

He said to them, "You are the ones who justify yourselves in the eyes of men, but God knows your hearts. What is highly valued among men is detestable in God's sight."

ꟹ Luke 16:15 ꟹ

There are many people who choose money and possessions rather than God. Even many church members and spiritual leaders, like the Pharisees. When Jesus said that they had to make a choice between God and Mammon, they laughed derisively at Him. The Bible tells us that they were very fond of money. To other people they looked like good people and sincere spiritual leaders, but their hearts were filled with a love for Mammon.

We cannot hide our hearts from God. When the Bible talks about people's hearts, it refers to the very center of our being, the focal point of our existence; that which makes us essentially who we are. God always makes an appeal for our hearts. Proverbs 23:26 says, *"My son, give me your heart and let your eyes keep to my way."* Our hearts are often deceitful, but God knows what goes on in every person's heart.

Jesus also knew what was going on in the hearts of the Pharisees. They looked so good on the outside, but inside, they served Mammon. Money and possessions were far too important to them, but God says that He is not interested in how much we own. In fact, He says that their riches were an abomination to Him. Through their love of things they showed what was in their hearts.

Beloved, let us hold our possessions lightly. They are all gifts from the hand of God that He has given us to use in His Kingdom. Do not bow before things. Our hearts should be filled with a passion for God.

March 13

Divorce

"Anyone who divorces his wife and marries another woman commits adultery, and the man who marries a divorced woman commits adultery."

℘ LUKE 16:18 ℘

Divorce has reached epidemic proportions in our society. Even Christians go through the heartache of broken marriages and divorce. Jesus spoke out against divorce. It was important for Him that people who marry realize that they have made a vow before God and that they should do everything they can to honor this covenant. The bond of marriage is so important to God that we should never regard it as trivial or insignificant.

The Pharisees in New Testament times tried to bend the law of God to make it easier for them to get divorced. It got so bad that Hillel, a rabbi who taught during the reign of Herod the first, taught that a man could divorce his wife if she burned his supper. Another rabbi, Akiba (in approximately 110 AD) said a man could divorce if he met a prettier woman. But Jesus taught that divorce should not be so quick and easy.

In Matthew 5:32 Jesus said that there was really only one acceptable reason for divorce, and that was unfaithfulness to the marriage vows. The act of adultery already breaks the covenant of marriage, which means that when a husband or wife commits adultery the marriage is already broken. Of course God is still able to restore and heal a broken marriage when a husband and wife repent before Him.

We should not take divorce lightly, and we should not enter into divorce proceedings too hastily. Let us seek God's heart and make the most of marriage.

Remarriage: Adultery?

"Anyone who divorces his wife and marries another woman commits adultery, and the man who marries a divorced woman commits adultery."

Luke 16:18

These words of Jesus are difficult to understand. Many divorced people who have asked God to forgive them and who have remarried, find this verse distressing. If they are remarried, are they committing adultery in God's eyes?

We know that God desires that a husband and wife should stay together, and that they should not divorce, especially for shallow and trivial reasons. A man and a woman become one when they marry and that is how they should remain. But if they do divorce because of unfaithfulness, it becomes easy for the two newly single people to commit adultery again.

Matthew 5:32 can be literally translated as "whoever divorces a woman, except for unfaithfulness, exposes her to the temptation of adultery or sexual sins." If we do divorce for trivial reasons, then we need to bear the responsibility that our ex-wife or ex-husband, who is now a single and needy person, can give in to the temptation of sexual relations with another person, without being married to them. We should rather try to bring about a reconciliation between a husband and wife. We should also not enter new relationships too hastily.

Divorce is always hard. We really need to be sure that we have heard God before we do anything rash. There is forgiveness of sins and healing for everyone who comes to the Lord, even for divorcées. If you are divorced, pour your heart out to God, ask His forgiveness for your part in it, and receive His peace and blessing in your life. If you are in the process of getting divorced, think twice before rushing into it, and humbly seek God's will.

March 15

Keep on praying

Then Jesus told his disciples a parable to show them that they should always pray and not give up.

ᘓ LUKE 18:1 ᘐ

People talk about arrow prayers to describe the short, impulsive prayers they pray in an anxious moment. Of course it is not wrong to call on God in any situation we face, but prayer – or conversation with the Living God – is more than arrow prayers.

Jesus told a parable to make it clear that we should always pray and not give up hope. Have you ever become so discouraged that it becomes hard to keep praying with intensity and purpose? We live in a society of instant solutions. We use instant porridge, instant mashed potato, and instant coffee. The faster the better, we think. We don't have time to waste. But prayer does not follow that pattern. We need to be prepared to persevere in prayer, even when we sometimes begin to feel discouraged because it looks as if we will never see the answer to our prayer.

There was a judge who did not believe in God. He was a hard man and treated people badly. A widow came to him for help. Someone had cheated her out of some money. At first the judge did not want to help her, but she kept on and on at him until he finally decided that he would help her just to get her off his back. And then Jesus said, *"And will not God bring about justice for his chosen ones, who cry out to him day and night? Will he keep putting them off?"* (v. 7). With this illustration God encourages us to keep on praying and not to lose heart. Don't be so quick to give up hope in your prayers! Keep on knocking until the door is opened for you. Pray your case through, but pray in faith. Praying without ceasing is really praying in faith. Someone who really believes that God hears prayers and answers keeps on praying even when he can see no possibility of the prayer being answered. *"However, when the Son of Man comes, will he find faith on the earth?"* (v. 8). Let's keep on praying in faith. The answer will come when the time is right.

A wrong thank you

"The Pharisee stood up and prayed about himself: 'God, I thank you that I am not like other men – robbers, evildoers, adulterers – or even like this tax collector.'"

☙ Luke 18:11 ❧

To look down on others in self-righteousness is a horrid sin. God hates it. And other people don't like it either. When someone is condescending to you, you can sense it instinctively. When someone looks down on you, they have raised themselves up to a place that God did not intend for them to have.

A Pharisee came to pray. He was arrogant and made a great fuss and show of what he was doing. He raised his hands and his eyes to the heavens. He addressed his prayer to God, but only his tongue moved. His heart was stone cold dead. He described how good he was. He thanked God, but his thanks were inappropriate, because he thanked God that he was not like other people – like the thieves and robbers, the adulterers, and certainly not like the tax collector who had come to mumble near him. He reminded God that he fasted twice every week, and that he gave a tenth of everything he had. Not once did he ask God to forgive him, because there was no awareness of his own sinfulness. In comparison with other people, he thought the scale was balanced 100 percent in his favor.

But the tax collector stood off to one side, where no one could see him. He did not even lift his eyes to heaven, but struck himself on the chest and begged for mercy. He knew he was a sinner, and he knew that he was broken and lost. He grieved over his spiritual condition. God can do something with someone like that. That is why Jesus said that the tax collector, not the Pharisee, went home justified by God. Jesus concludes, *"For everyone who exalts himself will be humbled, and he who humbles himself will be exalted"* (v. 14). Rather be like the tax collector in your thoughts, words and attitude.

March 17

Jesus' question

"What do you want me to do for you?" "Lord, I want to see," he replied.

LUKE 18:41

Jesus was on the road from Jericho. His disciples and a very large crowd of other people followed Him. They walked past a blind beggar, Bartimaeus, sitting at the side of the road. He heard that Jesus of Nazareth was going past and so shouted out as loudly as he could, *"Jesus, Son of David, have mercy on me!"* (v. 38).

Many people scolded him and told him to keep quiet. But, Mark tells us, he simply shouted even louder and refused to keep quiet. He was a desperate man. Jesus suddenly came to a standstill. Against the expectations of the crowd, Jesus said that they should bring the blind man to Him. He jumped up and ran to Jesus. And then Jesus asked him an important question. *"What do you want me to do for you?"*

Jesus asks you and me the same question today, because He truly cares about the problems we have in life. The blind man answered, *"Lord, I want to see."* Because of his faith, Jesus opened his blind eyes. He was able to see clearly straight away, and he followed Jesus.

At first, the people had tried to keep him quiet. Why? In those days the rabbis would teach people as they traveled from one town to another. The travelers would walk with Jesus and listen attentively as He spoke. They did not want to be interrupted and that is why they tried to silence the blind man. They were so busy having "church" that they didn't even see the problem the man sitting at the side of the road had. Don't we also do this? Sometimes we close our ears to the cries of the people who call to us from the sidelines. We are too busy with our church life. But Jesus is different. He stopped when He saw someone in need. And He helped him when others would have ignored him.

We must guard against becoming so busy with the things of Jesus that we do not hear the cries of people who need a touch from God.

Save or judge?

"As for the person who hears my words but does not keep them, I do not judge him. For I did not come to judge the world, but to save it."

ꟸ John 12:47 ꟸ

In John 12 Jesus said that He is the Light that came into the world so that those who believe in Him no longer need to be in darkness. He also said that if someone hears His words and ignores them, then He will not judge them. Could this really be true?

Jesus said that His purpose in coming to earth was not to judge people. He did not come to damn people for being sinners and for not living according to God's will. He came, instead, to save the world. He is, after all, the Savior and Redeemer. His name carries within it the reason for His being on earth. He told people how to be set free from Satan, self, and sin. Jesus is first and foremost the Savior, not the judge. And, as His followers, you and I should also be careful that we do not judge others. We are not called to judge other people, but to bring them to salvation in the Name of Jesus.

But what happens when people choose to reject the words of Jesus? If they turn their backs on God and ignore what Jesus says, does that mean that everything's okay for them and they can continue doing what they please without any consequences? Not at all. Jesus said, *"There is a judge for the one who rejects me and does not accept my words; that very word which I spoke will condemn him at the last day"* (v. 48). Jesus did not judge people when He was on earth. But on the Day of Judgment when God will review every person's life, He will evaluate everything in the light of the words of Jesus. These people heard, but refused to respond. And His words will be the deciding factor.

We must be careful not to be judgmental here on earth. Let us rather bring words of salvation to people. On that final day there will be a judgment – but it will not be a task allocated to you and me.

March 19

Back stabber

"I am not referring to all of you; I know those I have chosen. But this is to fulfill the scripture: 'He who shares my bread has lifted up his heel against me.'"

༄ JOHN 13:18 ༄

Jesus suddenly became deeply heart sore. His soul was overwhelmed by sorrow and He said, *"I tell you the truth, one of you is going to betray me"* (v. 21). This was shortly before He was arrested and began to suffer for the sins of humanity.

The disciples looked at each other in shock because they did not really know what He meant. Simon Peter urged John to ask Jesus what He meant by this. So John asked, and Jesus replied, *"It is the one to whom I will give this piece of bread when I have dipped it in the dish"* (v. 26). He gave the piece of bread to Judas, and Satan entered him.

Jesus was deeply upset because for three full years He had shared the wonderful message of His kingdom with His disciples, including Judas. Judas had seen each day how He did all things motivated by the love of God. He must have been amazed by some of the miracles he had seen. He must have, on occasion, hung on every word of wisdom that came from Jesus' mouth. But Judas never fully committed his heart to Jesus. He took the words of Jesus with a pinch of salt. The miracles did not move him. And when his heart was completely hard, Satan took complete control of his life. And so he chose to do the unspeakable, horrendous thing. To hand Jesus over to be tried and crucified.

Jesus' heart was broken because someone with whom He had shared bread, with whom He had eaten and laughed and enjoyed time together, with whom He had sung praises to God, stabbed Him in the back.

It remains incomprehensible that people can hear the gospel, and walk with Jesus for a while then later turn around and stab Him in the back. May this never be true of you and me!

His tears

"Where have you laid him?" he asked. "Come and see, Lord," they replied.

ꟷ John 11:34 ꟷ

Jesus began to cry. He burst into tears is closer to the meaning in Greek. This is the only place in the New Testament where this particular Greek word is used. There were many times that Jesus wept. The tears were the result of the intensity of His love for lost humanity. They were tears of heartbreak because of the pain and suffering that people endure because of the sinfulness of humankind. Hebrews 5:7 says, *"During the days of Jesus' life on earth, he offered up prayers and petitions with loud cries and tears to the one who could save him from death."*

In John 11, Jesus wept because of the love He had for His friend Lazarus who had died. And He cried also for Martha and Mary and the other mourners. His tears were an expression of His sincere sympathy. He is, indeed, truly Man and truly God. His tears were not sentimental posturing. His tears were heartfelt and holy, cried by the compassionate Son of God. He asked where they had buried Lazarus. They showed Him where the grave was, and He went to it. When He looked at the grave He was once again deeply moved in His heart. According to human opnion, the situation was hopeless since Lazarus had been in the grave for four days. Martha warned Him that if they opened the grave, the stench would be overpowering. But Jesus was ready to show the glory of God to them.

Jesus prayed, and His prayer was a prayer of faith. He prayed for the sake of those who would see this miracle. Then Jesus called loudly for Lazarus to come out and suddenly Lazarus, still swathed in the grave clothes, walked out of the tomb. The glory of God was visible for all to see.

Jesus has the same compassion and sympathy for your pain today.

March 21

Climb down, Zacchaeus

When Jesus reached the spot, he looked up and said to him, "Zacchaeus, come down immediately. I must stay at your house today."

ഗ Luke 19:5 ജ

Jericho was an attractive town. This town with its palm trees and rose gardens was called Little Eden. Herod the Great built a large winter palace for himself there. And Mark Anthony gave the city to the Egyptian queen Cleopatra as proof of his love for her.

A man named Zacchaeus lived in the city. He was in charge of the tax offices, and was a very wealthy man. He heard that Jesus was coming through the town and he wanted to see what He looked like so he clambered up a tree because he was not very tall. Zacchaeus was very inquisitive about Jesus, but his curiosity very quickly turned to admiration. Jesus stopped under the fig tree, looked up at Zacchaeus, and said to him, *"Zacchaeus, come down immediately. I must stay at your house today."*

Jesus *must*. He did not ask if He *could* go to Zacchaeus's house. He had received an instruction from His Father and had to go there. This was the day appointed for Zacchaeus to meet his Redeemer and to make peace with God the Father. But other people began to moan and complain. Tax collectors were considered the scum of the earth. People thought of them as rogues and traitors because they were Jews who worked for the enemy. But Jesus went into Zacchaeus's house.

Zacchaeus was so profoundly moved by Jesus that he declared that he would give half of everything he owned to the poor, and he would pay back four times the amount that he had extorted from others. Jesus was delighted that salvation had come to the house of Zacchaeus because he understood how the kingdom of God works.

God still makes appointments with lost people. Be prepared to welcome Him into your home.

The river

"Father, the time has come. Glorify your Son, that your Son may glorify you."

ꟃ John 17:1 ꟃ

In John chapter 17, Jesus prayed for His disciples. He interceded on their behalf because He knew that He was about to be arrested. When He had finished praying, He went to the Kidron River with the disciples (18:1).

The Kidron was a little brook that usually flowed strongest through the winding valley outside Jerusalem during the rainy season. Jesus crossed this little river on His way to Gethsemane. There was an olive grove there, and a press where olives were crushed to produce oil, which is why the Garden had been called "the olive press".

He knew that His last hours of freedom were at hand. Judas had gone to betray Him and very soon the soldiers would come and arrest Him. He was about to die. Jesus had no illusions about this. He knew that He had to die for the sins of the world.

As Jesus crossed the river He could see the dark water beneath His feet. Some commentators believe that the blood from the animals offered in sacrifice by people who wanted God to cleanse them from their sins, flowed into this river. The animals were sacrificed in the temple, and their blood flowed into the surrounding rivers, including Kidron. So when Jesus stepped over this little river He could see the blood shed in sacrifice, and would, perhaps with a twinge in His heart, have thought that He as the Lamb of God would soon be sacrificed for the sins of all people. Soon His blood would flow to wash people clean of their sins in the eyes of God. It must have made a deep impression on Him. And yet He, with courage and conviction, did not back off, and later, when He needed new courage, His sweat fell to the ground as drops of blood. Oh, let's thank God for the blood of Jesus, the Lamb of God.

March 23

"Who are you looking for?"

Jesus, knowing all that was going to happen to him, went out and asked them, "Who is it you want?"

ꟷ John 18:4 ꟷ

The time had come for Jesus to be arrested. In the distance He could see Judas leading a troop of soldiers and the guards who served the priests in the temple and the Pharisees carrying lanterns, torches and bearing weapons.

Jesus knew everything that was going to happen to Him, and so He walked forward to meet the commandoes. Before they could say anything, He asked who they were looking for. Our Lord and Master did not run and hide in fear of all that was about to happen to Him. That does not mean that He did not feel some trepidation, but He was so completely committed to fulfilling the will of God that He took the initiative when things began to happen. He was in control in a very difficult situation.

They answered that they were looking for Jesus of Nazareth, and He replied, *"I am He!"* As He spoke these words, they came forth with such majesty and power and glory that they all drew back and fell to the ground. Was this because of the power of Jesus' words? Was it because of their amazement that He acted with such strength and such confidence? Did the Spirit of God strike them down? We do not really know, but we do know that they fell on the ground. Again Jesus asked who they were looking for. And again they said they were looking for Jesus of Nazareth. Jesus said, *"I told you that I am he."* And so they arrested Him.

The way Jesus approached His death is an example for all of us of indescribable power and faith. Let us serve Him with the same commitment and surrender when circumstances are against us.

The pull of the flesh

This happened so that the words he had spoken would be fulfilled: "I have not lost one of those you gave me."

☙ JOHN 18:9 ❧

When the soldiers who had come with Judas arrested Jesus, He made only one request. He asked that those who were with Him should be left alone. Jesus did not want His disciples to face the persecution that He was about to go through at that time. He had prepared them to carry His message of salvation to the world. By leaving them alone, the soldiers would also fulfill the words Jesus had previously prayed to His Father. *"I protected them and kept them safe by that name you gave me. None has been lost"* (Jn. 17:12).

Jesus made a way of escape for His disciples. They had to flee as quickly as they could. The road He had to walk now was a lonely road, even though it was the road God had set before Him. But Simon Peter did not concern himself with Jesus' words in this dreadful moment. He didn't seem to have heard anything of what Jesus had said. He was so upset that he felt he had to do something to try to save the situation. So he unsheathed his sword – something like a dagger – and hit out wildly in the direction of the servant of the High Priest. In so doing, he cut off his right ear. Imagine the consternation when they saw Malchus's ear on the ground. But then Jesus' words pulled Peter back to the necessity for obedience. *"Put your sword away! Shall I not drink the cup the Father has given me?"* (v. 11).

How often do we react in impulsive and fleshly ways in an attempt to set spiritual things right? We think that we are doing Jesus a favor, but we actually just get in the way and become a stumbling block in the execution of His will. If we listen more carefully to Jesus' will then perhaps we won't behave so inappropriately as Peter in a crisis situation.

March 25

Transparency

"I have spoken openly to the world," Jesus replied. "I always taught in synagogues or at the temple, where all the Jews come together. I said nothing in secret."

ꙮ John 18:20 ꙮ

Jesus was taken prisoner and brought before the high priest, Annas, the father-in-law of the head of the Sanhedrin – Caiaphas. Caiaphas had been the first one to suggest that Jesus had to be killed. His motives were anything but pure. He was devious through and through.

When Jesus stood before Annas he began to cross-examine Him. He questioned Him about His disciples and the things He had taught. Jesus informed him that He had always preached openly and that He had taught publicly in the temple and in the synagogues where all the Jews came together. He had said and done nothing in secret. There was really no need to interrogate Him since everything had been done in the open.

This was in strong contrast with the way the Pharisees and Scribes formed cliques and came together secretly to devise conspiracies. The more that we give in to the flesh, the more there is a tendency to form groups that function in secret. The devil always works in secret. And the effect is like the yeast that Jesus spoke of – that works its way through the whole lump of dough. Jesus, on the other hand, wants His truth to be always in the light. It should be declared openly because there is nothing to hide.

There is no place for secret meetings and hidden agendas in His kingdom. Everything is laid open before God and people. There is no place in Christianity for exclusivity, for tightly knit huddles that keep others out. Secret meetings and decisions made behind closed doors are out. Transparency is the mark of the kingdom.

Bread and wine

And he took bread, gave thanks and broke it, and gave it to them, saying, "This is my body given for you; do this in remembrance of me."

ꕥ LUKE 22:19 ꕥ

When Jesus and His disciples enjoyed the Last Supper together, He made a very special occasion of it. Today we refer to that meal as the induction of the Holy Communion. It was an ordinary Passover meal, but Jesus said things at this dinner that penetrated so deeply into the hearts of the disciples that it gave the celebration a whole new perspective.

Jesus broke the bread, as was His custom, and gave it to His disciples. When each one of them had a piece in his hand He told them that the bread represented His body that was about to be broken when He died for them on the cross. Therefore, each time when they came together again and they broke bread and ate it then they should remember that Jesus' body was broken for them so that they could be set free and receive life.

Then He took the wine, and He explained that His own blood would soon be poured out. As He bled to death, He would make it possible for people to receive His life. Therefore, each time that they came together and drank wine like this, they should remember the things that He said and praise and worship God because He died for them. Later Paul also wrote about the bread and the wine and said that Jesus instituted this practice so that when we take Communion with other believers, we will remember what our Savior has done for us (cf. 1 Cor. 11:23-26).

Communion is such a special occasion. It is then that we can remember in a tangible way that Jesus died in our place. In our mind's eye we can picture Him hanging on the cross and we understand that His body was broken and His blood shed for our sake. Then we take the bread and the wine and our hearts overflow with gratitude.

March 27

A powerless God?

"Do you think I cannot call on my Father, and he will at once put at my disposal more than twelve legions of angels?"

Matthew 26:53

When Jesus was arrested in the Garden of Gethsemane, Peter didn't quite understand that His hour of suffering had arrived. That is why he grabbed his sword and cut off Malchus's ear. Jesus rebuked him and said that all those who live by the sword will also die by the sword. How often do we grab a sword in an effort to settle things, and in the process there is always someone who comes off second best, who is wounded and suffers. As Christians, grabbing the sword should be the last of our options. A person who reaches for a sword sows discord.

Jesus told Peter to put his sword away because God was not powerless to intervene. The Lord does not need our strength and ability with the sword to protect His kingdom. Was this not the great heresy of the Crusades? The armies of Western Europe decided that they could do God's work better if they wielded swords in His name. And the church is still reeling from the effects of this heresy.

God is not powerless. Jesus said that the Father could send twelve legions of angels to help Him if the Father thought it was necessary to do so. That would be twelve times 6,000 angels. More than enough to deal with a handful of soldiers. No, we do not need to build His kingdom through might and violence, but by the Spirit of the Lord of Hosts (cf. Zech. 4:6).

Why then does God sometimes not intervene when you seem to be helpless? Perhaps God has a greater plan in mind with what you are going through. Keep trusting Him. God is not powerless, but is El Shaddai: God Almighty.

Care for each other

When Jesus saw his mother there, and the disciple whom he loved standing nearby, he said to his mother, "Dear woman, here is your son," and to the disciple, "Here is your mother."

℘ JOHN 19:26-27 ℘

We cannot fully understand or identify with everything that Jesus went through on the day of His crucifixion. A day of being beaten, cross-examined, rejected, and abandoned at the hands of His enemies. Then He had had to carry the cross until His knees buckled under Him and His ankles gave way. He just couldn't take another step. And then the nails smashed through His hands. The pain was horrific.

Some people had gathered at the foot of the cross. His aunt Mary, the wife of Cleopas, Mary Magdalene, and also Mary, the woman from Nazareth who had brought Him into this broken, fallen world. The blood poured out of the wounds the crown of thorns had made on His head and everything before His eyes was hazy and vague. And yet Jesus recognized His mother standing beneath the cross. John was standing with her and the other women – John, for whom Jesus had a particularly soft spot. He was not so caught up and focused on His own suffering that He was unable to see how distressed others around Him were. He realized that His mother would need to be cared for, and so He asked John to look after her. John would probably also be very sorrowful once Jesus had returned to His Father. And so He asked His mother to care for John. Jesus said that they should be like family to each other. Mother, here is your son, son, here is your mother. Now look after each other and love each other.

We too need to learn to care about what others are going through. The best way to follow Jesus is to show His love to others. Do not be so caught up in your problems and so focused on your own pain that you do not see the needs around you. Let us care for one another – spiritually, emotionally, and physically.

March 29

It is finished

When he had received the drink, Jesus said, "It is finished." With that, he bowed his head and gave up his spirit.

JOHN 19:30

From the moment that God said that He would send Someone who would crush the head of the serpent in Genesis 3:15, the devil knew that his days were numbered. And so he tried to wreck God's plan of salvation through Jesus Christ. More than once he tried to stop the promises God had made concerning Jesus' advent into the world from being fulfilled.

Think about the days of Esther. The enemy stirred up hatred in Hamaan's heart toward Mordecai and so formulated a plan to kill all the Jews who were in exile. If he had succeeded then he would have destroyed the bloodline of Jesus and He would never have been born. But God stepped in through the young woman Esther, and the Jews were saved.

And think about when Jesus was born. The devil worked in Herod's heart and he decided to kill all the baby boys in the surrounding area. In this way he hoped to get rid of the new King of whom the wise men had spoken. But God sent an angel at night to warn Mary and Joseph to flee. And so Jesus was rescued and our Redeemer grew to be a man.

Then there was the time when Jesus was in the wilderness and the devil tempted Him. He literally offered Jesus everything in the world if He would only not go to the cross. If Jesus had succumbed to the devil's temptations, there would have been no cross on Golgotha on which the price for our sins was paid. But Jesus did not succumb and so He could cry out from the cross, "It is finished!"

When God makes a promise then He sees it through to completion. When He gives His Word, He does what He says He will. You can trust each one of His promises for He will bring them to pass.

Thirst

Later, knowing that all was now completed, and so that the Scripture would be fulfilled, Jesus said, "I am thirsty."

JOHN 19:28

Jesus was dehydrated because of the horrendous pain and suffering He went through on the cross. He developed a fever because of all the wounds to His body and His tongue cleaved to the roof of His mouth. He called out, *"I am thirsty!"*

A jar of sour wine stood near the cross. When the soldiers heard Jesus say that He was thirsty, they dipped a sponge into the jar and used a long stick to push it against His mouth. This had been foretold in Psalm 69:21 where it says, *"They ... gave me vinegar for my thirst."* This would not in any way have lessened His thirst, and with this unquenchable thirst, He died.

When we hear these words of Jesus on the cross, we can't help but think that Jesus Himself said that He is the Living Water and if anyone drinks the water that He offers, he or she will never thirst again (cf. Jn. 4:13-14). We remember, too that He said He would send His Holy Spirit and those who are filled with the Spirit will have streams of living water flowing out of them (cf. Jn. 7:38).

Jesus had to suffer agonizing thirst so that we could be filled with the Living Water that quenches the thirsting in our souls. If He had not suffered thirst, we would not have had our thirst quenched. We remember too that Jesus, when He instituted the Holy Communion, said that whenever we drink the wine we should remember that His blood was poured out for us so that we would no longer thirst spiritually.

"Come, all you who are thirsty, come to the waters; and you who have no money, come, buy and eat!" (Is. 55:1). Let's come and drink deeply of the fountain of Living Water that Jesus opened on the cross for us.

March 31

Forgive them

Jesus said, "Father, forgive them, for they do not know what they are doing." And they divided up his clothes by casting lots.

ꕤ Luke 23:34 ꕤ

The first words Jesus spoke after He had been nailed to the cross, were a prayer for forgiveness for those who had persecuted Him. What amazing love! He was dying and suffering even though He was innocent, but pleaded for the sins of those who persecuted Him to be washed away in the eyes of the Father.

These words express the heart of the gospel message. The good news of Jesus Christ is that He came to set people free from the burden of sin. God the Father wants to forgive people and so He let His own Son pay the price for sin, and made forgiveness possible. Jesus asked His Father to forgive those who persecuted Him because they did not know what they were doing. How could they have not known? They knew something about Jesus, but they had not seen the full picture. They were spiritually blind and their understanding was dimmed and so they could not really see that they were crucifying the Son of the Living God.

If Jesus was so willing to forgive, should we not also have the same attitude? Christians do not keep a record of the wrongs of others. They forgive and acquit people who have harmed them. That is why Stephen, when he was being stoned for his faith in Jesus, used almost the same words that Jesus had spoken on the cross. *"Lord, do not hold this sin against them"* (Acts 7:60). When he had said this, he died.

We can never be thankful enough for the forgiveness we have from God through Jesus Christ. Even in this most unjust moment, He still interceded on behalf of His murderers and asked for forgiveness for them. Then He died in their place. Let us receive His forgiveness and also set others free!

April

April 1

In Paradise

Jesus answered him, "I tell you the truth, today you will be with me in paradise."

so LUKE 23:43 cs

On Golgotha Jesus hung between two criminals. One of them mocked and scorned and insulted Him with words such as, *"Aren't you the Christ? Save yourself and us!"* (v. 39).

But the other criminal rebuked him and asked if he did not fear God. And then he made an exceptional statement. He admitted that both he and the other criminal were only receiving their due punishment. They deserved to be nailed to the crosses. But Jesus had done nothing wrong and yet He had been nailed to the cross. This was an extraordinary confession of his own guilt, as well as a declaration that he realized Jesus was innocent and did not deserve to be crucified. Perhaps he had seen how Jesus was suffering on the cross. He saw with what dignity and strength and majesty He endured the pain. Perhaps he had been aware of how calm and in control Jesus was and was deeply moved by this. But the Holy Spirit was also at work in his heart. So he turned to Jesus and asked Him an unusual question.

He said, *"Jesus, remember me when you come into your kingdom"* (v. 42). With these words he acknowledged Jesus as King and he asked if Jesus would prepare a place in His kingdom for a sinner such as him. Perhaps he had heard Jesus teach once or twice and had seen how He forgave sinners who wanted to give their lives to God. And now he appealed to Jesus. And Jesus gave him the wonderful assurance that he would be together with Him in Paradise on that very day.

It is never too late to give your life to Jesus. This man was in the final minutes of his earthly life; he was dying. But he cried out for salvation and mercy, and God answered him. Praise the Lord!

Forsaken by God

And at the ninth hour Jesus cried out in a loud voice, "Eloi, Eloi, lama sabachthani?" – which means, "My God, my God, why have you forsaken me?"

Mark 15:34

Many people have, at some stage or other in their lives, said, "I feel as if God has forsaken me." What they most likely mean is that they feel isolated and alone, and as if no one cares for them or is able to help them. With due respect for the people who feel this way, we can honestly say that they do not really understand what they are saying. There has only ever been one person who was truly forsaken by God while He was on earth, and that was Jesus.

God the Father had been with His Son through every day of His life on earth. He had been present with His Son in a special way when He began to suffer. He was there when Jesus was arrested in Gethsemane. He was there when they dragged Jesus before Annas and Caiaphas. He was there when Pontius Pilate found Him not guilty. He was there when the lashes of the whip fell on Jesus' back. He was there when He stumbled as He carried the cross along the Via Dolorosa. He was with His Son when nails were driven through His hands and He was pinned to the wood of the cross. He was with Jesus when darkness fell from noon until three o' clock. But now suddenly, at three in the afternoon the Father turned away from His Son. In that one fleeting moment Jesus realized that His Father's presence had been withdrawn. Yes, the Father turned His back on the Son and He endured the worst of the worst agonies. Forsaken by God. In those moments Jesus was literally godforsaken.

He endured this for you and me, so that we need never again feel abandoned or forsaken by God. He did it so that we could always feel God's presence in and with us. Even though we sometimes feel lonely and alone we have the assurance that God said, *"Never will I leave you; never will I forsake you"* (Heb. 13:5).

April 3

Into Your hands

Jesus called out with a loud voice, "Father, into your hands I commit my spirit." When he had said this, he breathed his last.

ℬ Luke 23:46 ℭ

As far as we know these were the last words Jesus spoke on the cross. And in them we hear the note of victory. He was about to surrender His life, but He was not giving it to the forces of darkness. He committed Himself into the hands of His Father. The devil had no hold on Him and could therefore not drag Him into everlasting death. Jesus is the true Life, and when the Living One had to walk through the Valley of Death, He stood on the promises of God's words, confident that death can never swallow life.

"Into your hands I commit my spirit." This shows us that Jesus laid down His life voluntarily. No one took His life from Him. He gave His life as a freewill offering. Freely He chose to come to earth to make this sacrifice, and freely, for the sake of many He chose to die. But He committed Himself into His Father's hands.

In John 10 Jesus had already said that He was the Good Shepherd who gave His life as a ransom for many, and in verse 17-18 He declared, *"The reason my Father loves me is that I lay down my life – only to take it up again. No one takes it from me, but I lay it down of my own accord. I have authority to lay it down and authority to take it up again."*

Every person will die someday. How it will happen we cannot know, but we can be certain that we will die. But as Christians we know that when we lay down our lives, we, like Jesus, commit ourselves into the hands of our Father in heaven.

See and do

"Whoever has my commands and obeys them, he is the one who loves me. He who loves me will be loved by my Father, and I too will love him and show myself to him."

JOHN 14:21

Jesus described what a person who loves Him looks like. Such a person listens to the words of the Lord, hears the commands of Jesus, and then goes and does them. True love for the Lord is not mere lip service, but obedient action. The measure of the love we have for the Lord can be seen in the way that we obey the commands of Jesus.

And when we demonstrate our love for the Lord by doing as He says, then the Father will reveal His love to us. The Father sent His beloved Son to us to show us the Way and the Truth and the Life. Because the Father loves us, the Son naturally loves us too. And then something wonderful happens. The Father and the Son show themselves to those who love them.

There are many people, including some Christians, who do not have a strong love relationship with the Lord. Therefore they have a very limited understanding of God. They stumble around spiritually like someone with a flickering flashlight in a dark, stormy night. They have little or no spiritual insight. But something wonderful happens to those who obey God's commands and are filled with the Holy Spirit. God opens their spiritual eyes so that they can gaze deeply into the unfathomable wisdom of God (cf. 1 Cor. 2:9-10).

The more faithfully we obey His Word, the closer we are to His heart and we gain a richer and deeper wisdom and understanding. Let us willingly obey Him today! And He will reveal Himself to us.

April 5

The gardener's joy

"This is to my Father's glory, that you bear much fruit, showing yourselves to be my disciples."

JOHN 15:8

This well-known passage of Scripture about the vine and the branches, gives us insight into our intimate relationship with God and the fruit that grows as a result of it.

Jesus said that He is the True Vine. Every vine has branches and the branches are expected to bear fruit. When the life-giving sap of the vine flows through the branches, bunches of grapes are formed. Every Christian must ensure that he or she is always connected to the Lord Jesus Christ so that the life-giving sap of the Holy Spirit can flow through our lives and produce wonderful spiritual fruit. We must remain in Him so that we can hear His commands and carry them out. If we are not intimately connected to our Heavenly Father we will not be able to bear spiritual fruit.

When something disrupts the flow of sap the branches should be getting from the Vine, they do not produce fruit and are cut off and thrown away to dry out. Later on they are used as firewood.

Branches that produce good fruit will be pruned so that they can produce more fruit. Sometimes it isn't very pleasant when our Heavenly Father prunes us, but when we see the new and more abundant fruit we know that the pruning was worthwhile. We should not shy away from the pruning shears.

An important point to remember is that Jesus said that His Father is the gardener. He is the one who expects us to bear fruit, who works in His vineyard, and is delighted when He sees the fruit in our lives. He is glorified when we produce much fruit. When do we bear fruit? When we obey Jesus. Let's make the heart of the Heavenly Gardener glad through the righteous fruit that we bear.

A dead Bible?

"Nor does his word dwell in you, for you do not believe the one he sent."

JOHN 5:38

Is it possible to read the Bible, the living Word of God and not be affected or changed by it? Sadly, it is possible. We know that the Bible says that God's Word will never return to Him without accomplishing His purposes, but this is only true when the Father sends His word with a specific goal in mind and it is received in faith by the one who hears it. The Bible is living and active, but not for those whose hearts are hard and cold.

The Scribes and the Pharisees had the Old Testament. That, too, is the Word of God. There is the promise of life and life eternal in its pages too. And yet this word did not live in them because they did not believe the one whom God sent. They did not recognize Jesus in the pages of the Word of God. And so when they rejected Jesus, they also rejected God's Word. They had studied the Scriptures because they thought that they would find eternal life in it, but they did not realize that the Bible actually testifies of Jesus Christ, who is the true and eternal Life.

Take heed. We should not take the Bible in our hands and casually read it and think that we will have a living relationship with God. If the Bible does not bring us to the point where we acknowledge and honor Jesus Christ as Lord, then it will remain a lifeless letter to us. Those who find Jesus in the pages of the Bible, find true life. The Bible is the map that points us in the direction of Jesus Christ our Savior.

Take the message of the Bible to heart. You will find Him who is Life and who gives us Life.

April 7

Are you sleeping?

"Why are you sleeping?" he asked them. "Get up and pray so that you will not fall into temptation."

ꕤ LUKE 22:46 ꕤ

In Jesus' darkest hour, just before He was arrested in the Garden of Gethsemane, He wanted His disciples to keep watch with Him. Here, on the slopes of the Mount of Olives, He knew that His last hours of freedom on earth had come. And so He asked His disciples to pray that they would not be tempted (cf. v. 40). Why did Jesus say this to them? He knew that He was about to be arrested and that they would be sorely tempted to distance themselves from Him, their leader. What would happen to them when He was persecuted and abused at the hands of the Scribes and the Pharisees? Would they turn their backs on Him? Bear in mind that they were God's plan for the future. They had been chosen to spread the gospel message throughout the known world. And so Jesus asked them to pray so that they would not yield to temptation. They would only be able to hold fast to Jesus' words when others abused Him if their relationship with God was strong.

He went a little way away from them to pray. After He had wrestled in prayer He went back to where they were, and found them all asleep. It was very late and they were extremely tired, but Jesus had expected them to stay awake, and so He woke them and asked them again to pray so that they would not be tempted. We do need to sleep, but sometimes it is more important to pray, and then we need to resist the urge to sleep.

There are times when we need to pray very focused and purposeful prayers. God, through His Holy Spirit, will let us know when we need to sacrifice other things so that we can commit ourselves to prayer. We must guard against falling asleep when God expects us to go down on our knees and intercede for people and specific situations. We must not be sleeping disciples.

My will, His will

"Father, if you are willing, take this cup from me; yet not my will, but yours be done."

ᘓ LUKE 22:42 ᘐ

Jesus went a stone's throw away from His disciples and began to wrestle in prayer. The disciples fell asleep, but before they did they must have seen how Jesus was praying, how He struggled in prayer before the Father. In great distress and with tears and loud cries He committed Himself to His Father's will (cf. Heb. 5:7).

He prayed that the cup of suffering could be taken from Him. The cup that had, symbolically, been given to Him to drink, was as bitter as gall. It was sheer hell. The weight of the burden that had been placed on Him, the massive responsibility that He had to carry, literally crushed Him to the ground. His sweat was like drops of blood.

It is possible that Jesus literally sweated drops of blood. The medical term for such a phenomenon is *hematidroses*. Luke, who wrote this passage of Scripture, was a doctor and doctors will tell you that it is possible when someone is placed under intense stress and pressure that some veins can burst, and if they are near sweat glands, blood and sweat can be excreted simultaneously. It is possible that this is what happened to Jesus.

An angel came to strengthen Him. Oh, the ministry of angels! One day, in heaven, we will see how often they came to strengthen us when we were least aware if it. Jesus needed the strength the angel came to give Him, and so the Father sent an angel to minister to Him. And then He spoke the courageous words, *"Not my will, but yours be done"* (v. 42).

Are you prepared to set aside your own will? Thank God that Jesus was.

April 9

Mountains and hills

Jesus turned and said to them, "Daughters of Jerusalem, do not weep for me; weep for yourselves and for your children."

☙ Luke 23:28 ❧

Jesus was taken away with two criminals to be crucified on Golgotha. On the way there, the soldiers grabbed hold of Simon of Cyrene, who had just arrived in the city. They placed the cross on his shoulders and ordered him to carry it for Jesus because He had no more strength. Did Simon's life change radically on that day?

A large, motley crowd followed Jesus. There were some women who walked behind Him weeping and mourning. And in spite of all that had happened to Him, Jesus still took a moment to speak to them in love and to warn them, saying, *"Daughters of Jerusalem, do not weep for me; weep for yourselves and for your children."* He told them that the day would come when they would call out to the mountains to fall on them and to the hills to cover them.

Jesus was referring to the destruction of the temple and a large part of Jerusalem that took place in 70 AD when the Roman general Titus besieged the city. But He was also referring to the Day of Judgment that is still to come. John, in the book of Revelation, describes it, saying, *"'They called to the mountains and the rocks,' Fall on us and hide us from the face of him who sits on the throne and from the wrath of the Lamb! For the great day of their wrath has come, and who can stand?'"* (Rev. 6:16-17).

Jesus was saying that they need not mourn for Him and His suffering, but they should rather weep over what will happen to people who do not repent and turn from their wicked ways.

Make sure that you hold onto Jesus so that on that day you will remain standing!

The snake on the pole

"Just as Moses lifted up the snake in the desert, so the Son of Man must be lifted up."

ꕤ JOHN 3:14 ꕤ

Israel once again rebelled against God. The people had defied God and said to Moses, *"Why have you brought us up out of Egypt to die in the desert? There is no bread! There is no water! And we detest this miserable food!"* (Num. 21:5). And the Lord was angry. He sent poisonous snakes in among the people to strike them. Many Israelites died that day.

Then the people began to repent and they confessed that when they had said those things they had sinned against Moses and against God. And they begged Moses to intercede with God on their behalf and ask Him to remove the snakes.

The Lord told Moses to make an image of a snake and set it on a pole in the middle of the camp. Anyone who had been bitten could simply look at the bronze snake and live.

The full meaning of Moses' prophetic action was only revealed and understood when Jesus Christ was lifted up and nailed to the cross on Golgotha. He died on the cross so that people who were dying in their sins could be given new life. Jesus said that He, as the Son of Man, would be lifted up so that everyone who believes in Him will have eternal life.

We are dying in our sins until we look up at Jesus on the cross and in faith receive new life.

April 11

So loved

"For God so loved the world that he gave his one and only Son, that whoever believes in him shall not perish but have eternal life."

ഇ John 3:16 ω

Billy Graham described these words of Jesus as the gospel in a nutshell. If we do not have a lot of time to tell someone all about the Bible, we can simply quote John 3:16 to them, and thereby share the essence of the whole Bible with them.

What is the central message of Christianity? It is that God loves people, all people, every person in every farflung corner of the world. God's love for people crosses all boundaries and reaches every person who has ever lived. If ever we need proof that God is love, we need only look at Jesus on the cross. That is all the evidence we need.

The God who loves so much is the Father of Jesus Christ. He is not just any god. He is the God of the Bible, Jehovah, the Great I AM. And Jesus came to reveal the Father to us, making it possible for us to be reconciled to Him.

The love of God compelled Him to sacrifice His only Son. He sent Him to earth to become a man and live among us. He sent His own Son, He who is holy, spotless, without sin, and filled with the love of God, to offer His life as a sacrifice for the sins of all people. And those who believe in Him will not perish but will receive eternal and abundant life.

The gospel in a nutshell is: Incomprehensible Divine love, the sacrifice of Jesus, and eternal life as the gift of faith. Do you believe? Then you truly live!

A Bethesda miracle

Then Jesus said to him, "Get up! Pick up your mat and walk."

ꕥ John 5:8 ꕥ

The Pool of Bethesda lay just inside the Sheep's Gate. There were five colonnades there where many disabled people used to lie – those who were lame, and crippled and blind. Sometimes the waters in the pool began to move. People believed it was an act of God and would jump into the water to be healed. According to tradition, the first person into the water would be fully healed.

There was a man who had been an invalid for 38 years. It was just not possible for him to get near to the water. He was always too slow, and nobody would help him because it was every man for himself. Jesus knew how long he had suffered. He asked the man if he really wanted to be made well because He wanted the man to express his desire to be healed out loud.

Then Jesus said to him, *"Get up! Pick up your mat and walk."* Immediately the man was healed. It was a Sabbath day, and the Pharisees rebuked the man because according to their tradition he was not allowed to carry anything.

The Pharisees had their knives out for Jesus. They were looking for a reason to kill Him. And so they grabbed this man and began to interrogate him. All that this man knew was that something miraculous had happened to him. He had been lame for 38 years, and now here he was walking around like a young man!

Once again we see the passion and compassion Jesus had for people in desperate circumstances. When everything seemed impossible for this man, Jesus came into his life. How privileged we are to have such a Jesus with us every day!

April 13

Ulterior motives

"Do not work for food that spoils, but for food that endures to eternal life, which the Son of Man will give you. On him God the Father has placed his seal of approval."

ꕤ JOHN 6:27 ꕤ

After Jesus performed the miracle of feeding the 5,000, news spread like wildfire that He was handing out food for free. The very next day masses of small boats set out from Tiberius and landed near where Jesus was. The people searched for Jesus but at first He kept His distance from them.

The words Jesus eventually spoke clearly showed that He knew why they had come looking for Him. They were not there because they were awed by the great things that God was doing, but because they had received food from Him. The hearts of people are often so corrupt that we will do anything to enrich ourselves and to have our appetites satisfied. We will even try to use God to suit our purposes. But the Lord does not allow Himself to be used or abused by people.

That is why Jesus said that they should not work for food that spoils, but rather for the food that never perishes and that gives eternal life. Boatloads of people had come to Jesus in the hope of getting some free food, but He said that they needed to make sure that they received the bread that lasts forever and that is eternal. Spiritual food that would completely satisfy their hearts and their lives.

Do you perhaps have ulterior motives for serving God? Do you serve Him because you want Him to bless your business? Because you want Him to give you all kinds of things? What is the motive behind your service to Him? Are you trying to get something from Him? Or do you love Him because of who He is and not what He can give you? If this is so, then you will be truly satisfied.

What God wants

Jesus answered, "The work of God is this: to believe in the one he has sent."

℘ JOHN 6:29 ℘

By now we have a fairly good idea of what Jesus wants from us. He gave clear commandments and instructions and so much teaching on how we should live that we have no doubt what He expects from us.

Of course we could say that the whole of the Old Testament is filled with God's commands. As we read it we begin to understand something of His character. We see that He spoke to His people, the Israelites, and gave them very clear instructions about how to live their lives. We also know the Ten Commandments and acknowledge that they provide good guidelines by which to live a successful spiritual life. But here Jesus tells us that God has one primary desire in His heart. What He truly wants from us is to believe in the One whom He sent to us.

Here, in a short phrase, Jesus tells us what God expects of you and me. He Himself took the initiative to send His only begotten and clearly Beloved Son from heaven to earth to die on a cross for the sins of mankind. This was the loving and merciful action of the Almighty God. And now He simply waits for us to believe Him. The Messiah, Jesus, died for us and paid our debt of sin. The Messiah then rose from the dead and so broke the power of our greatest enemy. Now the ball is in our court.

God wants us to believe in Him, the Messiah. He wants us to say *yes* to the One who, through His life showed us God's love. Faith is taking cognizance of the truth and trusting Him. We acknowledge that Jesus is the Messiah and then we entrust our lives to His care. And when we do so, the Father rejoices. Then we please Him because we do what He truly wants.

April 15

Who is He?

"But what about you?" he asked. "Who do you say I am?" Peter answered, "You are the Christ."

ℰ𝒪 MARK 8:29 ℭℛ

Many people have very different opinions about who Jesus really is. People who spend a lot of time really studying what the gospels tell us about His life, discover that He was a multifaceted and fascinating Person. We know Him as the Son of God, and in saying that we proclaim that He is holy and perfect and was not contaminated by sin in any aspect of His life. On the other hand He was truly a Man, one that showed His humanness in so many and in such colorful ways that we are sometimes astounded by Him.

Some people like to think of Jesus only in terms of a gentle, amiable person whose love for people was so tender that He never said a harsh word to anyone. Others say that Jesus was a dynamic leader who did not kowtow to any devil or person who stood in His way. He set about achieving His goals with determination and performed mighty miracles. And yet others see Him as a friendly, sociable person who made friends easily with anyone He met, from the high to the low. He spent time with the down and outers, the dregs of society. Others see Him as the one who taught and preached and spoke wise words. Still others emphasize His deeds of compassion.

He is very likely all of the above and far more. He was both gentle and strong, both compassionate and a wise teacher. At times He used strong words but His words were always filled with love. Sometimes we do not quite know what to make of the hard things He said, like when He called the Pharisees a brood of vipers. And then we stand amazed as the tears roll down His cheeks when He looked at lost and broken people. Who is this Jesus? Let's ask Him to help correct any wrong impressions we might have of Him, and to let us see Him as He really is.

Bread

"I am the bread of life."

JOHN 6:48

In John 6 Jesus called Himself the Bread of Life. Bread was the staple food of the Jews in Bible times. It kept them alive. When they came together to fellowship and visit with each other, they would break bread together. And Jesus broke bread with His disciples too. He is the Living Bread that came from heaven and yet when He was on earth He also needed earthly bread in order to live.

Jesus drew on the history of the Israelites to explain what He meant. He said that Moses had prayed to God and asked that the hungry people would be given food to eat. And God sent them manna. Just as the Father fed the people with bread from heaven so He sent Jesus from heaven as the true Bread to give true life to people.

Jesus said that any one who comes to Him will never again be hungry. What Jesus meant by this was that people who come to Him will find that their hearts and spirits will be filled. He is the Bread that will satisfy the inner hunger of our hearts. The forefathers of the Jews ate manna in the wilderness, and still they died. But He is the Bread that came down from heaven and is given to people to eat so that they can live forever. When you eat of Him you will have eternal life.

Some time later, Jesus broke earthly bread with His disciples and said that each time that they eat of this bread they should remember that He gave His Body to us as the Living Bread.

Day by day we eat food, but soon we are hungry again. And at times we find ourselves spiritually starved as well. Let Jesus be as Living Bread to you so that your spiritual hunger may always be satisfied.

What gives life?

"The Spirit gives life; the flesh counts for nothing. The words I have spoken to you are spirit and they are life."

ꟷ John 6:63 ꟷ

The Bible teaches us that people are spiritually dead until they are born again and receive a new life that will help them to live a godly life. According to God, living is more than simply breathing. To be truly alive means that your spirit has awoken to the things of God and wants to honor and serve Him.

Paul explains, *"As for you, you were dead in your transgressions and sins"* (Eph. 2:1). You were dead even though you breathed and worked and played and ate and were involved in all kinds of activities. Spiritually you had no life and so you were dead. But then something wonderful happened. *"Because of his great love for us, God, who is rich in mercy, made us alive with Christ even when we were dead in transgressions"* (vv. 4-5). Therefore we see that the definition the Bible gives of life is far more than simply breathing. It is to be spiritually alive in Christ.

Jesus was very clear when He said that it is only the Holy Spirit who can give a person life. No person can do it for him or herself. Oh, how we long for people who are spiritually dead, and who walk around like breathing corpses, to find true life in Christ! Sometimes we feel like taking people by the shoulders and shaking them until they wake up spiritually. But that will not help. Only the Spirit of God can give life to people.

Therefore we need to spend more time in prayer, asking the Holy Spirit to work in people's hearts and bring life to them. We need to trust more in the Spirit of God and less in human efforts and human activities.

Offence

Aware that his disciples were grumbling about this, Jesus said to them, "Does this offend you?"

JOHN 6:61

Jesus spoke out strongly against people who had ulterior motives for following Him. After He had multiplied the bread and the fish, there were many people who followed Him simply because they had been fed, and were looking for more free food.

Jesus went on to say that in fact they needed to eat His body and drink His blood so that they could receive eternal life. This was a difficult thing to understand. It was a strange thing to say, and they didn't really understand what He meant. How could they eat His flesh and drink His blood? After all, they weren't cannibals!

Of course, Jesus did not mean what they thought He was saying. He was talking of spiritual matters. He is the Living Bread and those who believe in Him and follow Him eat of the living bread and receive eternal life. And they will never again be spiritually hungry.

And so they were offended by the gospel message. They said, *"This is a hard teaching. Who can accept it?"* (v. 60). Jesus asked them, *"Does this offend you?"* He spoke to them about their lack of faith, but, the Bible says, *"From this time many of his disciples turned back and no longer followed him"* (v. 66).

How many people through the centuries have turned away from Jesus because they have been offended by the Word of God that has been preached to them? Sometimes the things that Jesus said were difficult to understand. Be open to receive correction and to be taught by the Lord. Do not harden your heart and reject the Word of God in your life. That would be to play with fire!

April 19

Build or fall

"You do not want to leave too, do you?" Jesus asked the Twelve.

ꟃ John 6:67 Ꟃ

When Jesus said things that were difficult for His followers to understand, many of them were offended. Jesus was not going to pamper them any longer. He was not going to sugarcoat the truth for them. He clearly said that many followed Him who did not really believe in Him. They had their own ulterior reasons for following Him.

When He said these things many of His followers turned away and went home. They no longer wanted to follow Him. Then Jesus turned to His twelve disciples and asked, *"You do not want to leave too, do you?"* Peter quickly voiced his viewpoint, and that of the rest of the Twelve when he said, *"Lord, to whom shall we go? You have the words of eternal life"* (v. 68). Through these words Simon Peter made a definite choice for Christ, even though He sometimes said things that were difficult and hard to understand. He knew that Jesus' words were trustworthy and true and so he opened his heart to receive them.

We can either build our lives on Jesus Christ or stumble over Him and hurt ourselves spiritually. Peter compares Jesus to the cornerstone of a building. Either you build your life on Him and enter heaven, or you stumble over Him and go to hell. The choice is yours. Jesus is the precious cornerstone, but what you do with Him determines your future. Peter said, *"See, I lay a stone in Zion, a chosen and precious cornerstone, and the one who trusts in him will never be put to shame"* (1 Pet. 2:6). But he also says, *"A stone that causes men to stumble and a rock that makes them fall"* (1 Pet. 2:8).

Let us, in faith, build our lives on Jesus. Those who do not will stumble over Him and fall.

Righteous judgment

"Stop judging by mere appearances, and make a right judgment."

JOHN 7:24

When Jesus healed the invalid at the pool of Bethesda, the Pharisees finally decided that they wanted to have Him killed. They came to this decision because He worked this miracle on the Sabbath day. Jesus entered into a discussion with the Pharisees, the Scribes, and the crowds that stood around Him. He pointed out that they had the wrong perspective because they thought that people should not be healed on the Sabbath day. They were so obsessed with rules and regulations that they could not always clearly see the purposes of God.

And then Jesus said something very important. He was concerned about the fact that they judged Him unfairly. They had already clearly made up their minds and judged Him based on their own opinions and not on the facts. They had prejudged Him and condemned Him without cause. Jesus said, *"Stop judging by mere appearances, and make a right judgment"* (v. 24).

Is this perhaps why there is so often strife between people, even in the body of Christ? Do we not also too easily and too readily condemn things without looking at them objectively? We let all kinds of people fill our ears with all kinds of ideas and are influenced by all kinds of things. And so we do not see clearly. Don't make judgments based on what you hear and see. Jesus says that we should first gather all the appropriate information so that we can make the right judgments. Beware of personal perceptions that are not based on the truth. Don't be too quick to state an opinion about another person or situation. First make sure that you see the big picture and find out what lies behind what you hear and see.

April 21

With Me

"The one who sent me is with me; he has not left me alone, for I always do what pleases him."

JOHN 8:29

There is no safer place in all the world than being in the center of God's will. When you are in the place where God wants you to be, you have the best protection from your heavenly Father.

The Christian life is not for the faint of heart. We live in the lion's territory. The roaring lion that Peter talks about walks around looking for someone to devour (cf. 1 Pet. 5:8). Life is not a kid's game. Life is sometimes very hard and dangerous. Jesus knew this, which is why He was also careful always to do the Father's will. He knew that if He obeyed His Father nothing could in any way harm Him, unless it were in His Father's will for Him. More than once Jesus said that He did nothing on His own but only those things that the Father showed Him to do.

And then He assured His listeners that the God who had sent Him was always with Him. He had never left Him alone. Why? Jesus explains, *"I always do what pleases him."*

Beloved, if you want security and to be safe in God, do what He asks you to do and you will be able to live your life free from fear. Even if you walk through the valley of the shadow of death, you can be assured that He is with you (cf. Ps. 23:4). The safest place on earth is in God's will.

You are free!

"Then you will know the truth, and the truth will set you free."

ꟷ John 8:32 ꟷ

Every person is caught in the grip of sin. When you accept Satan's lies as true in your life, then you are his prisoner. You need to be set free, to be saved from the lie the devil has spoken over you.

Jesus, our Savior, came to set us free. He did this through His words and through obediently laying down His life on the cross to pay the price for our sin. He truly sets people free. Only when the Son sets us free can we be really free. Everyone who sins is actually a slave to sin. But Jesus came to set the slaves to sin free. How?

When we hear the words of Jesus and faithfully follow them we become His true disciples and then we will know the truth and the truth will set us free. Jesus' words are the truth and each time we deliberately choose to obey them, we experience freedom in our lives.

We are free from guilt, free of self and Satan, free to live for Christ. And no one can take this freedom away from you, even if they send you to prison in chains. They could even kill you, but the freedom that is deep in your heart cannot be taken from you by anyone or anything. You are free, free, free, forever free!

That is why it is imperative to hear the truth regularly. That is why we need to desire to hear the truth each day. Then we will live in freedom. Unfortunately, our ears are assaulted each day by a package of lies.

April 23

Children of the devil

"You belong to your father, the devil, and you want to carry out your father's desire. He was a murderer from the beginning, not holding to the truth, for there is no truth in him. When he lies, he speaks his native language, for he is a liar and the father of lies."

ꕤ John 8:44 ꕤ

On one occasion when Jesus spoke to the Pharisees, He told them that He only said the things His Father told Him to say. The snide reaction of the Pharisees was that Abraham was their father. Jesus responded by saying that if they really were children of Abraham then they would do what Abraham did. But they wanted to kill Jesus, which showed that they were not Abraham's children. Jesus said that they had deceived themselves.

The Pharisees insisted that they were God's children, but Jesus said that they were confused. If they were God's children they would have loved Jesus, because He came from God. And then He clinched it with these shocking words, *"You belong to your father, the devil, and you want to carry out your father's desire"* (v. 44). This was an outrageous thing to say. But it was unfortunately true.

People have only one biological father. It is impossible to have two. And people can also have only one spiritual father. It is impossible to have two. Either the heavenly Father is the father of your spirit, or the devil is. And the devil is, of course, a murderer. He is also the father of lies. That's what Jesus said.

But, those of us who have been born again, have God as our Father because we have been born from the seed of His Word.

Spiritual Blindness

Jesus said, "For judgment I have come into this world, so that the blind will see and those who see will become blind."

JOHN 9:39

Jesus healed a blind man's eyes. Suddenly he was able to see. And he believed in Jesus. Later on he told the Pharisees that if Jesus were not God He would not have been able to heal him. But the Pharisees remained spiritually blind, even though they had the evidence of this man's healing right before their eyes. Their hearts were hard, and they rejected Jesus.

The previously blind man worshiped Him with sincere humility. And the Pharisees rejected Him with coldness and hatred. Jesus, always had diametrically opposite effects on people. Some received Him with joy and were blessed; others rejected Him and were judged. That is why Jesus said that He came to earth to offer people a choice.

People can pretend that Jesus does not exist. They can block their ears to His words. But they cannot ignore Him. He is the Son of God and He came to live among us. The very fact that He came to earth means that people have to make a decision regarding Him. Either you are for Him or against Him.

In Matthew 25:33 Jesus explained that a great division will take place. This division will occur on the Day of Judgment when God will sit on His throne and separate the goats from the sheep. Jesus asks us to make a decision right here and now. People must make a choice and ask themselves where they stand regarding Jesus Christ.

Jesus is not just vaguely near where we are. He does not stand on the sidelines of our lives. He stands right in front of each one of us and asks us to make a decision. Those who think they can see, says Jesus, are actually blind if they do not accept Him. Those who realize that they are blind and want to be able to see clearly will have the eyes of their spirits opened when they accept Him in faith.

April 25

The Shepherd

"I am the good shepherd. The good shepherd lays down his life for the sheep."

ꚛ JOHN 10:11 ꚛ

The parable Jesus told of the Good Shepherd is filled with beautiful spiritual truths. We are His sheep and the sheep follow Him because they recognize His voice. When they hear strange words that are not in line with the words of the Shepherd then they refuse to go that way. Verse 5 says that they will never follow the voice of a stranger.

This parable also tells us that the Good Shepherd calls each sheep by name. Many centuries previously, in the days of Isaiah, God had already confirmed that He knows each of us by name and that He calls us His own. How wonderful to know that your name is in God's thoughts today.

Not only do the sheep listen to Him, but they also follow Him. In the words of the old song, "Where He leads they will follow." Where does the Shepherd want to lead you today? It isn't always clear, but it is always safe to follow Him.

The Shepherd also brings us to the place where there is much grass to be grazed. This symbolizes His care for us, and the peace that He gives us so that we no longer have any reason to be anxious. There are thieves who want to kill, steal, and destroy, but our Good Shepherd gives us life, and life that overflows. What joy to know that whatever you need today, your heavenly Father can give you!

Not only do the sheep recognize the voice of the Good Shepherd, but He also knows His sheep. Praise the Lord because He knows me. He knows everything about me and still He loves me.

Finally, the Good Shepherd promised that He would lay down His life for His sheep. He did this for us on the cross on Golgotha. And that is why He is able to give you, and all His other sheep, eternal life. Through all eternity they will never be lost. No one will be able to take us out of His hand.

Compelling Jesus

"When I am lifted up from the earth, will draw all men to myself."

JOHN 12:32

In a wrestling match, the wrestlers try to throw each other to the ground and the one tries to prevent the other from overpowering him by lying on top of him. The wrestler that can pin his opponent to the floor by lying on top, wins. In John 12:31-32, Jesus says, *"Now is the time for judgment on this world; now the prince of this world will be driven out. But I, when I am lifted up from the earth, will draw all men to myself."*

Jesus refers to two different movements: He will move up and the devil, His opponent, will be pushed under. The time had come to pin him down on the ground. And in the process Jesus will be lifted up. He is the victor in this battle between light and darkness. The power of the devil over the nations of the world was broken by the death and resurrection of Jesus. That is why Jesus said that He would be lifted up and all people from all nations who believe in Him will be drawn to Him. His victory will be like a magnetic force field that draws people into an intimate relationship with their Savior.

In the verse that follows we are given an explanation of what Jesus meant when He said that He would be lifted up. This was a reference to the cross that would be raised on Golgotha and on which Jesus would hang. People who, in faith, accept His death on the cross on their behalf become His followers. More than that, they partake of His very nature. Jesus was lifted up on the cross, and then He was raised up from the dead. Then He ascended to heaven where He now rules and reigns. His work of victory lifted Him up while the devil's defeat sent him under. In the great wrestling match he was pinned down by someone stronger than him. Today turn your eyes toward the Lord who was lifted up from the earth.

April 27

Neither do I

"No one, sir," she said. "Then neither do I condemn you," Jesus declared. "Go now and leave your life of sin."

℘ JOHN 8:11 ℘

If we look at all the so-called heathen gods that exist, the gods and idols of the Hindus and Muslims and Buddhists, and a whole collection of others, then we notice that the people who serve these gods do not just respect them. They are terrified of them. They believe that if they do anything wrong then the gods will punish them. Is Jesus like that too?

Of course Jesus sets high standards for His disciples, but He also gives us the means to attain His standards. He empowers us through His Holy Spirit. Every person on earth will be judged at the end of their lives, but the true children of God do not need to fear because there is no condemnation for those who believe in Jesus (cf. Rom. 8:1).

When the Pharisees dragged the woman caught in adultery to Jesus, He handled her with tenderness and love. It isn't what we would really expect from God. We expect God to pronounce judgment on a sinner. Shouldn't He have pointed out what was morally right and wrong? At the very least He could have told her that it was her own fault she had ended up in such a mess. He should have done something to make her believe and feel that she had done wrong.

But He didn't do that. There was no word of condemnation. No judgment. In fact, He spoke sharply to the Pharisees who with indignant and self-righteous hearts had dragged her to Him. *"Where are they? Has no one judged you or condemned you?" "No one, Lord," she answered quietly. And then Jesus said, "Neither do I. Go, and sin no more."* I'm pretty certain that she never again sinned in this way. A Lord who sets us free from sin, who forgives, who loves us so much, is a God that is worth serving.

Skeletons in the closet

When they kept on questioning him, he straightened up and said to them, "If any one of you is without sin, let him be the first to throw a stone at her."

ꕤ John 8:7 ꕤ

Before she knew what was what, they were in the room where she was with her lover. Chaos, shame, fear burst lose inside her. The Sanhedrin! The rigid religious leaders! She realized she was as good as dead. They pulled her up roughly, called her a slut and ordered her to get dressed. Then they grabbed hold of her and dragged and pushed and shoved her all the way to the synagogue where a Man was standing teaching. They formed a ring around her and shoved her into the middle. And then they spoke to the Man. *"Teacher, this woman was caught in the act of adultery. In the Law Moses commanded us to stone such women. Now what do you say?"* (vv. 4-5).

The Man was quiet. Everyone's attention was focused on Him, but He said nothing. Then suddenly He bent forward and began to write something in the dust of the ground. The accusers kept on insisting that He answer them, and finally He looked at them and said, *"If any one of you is without sin, let him be the first to throw a stone at her."* And then He continued writing.

Whatever He wrote and said, caused all of them, one by one, to turn away in shame.

Suddenly she realized that she was free. A sense of relief swept through her, and a deep sense of gratitude to this Man. There was no judgment or condemnation in His eyes. She found only sympathy and compassion in Him. And then He spoke to her, asking where her accusers had gone, and whether anyone had condemned her. As if He didn't know! And then her heart melted before Him. She knelt and called Him Lord. And He said that He did not condemn her.

She never forgot Him and His compassion.

April 29

A den of thieves

"It is written," he said to them, "'My house will be a house of prayer'; but you have made it 'a den of robbers.'"

LUKE 19:46

When He walked into the temple that day, He was immediately angry. It was like a madhouse in this holy place where people came to worship His Father. It was worse than market day in the streets of Jerusalem. And this was His Father's house where people came to pray. He could not tolerate it anymore.

The Passover was at hand and it was a busy time for those who sold animals to be offered in sacrifice, a time when they could make good money. Of course people could bring their own animals to be sacrificed but the chances were good that the priests would find some reason or other to reject the animals they brought. Of course, the priests got a cut of the business deals!

No wonder Jesus was upset. These people were like robbers who exploited the worshipers. And all in the name of religion. They made it difficult for people to bring their offerings to the temple because many of them couldn't afford to pay the prices the traders charged.

Jesus' eyes flashed with indignation, and with the wrath of God in Him, He drove the traders and animals out of the temple. While He was doing this He reminded them that His Father's house was supposed to be a house of prayer for all nations (cf. Mk. 11:17) and not a den of thieves.

Today you and I are the temple of the Holy Spirit. God no longer lives in temples made with hands (cf. 1 Cor. 6:19; Acts 17:24). We should approach worship with sincerity and soberness. We must avoid presenting worship, prayer, and the gospel in commercialized ways. The issue is not what we can get out of times of worship. It is reaching out in Spirit and Truth from within our inner hearts to the God who lives in us.

The best wine

Then he told them, "Now draw some out and take it to the master of the banquet."

℘ John 2:8 ℘

Jesus had been invited to attend a wedding feast. It was a wonderful time of celebration. The celebrations had been going very well, but the wine had been finished too soon. It was unthinkable to have a wedding feast without wine.

Mary knew in her heart that Jesus was the Son of God and could do anything. And so she asked Him to help in this situation. At first He was a little reluctant but Mary, in faith, told the waiters to do whatever Jesus said.

Jesus instructed the waiters to fill six large water jars, each of which could hold about twenty-five gallons of water. Then He said that they should take some of the water out and go and show it to the master of ceremonies. What a surprise he got when he tasted it. It was the best quality wine he had ever tasted. Usually the best wine was served first at weddings and when everyone had drunk that, the not-so-good wine was served. But here the best wine was being served at the end. The wedding celebration could go on. But more important was that this was Jesus' first public miracle and as a result of it His disciples believed in Him.

It is clear from this that Jesus honors the institution of marriage. At times the Bible refers to Him as the Bridegroom. And His disciples, those who believe in Him, are called the Bride.

He also demonstrated His desire to share His gifts and abundance with people. Not only to fulfill them spiritually but also to provide for their earthly needs. He even reaches out and helps us in moments that could otherwise be embarrassing for us. Trust that Jesus knows your situation well and, with a heart filled with love for you, can work a miracle in your life.

May

Legion

Jesus asked him, "What is your name?" "Legion," he replied, because many demons had gone into him.

ꕥ Luke 8:30 ꕥ

Jesus and His diciples were in the region of the Gerasenes. A heathen area. A man approached them. Children used to flee in terror when they saw this man. Everything he did indicated that he was demon-possessed, and he wore no clothes.

There had been a time when he had been normal. When he had lived normally among people in a house, and had earned his daily bread with dignity. But an evil spirit had overwhelmed him. Eventually people had tied him up, but time and time again he would tear the ropes off himself and flee into the desert. He refused to return home, choosing instead to live among the tombstones.

When Jesus saw him, He knew immediately what was wrong, and He rebuked the evil spirit in him. The evil spirit begged Jesus not to punish him. (It's interesting to note that the evil spirit knew that Jesus is the Son of God.) Jesus discovered that the evil spirit's name was Legion, because there were in fact a whole horde of evil spirits that had taken possession of this man. Jesus cast them out, sent them into a herd of pigs, and filled the man's heart with His peace and strength.

The next day the people of the town found the man sitting at Jesus' feet. He was calm, and dressed, and in his right mind. His eyes were full of worship and adoration for the One who had saved him from the hellish torment he had endured – and he had just one desire – to be near to Jesus forever.

Perhaps your circumstances were not quite so desperate. Or were they? Who can distinguish the degrees of being lost? You can't be more or less lost. And isn't every kind of spiritual lostness a desperate plight? But Jesus speaks into our situation and everything changes! We too go and sit at His feet and worship Him.

May 2

What are your priorities?

"Return home and tell how much God has done for you." So the man went away and told all over town how much Jesus had done for him.

℘ LUKE 8:39 ℘

The people of Gerasenes did not know what to do with the demon-possessed man. They left him to sleep in the cemetry.

And then one day the herdsmen that the pig farmers had appointed to look after their pigs came rushing into the town. Something awful had happened. Every single pig had drowned!

There must have been a vehement reaction to their news. Revenge! Who did this!? We'll sue for damages. Which of the herdsmen hasn't done his job properly? But the explanation that they gave was confusing. The mad man? What had he done now? No, it was another man. He spoke to the mad man and suddenly the pigs began charging around as if they were possessed. Before they could do anything the pigs hurled themselves off the edge of the cliff, fell into the sea, and drowned.

When the farmers arrived at the "scene of the crime" they saw that the mad man was sitting in front of Jesus, completely normal. There was definitely something strange on the go. And they were suddenly fearful. Those who had witnessed the whole episode told the others that the mad man was completely healed and restored. But instead of marveling at what had happened, the only thing they could think of was the financial loss they had suffered. Afraid of what else this stranger in their midst might do, they begged Him to leave them alone, *"because they were overcome with fear"* (v. 37). And so Jesus left.

Their earthly possessions were more important to them than a miracle that had brought heaven into their midst. Their pigs were more important than a poor, confused, pathetic, possessed man – a man who was one of their own. They were cold-hearted materialists.

"Welcome"

The crowds learned about it and followed him. He welcomed them and spoke to them.

ꟓ LUKE 9:11 ꟓ

People jostled each other in an attempt to get near to Jesus. As His ministry increased, the crowds following Him grew too. Think for a moment about how taxing it must have been to have to pay attention to so many people. That is why Jesus found it so necessary to set aside times when He could rest. Luke 9:10 says that He took His disciples with Him and set out for Bethsaida where they could be alone.

But then verse 11 says, *"But the crowds learned about it and followed him."* People were desperate to be fed spiritually. Many of them were also sick and really wanted to be healed. When they figured out where Jesus and His disciples were heading, they chased after Him.

We would probably think that when Jesus saw the large crowd that had followed Him, He would explain that He was very tired and that He and His disciples wanted a little time out. But that was not how He reacted when He saw them. *"He welcomed them."* He did this because He had pity on them and was moved by their plight. His heart went out to them (cf. Mk. 6:34). The need of the people – the sick, those who had lost hope and were discouraged, the hungry – meant more to Him than His own need for rest and relaxation. Therefore, He immediately began to talk to them about the Kingdom of God.

You and I do need times to rest, but we must guard against selfishly serving our own interests and ignoring the needs of those around us. Especially when somebody comes knocking on your door for help. Even if it is inconvenient for you, follow Jesus' example and welcome them.

May 4

The Kingdom of God

He welcomed them and spoke to them about the kingdom of God, and healed those who needed healing.

Luke 9:11

When Jesus and His disciples drew aside to get some rest the crowds did not leave them alone. We read yesterday how He welcomed them and began to talk to them.

Jesus spent much of His time teaching about the kingdom of God. In those days people lived under the heavy burden of Pharisaism and Rabbinical tradition. Day after day they were told how far they were from being able to have a relationship with God, about how badly they broke the laws of God, that they were doomed because they could not keep the law. But Jesus taught them from a completely different perspective. Firstly He emphasized that no one can be set free from his sinful nature by trying hard. A relationship with God is not entered into through following a long list of rules and regulations. The freedom to have a relationship with God is the product of His wonderful grace and the work that He does in people's hearts. They had never before heard anything like this.

The message He preached about the Kingdom of God was a message of hope. Jesus offered them freedom in the place of their fear. He offered joy for their broken hearts and His light for their spiritual darkness. And all this was possible because the Kingdom of God had come among people. When God reigns as King in the hearts and lives of people, a radical change takes place. The Kingdom of God is the realm over which God rules and where His rulership is accepted in the hearts of people. Then every aspect of their lives comes under His influence.

The words of Jesus still speak to us of the Kingdom of God. May you experience His Kingdom in your life today.

You give!

He replied, "You give them something to eat." They answered, "We have only five loaves of bread and two fish – unless we go and buy food for all this crowd."

ഌ Luke 9:13 ര

When the sun had set the twelve disciples came to Jesus with what they thought was good advice. *"Send the crowd away so they can go to the surrounding villages and countryside and find food and lodging, because we are in a remote place here"* (v. 12). The disciples pointed out that there was nowhere to get food. They could not be responsible for caring for all these people so they suggested that Jesus send them away.

But Jesus did not send them away. He looked His disciples straight in the eye and said, *"You give them something to eat."* These words must have sent them reeling. They surely thought that Jesus could not have been serious. What on earth could He have meant by this?

Perhaps Jesus wanted them to see that they should not shrug off their responsibility toward people too quickly. There are quite a few accounts in the gospels of the disciples trying to send people away from Jesus when they thought that He had had enough (cf. Mt. 15:23, Lk. 9:49-50). Jesus showed His disciples that simply getting rid of people does not provide any solutions.

Perhaps Jesus wanted the disciples to face the fact that faith has a different way of looking at problems. He wanted to show them how to operate by faith – to ask, to seek, to knock. He wanted them to learn that they could take the promises of God for themselves because the Lord can provide for every need that His people have.

Let us meet the needs of people, not with a shrug of our shoulders and hands thrown up in uncertainty, but in the faith that God can do wonderful things.

May 6

Our disappointment is God's opportunity

He replied, "You give them something to eat." They answered, "We have only five loaves of bread and two fish – unless we go and buy food for all this crowd."

Luke 9:13

Jesus said to His disciples, "You give them something to eat." But there were over five thousand hungry people and there was nowhere for them to buy food. The disciples did mention that a young boy had five small loaves and two fish. The only solution would be to buy food.

But Jesus told them to organize the crowds into groups of about fifty. He told them to seat them on the ground and get ready to eat. Then He took the five loaves and the two fish, looked up to heaven and asked His Father's blessing. After that He broke the bread and fish and gave it to the disciples to serve to the people. A miracle took place right before their eyes. As Jesus handed them the food, it just kept increasing. Everyone got more than enough to eat.

Our disappointment is often an opportunity for God to work a miracle. When we think that we have nothing, God can increase what we do have so that afterward we are amazed by the wonderful things that have happened.

The fact that this boy was prepared to share his food became an opportunity for Jesus to perform a miracle. The question we have to ask ourselves is what can we bring to God. Sometimes we think that what we can give is so insignificant that the Lord cannot use it. Let the lesson of the bread and fish motivate us to offer what we do have to the Lord for His use. A miracle can happen when we place things in His hands. Of course, God does not need what we have to bring, but He wants us to bring it to Him so that He can use it in His Kingdom. Give everything to God. He can use you.

Behind the miracle

(About five thousand men were there.) But he said to his disciples, "Have them sit down in groups of about fifty each."

Luke 9:14

This portion of Scripture relates the miracle that Jesus performed to multiply the bread and fish. Through this miracle 5,000 people had enough to eat from five loaves and two fish. In front of all those present, a miracle from heaven took place. And once again the miracle-working power of Jesus was confirmed. He was the one who was able to meet every need. This is still true today. He is unlimited in His power.

Behind this miracle we see the love and compassion that God has for mankind. The Lord is not interested only in our spirits, but He also wants our daily needs to be filled. Because He, as the Creator of heaven and earth, knows us whom He has created, He also knows what our daily needs are and how to provide for them. His loving concern for our needs is seen in this miracle.

We often tend to think that God is interested only in our spiritual welfare. But that is far from the truth! He knows when we are hungry. He knows when we feel lonely. He knows that we have a need to be touched by human hands. We see His concern illustrated in the father of the prodigal son, who welcomed his lost son extravagantly. This is how the heavenly Father feels about you and me.

This miracle also shows how generous Jesus is. *"They all ate and were satisfied, and the disciples picked up twelve basketfuls of broken pieces that were left over"* (v. 17). When God gives, He gives more than enough. He is not wasteful, but neither is He stingy. When He gave the fish and bread to the crowds He didn't give only enough to appease their hunger. When they finally stood up they were completely satisfied, and there were leftovers.

Our God is a great, wonderful, good Lord. He cares for His children. Trust Him.

May 8

Go!

"Therefore go and make disciples of all nations, baptizing them in the name of the Father and of the Son and of the Holy Spirit."

℘ Matthew 28:19 ☙

This is the Great Commission that Jesus gave to His disciples and His church. This was what He had spent three years training them for. He had taught them, and they had become His disciples in the fullest sense, and now they had a responsibility to fulfill. Once more Jesus emphasized that they were to go into all the world with the message of the gospel – that Jesus Christ is the Savior of the world.

In Matthew 10:5 Jesus told them not to go to the heathen nations, and He even stopped them from going into any Samaritan towns. Do His words in Matthew 28 indicate a change in His plans? Of course not. From the beginning it was clear that Jesus came for all people of the world. Think of the words of John 3:16. They refer to the whole world. Rather, the plan was that the Jews were to be the first to hear the good news and they should then share it with the rest of the world. The message should spread from Jerusalem to all the nations of the world. The disciples had to go, not stay where they were. You and I are also among those whom Jesus sends into all the world. We should constantly be looking for ways to reach others outside of our immediate community. We must develop the desire to take the Word of God to those who have not heard the good news.

This is a command that God has issued to us. In the command there is also the promise of the power and authority of Jesus that will enable us to obey. We obey because we are thankful for what He has done for us.

Go to all the nations. The passion of Christians should always be to spread the gospel to every corner of the earth. Everyone must hear. Let us today once again say *yes* to this great commission. What a privilege it is to carry this out!

Profit and loss

"What good is it for a man to gain the whole world, and yet lose or forfeit his very self?"

ꕥ LUKE 9:25 ꕥ

It is typical of human nature for people to so focus on themselves that they put their own interests first in all they think and do. They want to protect and preserve what they have at all costs. But God teaches us to live in a different way, to shift the focus away from ourselves, to live for others. He wants us to live for things that are bigger and wider than our own little I.

"What good is it for a man to gain the whole world?" (v. 25). Just think for a moment what it would mean if you could get everything that this world offers! Think of the diamonds, the gold jewelry, the fast, shiny cars and that giant yacht on the Meditteranean Sea. Think of the clothes, the houses, the vacations! Yes, think of owning all the world's glories, its prestige, its pleasures, its riches. But all of this means absolutely nothing, says Jesus, if you gain it all but lose your soul because of it.

There are people who are considered rich in terms of worldly possessions, but for various reasons they find no enjoyment in their possessions. It could be that such a person is so miserable within himself that the riches bring no joy, or perhaps he suffers from a serious or terminal illness. What does the glitter of this world have to offer then?

Jesus admonishes us to surrender our lives into His hands so that we can find ourselves and live a life of meaning and purpose. The joy of life does not consist in an abundance of worldly goods. It comes from your relationship with God. Are you filled with His peace? Do you know that you have been set free from the bonds of wickedness? To be in a right relationship with God is worth more than everything the world can offer you.

May 10

Ashamed

"If anyone is ashamed of me and my words, the Son of Man will be ashamed of him when he comes in his glory and in the glory of the Father and of the holy angels."

ꕤ Luke 9:26 ꕤ

Being a Christian means that you identify yourself with the person of Jesus Christ. In Him you find life, salvation, and the meaning and purpose of your whole existence. Identifying with Christ has certain implications for your life.

Jesus is not very popular with many people. The things He said were so radically different from the world's system that people who follow Jesus are often misunderstood. At the same time the work of the evil one behind the scenes is so intensely wicked that the conflict between light and dark leaves its mark on the lives of those who follow Jesus. There is currently much persecution of Christians around the world. Even as you read this there are Christians somewhere in the world who are suffering and dying just because they have identified themselves with Jesus Christ.

When things are so arrayed against Christians, it is quite possible that many people are ashamed to admit that they serve Jesus and agree with the things He said. To be ashamed of Him before people means that you do not wish to be completely identified with Him in public. This verse of Scripture refers primarily to people who want to keep control of their own lives and are too proud to follow Christ. They are ashamed of anything that has to do with the fact that Jesus Christ came to save people. Jesus says that He will be ashamed of the people who are ashamed of Him. He will reject and judge such people from His judgment throne in glory. They had their chance to choose to accept His offer of salvation and to receive new life but didn't.

Let us walk confidently next to Jesus, without being ashamed of Him or His words.

Christ the Anointed One

"But what about you?" he asked. "Who do you say I am?" Peter answered, "The Christ of God."

℘ Luke 9:20 ℘

Jesus asked His disciples who they thought He was. And we are all familiar with Peter's answer, *"The Christ of God."* Matthew says that Peter expanded on his answer a little. He added, *"the Son of the living God"* (Mt. 16:16). Jesus' response shows us that He approved of and agreed with Peter's answer. He confirmed Peter's statement with His own words.

The word *anointed*, or Christ, held a lot of meaning for Jewish people. Their history was rich with an understanding of the significance of being anointed. Prophets, priests, and kings in the Old Testament were all anointed when they were appointed to function in their position. Oil, which was usually used to anoint these people, symbolized that God had set the person apart to fulfill the function He had selected him for. It was also symbolic of the work of the Holy Spirit in his life – the fact that He enabled him to do the work God had called him to. So when Peter said that Jesus was the Christ he meant that He was the long awaited Anointed One of God who was chosen and appointed to be the perfect mediator between God and man. The Father had set Him apart for a very special task, and He was anointed by the Holy Spirit. Jesus was anointed as the great prophet, the perfect High Priest and the eternal King.

Like a Prophet, the anointed Jesus speaks His truth in our lives. As the High Priest He presented a perfect sacrifice on our behalf and now intercedes for us before the Father. As King, He reigns not only in our lives but also over His whole Kingdom.

May 12

Clothed in glory

"If anyone is ashamed of me and my words, the Son of Man will be ashamed of him when he comes in his glory and in the glory of the Father and of the holy angels."

ꕥ LUKE 9:26 ꕥ

Oh, what a day that will be when we finally see Jesus in all His glory! Some will see Him with their own eyes when He comes back to earth from heaven to fetch His people who are still in this world. Then the glory of the Father will be revealed to all of us and we will see the holy angels with our own eyes. This will be the most wonderful and most glorious event that anyone could ever hope to experience.

Jesus said that then those who were ashamed of Him on earth will realize in the blink of an eye that they will be lost for eternity. They will flee from the glorious presence of the Lord. They will not rejoice when His glory is unveiled, but they will weep and mourn. Christians look forward to the glorious day when they will see their Lord and Savior. But the unsaved hope against hope that He will not come again.

In the letter to the Romans, Paul writes that he is convinced that the suffering that we have to endure now cannot be measured against the glory of God that will be revealed that day. All of creation waits in breathless anticipation to see the fullness of God's glory revealed. And all of creation, together with the people on the earth, grieve because of the current sinfulness and brokenness and frailty in the world. But we all look forward to the day when God's glory will be visible in the earth because then we will be set free from bondage and imperfection. *"The creation itself will be liberated from its bondage to decay and brought into the glorious freedom of the children of God"* (Rom. 8:21). It will be glorious!

The Son of Man

And he said, "The Son of Man must suffer many things and be rejected by the elders, chief priests and teachers of the law, and he must be killed and on the third day be raised to life."

Luke 9:22

Jesus refers to Himself as the *Son of Man* approximately seventy times in the gospels. This wasn't really a well-known phrase in Bible times. The term was used on occasion in the Old Testament (cf. Dan. 7:13), but what did it mean? Why did Jesus use it?

Perhaps He used it because He did not want to use the term *Messiah* right from the start, as the Jews would not have accepted His using this title. He had to gently lead them to understand that He is God's Son who was sent to set the world free from sin.

When we look at all the instances where Jesus used this term, we see that it refers to two aspects of His life. In the first place it related to His humanity. It reminds us that although He is God He set aside His glory and humbled Himself. He chose to become a man and live among sinful, broken people. This points to His humility (cf. Phil. 2). He mentioned that as the Son of Man He had no place on earth to call His own home, that He would have to suffer, that He would be betrayed, crucified and buried.

But this term also points to the fact that He would be glorified and magnified. He would rise from the dead, ascend to heaven, and one day return to earth. When He comes again He will be seated on His throne as the Great Judge.

You and I know the Son of Man. He identified Himself with us in His humanity, but He will also come to rule us in His majesty.

May 14

Pray

"Why are you sleeping?" he asked them. "Get up and pray so that you will not fall into temptation."

ꟷ LUKE 22:46 ꟷ

One day Jesus took Peter, James, and John with Him when He went up a mountain to pray. It was most probably a place called Jebel Jermuk, which is north of Galilee. The summit of this mountain rises four thousand feet above the Mediterranean Sea and from its slopes one can see breathtaking views in every direction.

The Lord Jesus calls us, His followers, to pray with Him too. It is true, as the Word says, that He intercedes on our behalf. But He also wants us to be actively involved in praying for His Kingdom. Prayer is simply the way that the Kingdom of God functions. No prayer, no spiritual success. We must pray because the Father expects us to. Spiritual breakthroughs can happen only when we pray.

While Jesus was praying His appearance was transformed and glory radiated from Him. We know that the Lord is always present with His children whatever the place or circumstances, but when we purposefully seek His presence in prayer, and focus on Him with our whole heart, and listen with the ears of our spirit to hear His whisper, then we too are changed in the process.

People who pray often seem to radiate a kind of presence that is different from people who do not pray. They seem to be more gentle, more loving, more peaceful, and filled with a heavenly joy. True worshipers and prayers receive a kind of glory from the Father that is supernatural. That is not to say that they walk around with visible haloes – they don't become angels! They are ordinary people but the presence of God is visible in their lives. Yes, prayer changes things, but it changes people too.

More than powerless instruments

"O unbelieving and perverse generation," Jesus replied, "how long shall I stay with you and put up with you? Bring your son here."

Luke 9:41

A man called out to Jesus, asking for His help. His only child had a problem. He was only a young boy and it seemed that he suffered from some kind of epilepsy. But this boy suffered from more than just epilepsy. The Bible tells us that there was a wicked spirit that attacked him and assaulted him. The man mentioned something that upset Jesus very much.

He told Jesus that His disciples had been unable to cast out the demon. He begged them to help his son, but they just could not do it. The disciples had probably fallen behind as the crowds pressed forward to get closer to Jesus. When the man saw that he could not get close to Jesus he asked the disciples to help. After all, they were Jesus' followers, and if He could do such amazing miracles, then they should be able to as well. They had been taught by Jesus. But they could not do it, and Jesus was disappointed in them. That is why He said, *"O unbelieving and perverse generation, how long shall I stay with you and put up with you?"* (v. 41).

We could defend the disciples by saying that they were not yet filled with the Holy Spirit. That was so, but Jesus had already given them authority and power over the powers of evil (cf. Lk. 9:1). That was why Jesus was upset by their lack of faith.

The church of Jesus Christ on earth today is also often just talk. When it comes to action, they show little power. We have been equipped with the Holy Spirit and with power from on high and we ought to be effective instruments in God's Kingdom. Paul says that people of the Kingdom do not simply talk – they do (1 Cor. 4: 20). We should not drag our heels when people ask us to help them in their times of distress. Often, as it was with the disciples, it is our fear and doubt that hinder us from acting with authority and power. We must live out of and with the power of God.

May 16

Jesus bears with His disciples

"O unbelieving and perverse generation," Jesus replied, "how long shall I stay with you and put up with you? Bring your son here."

Luke 9:41

When Jesus found out that His disciples were not able to help the boy who was possessed by an evil spirit, He cried out, *"O unbelieving and perverse generation!"* We can almost see Jesus throwing His hands in the air in despair over the people He was dealing with and working with.

His comment was not directed only at His disciples but at the whole "unbelieving generation." His disciples had disappointed Him in this difficult situation, but the shallowness of the faith of all of humankind disturbed Him greatly. There was the father who did not have enough faith in the healing power of Jesus (cf. Mk. 9:22-24); the Pharisees who started arguing and debating with the disciples when they saw their lack of power (Mk. 9:14); and then there were the crowds of people who heard and saw, but did not really believe. They were so often more caught up in their own problems than concerned about the needs of others (Jn. 6:26).

Jesus was about to bring His earthly ministry to an end. It was not only the crucifixion and persecution by the Romans and the Jewish leaders that hurt Him but also, the lack of faith and the general depravity of the people He encountered daily.

Thank God! His grace always triumphs over condemnation. He never turns His back on those who struggle with unbelief. He heard the prayer of this desperate father, and reached out to the demon-possessed boy.

I often wonder that the Lord doesn't become discouraged at the way we go about doing His will. But His grace triumphs over our weaknesses. So let us try to live lives that will please Him.

The final attack

Even while the boy was coming, the demon threw him to the ground in a convulsion. But Jesus rebuked the evil spirit, healed the boy and gave him back to his father.

ཐ Luke 9:42 ཐ

Jesus had been asked to help a young demon-possessed boy. The Bible tells us that while the boy was still making his way toward Jesus, the evil spirit suddenly grabbed hold of him. Right there and then the demon hurled him to the ground and caused him to have violent convulsions.

How typical this is of evil! The devil knows when God has a plan to set someone free, or when a person is ready to surrender him or herself to the Lord. The devil will try anything to block our path so that we cannot meet with the Living Lord. Like with this boy – he sprang into action and threw him into a demonic fit. But this was the final attack as the end was in sight for the devil. So many times, just before people have an encounter with God or just as they are considering surrendering their whole life to God, they suddenly experience fierce attacks from the devil. It's almost as if the devil, who walks around like a roaring lion, tries his absolute best to keep people in his claws so that they will not come to Jesus.

But the good news is that God is more powerful than the devil. The power of the Holy Spirit is able to pluck people out of Satan's grip. Jesus sharply commanded the evil spirit to leave the boy and He healed the boy right there.

Don't be put off by the devil's attacks on your life. Follow the advice of Paul and put on the full armor of God, and having done all, stand. If, in the midst of the attacks and storms that the evil one brings into your life you can remain standing, then God, through Jesus Christ, will speak His Word of liberation in your life. Remain standing with your feet firm on the rock of the gospel message, and keep your eyes fixed on Jesus.

May 18

Too afraid to ask

"Listen carefully to what I am about to tell you: The Son of Man is going to be betrayed into the hands of men."

LUKE 9:44

Straight after Peter made the astounding observation that Jesus is the Messiah of God, Jesus told the disciples that He would have to suffer much. He would be rejected and killed, but on the third day He would be raised from the dead.

The disciples did not quite understand what Jesus was saying. They did not have the spiritual insight needed and they could not understand why Someone who was so successful and who was the Messiah of God should have to die. He was still so young and He had, after all, come to save the world. The Bible tells us that the meaning of Jesus' words was hidden from the disciples, which is why they could not grasp what He was saying. But then Luke continues, *"they were afraid to ask him about it"* (v. 45).

There are of course many things in this life that you and I are unable to understand. Spiritual issues are often the most difficult for us to fathom. We read the Bible and we have all kinds of questions. There are so many things we would like to ask about the deep secrets of God. Often we don't feel at liberty to discuss these issues with other people or with God, so we bury the questions in our hearts.

Perhaps we are afraid that other people will think we lack insight into the things of God. Perhaps we do not ask because we don't really think that our questions are important. And so we lose the opportunity to gain spiritual insight.

We should feel free to regularly search the deep things of God, and to ask when we do not know. We need to try to understand God's will for our lives. Let's not be too afraid to seek advice and to ask for help. But most of all we should kneel before God in dependence on Him and ask the Holy Spirit to teach us.

Who is number one?

They came to Capernaum. When he was in the house, he asked them, "What were you arguing about on the road?"

Mark 9:33

One evening Jesus arrived in Capernaum on the shores of Galilee, where He and His disciples were planning to spend the night and get some rest. Jesus looked His disciples in the eye and asked, "What were you talking about while we were on the road?" He hadn't been part of the conversation or near enough to hear, but He knew what they had been talking about.

The disciples had been arguing about which of them was the most important. It's hard to believe that this was such an issue for them. On the one hand they were humble enough to have given up everything to follow Jesus. They left their businesses, their homes and families because they wanted to serve Jesus. And yet here they were so self-centered. They wanted to know which of them had the highest position among the disciples. Luke tells us that not one of them answered Jesus' question.

Perhaps they were embarrassed because they suddenly realized that their discussion was not what was to be expected from disciples of Jesus. They had never seen Jesus wrangle for position and status. He never tried to be number one. He never competed with any person. His competition with the devil was because He is the Son of God. He was also not concerned whether or not people thought of Him as important. He came to serve. He came to earth because of His great love for mankind.

As Christians we should guard against jockeying for position. It isn't a matter of who is the most important in the Kingdom of God. Jesus is. We are simply His servants, and the ground is level at the foot of the cross. There are not more and less important people in His Kingdom. We are all servants, disciples, Christians. That's all. Each one simply has to do what God asks of him or her.

May 20

The first will be last

Sitting down, Jesus called the Twelve and said, "If anyone wants to be first, he must be the very last, and the servant of all."

℘ MARK 9:35 ℘

Jesus was upset that His disciples argued about which of them was the most important. He called the twelve to Him and told them that if anyone wanted to be first in life, he had to be prepared to take the very last place and to serve everyone else.

Jesus knew what was in the hearts of His disciples. He knew that they were fallen and broken people. He also knew that they had a longing to be recognized. They liked being patted on the back when they did well. But He was their Master, and they needed to learn to discern the fine line between a good self-image and pure selfishness. Perhaps they lived with a misconception. They had heard Jesus say that His Kingdom would come with power and they assumed that they would be given positions of authority in this important Kingdom. They would have power and status. Jesus had to set them right. Their idea of what it meant to be great on earth had to be changed. True greatness consists in losing yourself for the sake of others, sympathizing with them and doing everything that you can to help them in their times of need.

Any person, whether one of the twelve disciples or a person of high standing in the world's eyes, who wants to be first must be prepared to go to the back of the line. He needs to become the lowest ranked servant.

Proverbs 16:18 reminds us that pride goes before a fall. The main emphasis in leadership is to serve others; to wash their feet; to be the least of all; not to want to be helped first, but to let others go ahead of you. And Jesus was the best example of this kind of lifestyle.

Let us also serve more and expect less. Let us offer ourselves fully in the service of other people.

A little child

Then he said to them, "Whoever welcomes this little child in my name welcomes me; and whoever welcomes me welcomes the one who sent me. For he who is least among you all – he is the greatest."

Luke 9:48

When Jesus spoke to His disciples about no person being more important than any other in the Kingdom of God, He called a little child to Him. He asked the disciples to look at the child. It's great to note how often the Bible mentions that children were near Jesus, and how often His love for them is mentioned in the Gospels (cf. Mt. 9:18-19, 18:1-10). Grownups can learn many lessons from children. Just the way little children behave and respond to things around them speaks volumes to the hardness of grownups' hearts.

When Jesus showed this little child to His disciples, He said, *"Whoever welcomes this little child in my name welcomes me; and whoever welcomes me welcomes the one who sent me. For he who is least among you all – he is the greatest."* As children grow up they learn to compete with each other and to fight for the number one position. Younger children are not concerned about who is the best. They have no affectations and trust grownups implicitly.

When Jesus drew this child into the circle of disciples, He was showing them how they should live. He told them that if they were prepared to receive a child like that in His name, to love and care for the child, then they were beginning to understand what was important. Arrogant people, who are only focused on themselves and filled with pride, have no time for children. They push them aside and will even at times abuse children for their own personal gain. But a person who has a heart to serve others will bend to help the smallest child. He of least importance in society is great in the eyes of God.

May 22

Who is He?

"Master," said John, "we saw a man driving out demons in your name and we tried to stop him, because he is not one of us."

ꕤ LUKE 9:49 ꕤ

Some time back there was a very popular song that included the words "No man is an island, and I love you." The young man declared his love for his girlfriend by drawing on the general statement that no person can truly live without others. Yes, the singer was right, we need each other and are dependent on each other.

But the very human desire to be among others has a darker side. The negative aspect of it is that people are inclined to form cliques. In the midst of the mass of humanity, small groups form that become exclusive and so lock other people out. Something of this attitude was evident when John went to speak to Jesus.

John said that he and some of Jesus' other friends had seen someone casting out demons in Jesus' name. They tried to stop him because he wasn't part of the group that followed Jesus around the country. He was not part of the inner circle of disciples. Perhaps he wasn't even one of the general disciples of Jesus. Who was this man?

We do not really know the answer to that question but Jesus' reaction suggests that he was most probably someone who had listened to Jesus, who had come to the conviction that He was the Son of God and had decided to help build God's Kingdom. So he copied what he had seen Jesus do – and had begun to cast out demons as he had seen Jesus' disciples do.

Jesus wants all people to be involved with His Kingdom. The work of building His Kingdom is not the exclusive domain of any particular group or denomination. Jesus is delighted when someone believes in Him and is prepared to do His work. Even though we have no control over these people let us thank God that there are many people prepared to build the Kingdom of God.

An elitist attitude

"Do not stop him," Jesus said, "for whoever is not against you is for you."

LUKE 9:50

Jesus told John and the other disciples that they should leave the man who was casting out demons in His name. He was for them and not against them. This must have been hard for the disciples to understand because they were convinced that they were an elite group and the only ones whom Christ would use. Their fleshly nature rebelled against the thought of an outsider doing what they did, and possibly even more successfully. Jesus taught them that they had to develop a different attitude.

An elitist spirit is a dreadful thing in the body of Christ. There are so many churches, congregations, and denominations that point fingers at each other simply because they cannot accept that the Lord Jesus can use any other person or group. This is shortsighted exclusivism. People with this attitude think they have a monopoly on spiritual matters and want to keep others out because they think they alone have God's favor. If other people do not minister in the same way that they do, then they question the validity of their ministry. Even the disciples fell into this trap.

They could not accept the fact that another man outside their circle served Jesus effectively. This spirit of narrow exclusivity is often confused with loyalty to a denomination or church. We hear people say, "Our denomination is the purest expression of the body of Christ on earth." Should we not rather, while we are still in this world with all its sinfulness, found even within the Church of Jesus Christ, leave God to be the judge of such things? Let us learn to be more accepting of others in the body. Let us, like Paul, be more accepting of those whom God wants to use (see Phil. 1:14-18). Hold fast to what you believe to be the truth, but stop judging others for the way that they choose to serve God.

May 24

His unspoken words

"We are going up to Jerusalem," he said, "and the Son of Man will be betrayed to the chief priests and teachers of the law."

MARK 10:33

Jesus explained to His disciples that He would be put in the hands of the Scribes and Pharisees and that He would be rejected by them and suffer many things. Luke, in verse 51, goes on to observe that Jesus was resolutely determined to go to Jerusalem. He does not record the words of Jesus, but expresses what was in His heart. Jesus did not explicitly state His thoughts, but it was clear that He knew that He was about to set out on His final journey to Jerusalem where He would suffer and die (see Lk. 9:51).

Jesus must have spent much time weighing up the pros and cons of this final journey to Jerusalem. What exactly awaited Him there? He did not know the details, although He had a general understanding of what He was about to go through, and He knew it would not be easy. As the time for His return to heaven drew near, He purposefully set out for Jerusalem. He was determined to go there to give His life for the people He loved. His love for all mankind and the conviction that the Father had sent Him to do this work made His footsteps firm, His face shine, and His eyes focus on His goal. Nothing would prevent Him from carrying out His decision. No one would make Him deviate from the road He was walking. He had to go to the cross. What incredible, complete, wholehearted surrender and commitment!

In His heart of hearts Jesus knew that the time had come and His actions spoke louder than His words. When we look at the commitment of Jesus, we are stirred to commit ourselves to do all that the Lord requires of us. Let His words echo in our hearts: words of encouragement, words of decision, words that focus on our goal and purpose in life, which is to follow Him and serve Him.

Fire from heaven?

But Jesus turned and rebuked them.

ᘓ Luke 9:55 ᘐ

Jesus had decided that the time was right to begin His final journey to Jerusalem. His earthly ministry was drawing to a close. He had to die on the cross and pay the price for the sins of mankind. That is why He sent messengers ahead of Him to find a place for Him and His disciples to sleep over on their journey to Jerusalem.

The reason was clear: it was not that easy to arrange sleeping quarters for thirteen people and a few extra friends in a strange town. They had to make appropriate arrangements. Someone had to prepare a place. And now Jesus had to travel through Samaria to get to Jerusalem. Those who went before Him found place for the travelers in a Samaritan town. But when Jesus and His disciples actually arrived, the inhabitants of the town did not want Him to stay there simply because He was on His way to Jerusalem.

The Jews and Samaritans had been engaged in conflict even as far back as the end of the sixth century B.C. (cf. Ezra 4:1-3). When Jews traveled through Samaria, particularly if they were on their way to Jerusalem, they were often hindered by the Samaritans. Some travelers had even died in these conflicts.

James and John, the two sons of thunder, wanted to ask for fire to rain down mightily from heaven and obliterate the Samaritans. They really believed that this was possible, but Jesus turned round and sharply rebuked them. He did not come to judge people but to save them! And so they went on to a different village.

Let us follow the example of Jesus and walk in the way of His love. Let us not judge anyone, not even those who oppose and resist Him or us.

May 26

Pray for laborers

He told them, "The harvest is plentiful, but the workers are few. Ask the Lord of the harvest, therefore, to send out workers into his harvest field."

ꟸ LUKE 10:2 ꟹ

In Luke chapter 10 we read that Jesus appointed seventy-two of His disciples and sent them to every town and area that He was planning to visit. They went to prepare the way for Him. And then Jesus said to them, *"The harvest is plentiful, but the workers are few. Ask the Lord of the harvest, therefore, to send out workers into his harvest field."* If that was true when Jesus lived on earth then it is definitely true in our day.

The harvest is enormous. The field to be harvested stretches across the whole world. There are billions of people to whom we need to minister the message of salvation through Jesus Christ. Jesus gives us the same commission that He gave to His disciples. We need to earnestly pray first and foremost not for the harvest, but for laborers to go into the harvest fields. There are few laborers in God's Kingdom and that is why we need to pray that people will respond to the touch of God in their hearts and give themselves more fully to the building of God's Kingdom.

Note that Jesus said we need to pray for laborers to be sent. Who, then, does the sending? The Lord! It is only God who can change the hearts of people so that they will go where He sends them. But we are commanded to pray that this will happen. Only God can equip a person to be a laborer in the harvest field. It is God who sends people out. He uses all kinds of ways and methods to convince people to go. He equips them, prepares them, and confirms their calling. They go as laborers, not joy riders! Let us pray for more laborers.

Two by two

After this the Lord appointed seventy-two others and sent them two by two ahead of him to every town and place where he was about to go.

༄ Luke 10:1 ༄

In this passage Luke tells us about the seventy-two who were sent out in pairs so that they could work together. Luke 19:29-30 also mentions Jesus sending two men out together.

Way back in the Old Testament, Solomon had already pointed out that two are better than one because if one falls the other can help him up (cf. Ecc. 4:10). If the one becomes discouraged, the other can encourage him. Two can support each other. We find many similar references throughout the Bible. Even John the Baptist sent two of his disciples to Jesus (cf. Lk. 7:19). In Acts 3:1, and elsewhere, we read that Peter and John worked together when they witnessed for Christ. Barnabas and Saul were sent together on a missionary journey (cf. Acts 13:1-3). Other twosomes mentioned in the Bible are Jude and Silas, Timothy and Silas, and Timothy and Erastus.

There is a strength that comes when people work together in unity. The old maxim reminds us that unity is strength. When two followers of Jesus agree on an issue in prayer, then what they pray for will come to pass, so says the Word. There are no "lone rangers" in the Kingdom of God. Effectively establishing the kingdom requires working together, praying together, witnessing together, and serving together. If people go out two by two then the pairs should consist of a husband and wife, or two men, or two women. It is better, for obvious reasons, that a man and woman who are not married to each other should not go out to minister alone together.

Ask the Lord to send you a co-worker who will suit you so that you two can carry out His command effectively.

May 28

I am sending you!

"Go! I am sending you out like lambs among wolves."

Luke 10:3

Jesus selected workers and trained them. Then came the day when He said to them, "Go!" They were ready for action. But before they left Jesus warned them, "First listen, and listen carefully. I am sending you out like lambs among wolves."

Jesus' comment could hardly be regarded as a motivation. This didn't sound like an adventure, but more like a disaster waiting to happen. They would be like lambs among wolves? That sounded catastrophic! What could be more helpless than a lamb among wolves? It sounded as if unimaginable dangers were in store for them.

But let's shift focus and take note of the emphatic and definite, *"I am sending you."* Now that changes the picture somewhat. It is their Great Shepherd who is sending them out and He assures them that He is in control. Apart from Him this would have been a hopeless situation. But sent out by Him, as His apostles, the opposite becomes true. They must have thought of the words that the prophet Isaiah wrote, *"He tends his flock like a shepherd: He gathers the lambs in his arms and carries them close to his heart; he gently leads those that have young"* (Is. 40:11).

Those who are sent out by the Lord today sometimes do find themselves in difficult and dangerous places. Think of the many missionaries who place their lives on the line by working for Christ in far away countries and in foreign cultures. They are like lambs among wolves but they have the assurance that their Heavenly Shepherd is with them every second of the day. They go in response to His command because they know that He has been given all authority in heaven and on earth. We too can go out like lambs among wolves because the Shepherd is by our side.

Peace in this house

"When you enter a house, first say, 'Peace to this house.'"

ꕤ LUKE 10:5 ꕤ

When Jesus sent His disciples ahead of Him to the towns and cities where He was planning to minister, He instructed them to say, "Peace to this house" when they walked into a house.

For centuries the Jewish people have greeted each other with this blessing of the peace of God. We often find the words "Peace be to you" in the Bible. This was a kind of general greeting in those days, and is still so in the Jewish culture today. A greeting like this can become empty words, just as we ask people, "How are you?", often without really wanting to know.

But Jesus asked His disciples to speak peace over the homes they entered. He then explained that those people whose spirits were open and receptive to the blessing that was spoken would receive it as their portion. Their hearts and their homes would be flooded with peace. But those whose hearts were not really open would not experience peace in their hearts and lives, and the blessing of peace would not be fulfilled for them. Instead, it would return to the one who had given the blessing.

Perhaps, in this age of such unrest and violence, we should speak the blessing of peace over each other's lives more often. We need to say it with meaning, from the bottom of our hearts, trusting that the one who hears it will also truly receive it. In the same way we should also bless our neighborhoods, our towns, and our cities with the peace of the Lord.

God delights in giving His peace to His people, which is why He taught the Old Testament priests to speak this blessing over the Israelites: *"The LORD turn his face toward you and give you peace."* (Num. 6:26). And I pray today that you and your household will receive the peace of the Lord.

May 30

Jesus praises

At that time Jesus, full of joy through the Holy Spirit, said, "I praise you, Father, Lord of heaven and earth."

ꕤ LUKE 10:21 ꕤ

When the seventy-two disciples returned from the mission trip that Jesus had sent them on, they were full of joy and had exciting testimonies to tell of how the Lord had used them.

Suddenly Jesus began to sing a song of praise. *"I praise you, Father, Lord of heaven and earth, because you have hidden these things from the wise and learned, and revealed them to little children."* Jesus was overwhelmed when He considered the wisdom of God that touched the lives of ordinary, everyday people and made them into instruments He can use in His service.

Take note that it was the Holy Spirit who led Jesus Christ into this song of praise to God the Father. It did not originate in Jesus' intellect or in His feelings of gladness and excitement. There was only one source of His desire to praise and that was the person of the Holy Spirit in Him.

The Holy Spirit truly wants to bring us to the place where we will overflow with praise to God and Jesus Christ. He is the One who often inspires us to shout aloud with joy before the Father God, just as Jesus did here. We hear how Jesus praised His Father as the Lord of heaven and earth. He magnified His Father's name and was not ashamed to praise God publicly.

If Jesus, the Son of God, could be so moved by the Holy Spirit to offer praises to God the Father, how much more should you and I open ourselves to being filled with the Holy Spirit. Then we would be more willing to give God the praise that is due to Him. Then we would continuously praise Jesus for everything that we have received from and through Him. Praise the Lord!

What a privilege

Then he turned to his disciples and said privately, "Blessed are the eyes that see what you see."

LUKE 10:23

One day, Jesus turned to His disciples and said, "*Blessed are the eyes that see what you see.*" It was almost as if Jesus wanted to emphasize that His disciples should not take everything they saw and experienced for granted. Did they realize just how privileged they were? Did they have any idea how many people in previous generations had yearned to see the things that they saw on a daily basis?

There had been many prophets, priests, and even kings who, in the old dispensation, had been deeply moved by the things of God. Some of them spent nights reading and studying the law of God trying to determine more of God's purpose. Some of them dedicated their lives to uncovering the deep mysteries of God. They did receive a small measure of revelation from God, but they would have given everything they had to have experienced what the disciples went through with Jesus. Think of old Simeon who held the baby Jesus in His arms in the temple in Jerusalem. The Holy Spirit revealed to him that this little child was the Savior of the whole world.

We have not seen Jesus with our physical eyes as the disciples did. We have not touched His body with our hands but we have received the Holy Spirit who helps us to see the reality of the person of Jesus Christ in our hearts. Like the disciples, we have received revelation upon revelation. We stand in awe, amazed at all that He has revealed to us. The Lord Jesus Christ and the message of His kingdom are far more than theory for us. It has become our way of life. Let us thank God without ceasing and praise Him for allowing us to live in this time when so much has been revealed to us. And let us not be slack concerning the wonderful things that have been revealed to us.

June

The lawyer's question

"You have answered correctly," Jesus replied. "Do this and you will live."

ꟻ LUKE 10:28 ᘓ

The Jewish lawyers in Jesus' day knew the Pentateuch, the five books of Moses, very well. One day one of these experts in the law stood up. He wanted to humiliate Jesus and thought his knowledge of the law would enable him to squeeze Jesus into a corner. So he asked Him a trick question. He asked what he should do to obtain eternal life.

Jesus answered his question with another question. He asked him what the law of Moses had to say about it. He answered by reciting the verse that says that people should love the Lord their God with their whole heart, with all their strength and with all their soul and with their whole minds. And that we should love our neighbor as ourselves. Jesus said, *"You have answered correctly. Do this and you will live"* (v. 28). But the lawyer was still busy with his intellectual game and he wanted to justify himself before Jesus. So he asked another question. *"And who is my neighbor?"* (v. 29). In reply, Jesus told the parable of the Good Samaritan.

Through the parable Jesus showed that men and women who have the most sympathy and compassion for those in distress, and do what they can to lighten the load, are your neighbors. Not someone who talks about what should be done, or who makes philosophical observations, but the one who demonstrates love. The expert in the law understood exactly what Jesus was saying and he had no answer to Jesus' words, *"Go and do likewise"* (v. 37).

He heard the truth, that life does not consist of rules and regulations but of one heart reaching out to another. It's all about love that can be practically demonstrated. We can only hope that this lawyer went away and did what Jesus instructed him to do. His whole life would have taken on a new and wonderful purpose and meaning.

June 2

Look after him

"'Look after him,' he said, 'and when I return, I will reimburse you for any extra expense you may have.'"

℘ Luke 10:35 ℘

The parable of the Good Samaritan is probably one of the most famous stories of all time and carries a profound message.

A man was traveling from Jerusalem to Jericho when he was set upon by thieves. They stripped him naked, beat him, and left him to die. After a while a priest came along the road. He saw the man but quickly crossed to the other side and passed as far away from him as he could. The next traveler to come past was a Levite, also a religious man, and he also pretended not to see the man.

Finally, a Samaritan came along and when he saw the man, he immediately stopped. His heart was moved with compassion for him. Straight away he began to treat the man's wounds. With a great struggle he managed to lift the man onto the back of his donkey and transported him to a nearby hotel, where he continued to care for him.

The following day, he settled accounts with the innkeeper and left some extra money with him, asking him to carry on looking after the man. He had to continue with his journey, but should the money he had left not be sufficient to cover costs, he would settle the difference the next time he passed that way.

The message is clear and simple. The Father is looking for people who are prepared to reach out to others from a heart of sympathy and compassion. Are we sensitive to the needs around us? Many people in our communities are in desperate situations. But how often do we turn a blind eye to these people? How often do we walk on by on the opposite side of the road, while quickly trying to forget everything we have seen? Become involved with those people in need in your community!

The best food

"Martha, Martha," the Lord answered, "you are worried and upset about many things, but only one thing is needed. Mary has chosen what is better, and it will not be taken away from her."

Luke 10:41-42

Jesus and His disciples arrived in Bethany, a town about three miles from Jerusalem. Martha and Mary lived in this peaceful town with their brother Lazarus. Jesus was always welcome in their home.

It seems as if Martha was the elder sister. She warmly greeted Jesus when He arrived at their house. John tells us, "*When Martha heard that Jesus was coming, she went out to meet him, but Mary stayed at home*" (Lk. 11:20). Martha was the hostess. But as soon as Jesus had entered the house, Mary immediately went and sat at His feet. She probably had lots of questions she wanted to ask Him and listened carefully to His answers.

Martha was upset about this. She got quite angry with her younger sister. The Bible tells us that Martha was worried about all the preparations that had to be made. She really did need help, and yet Mary just sat talking to Jesus.

You and I probably have some sympathy for Martha. We also tend to think that Mary should have helped her sister. But Jesus' answer surprises us, "*Martha, Martha, you are worried and upset about many things, but only one thing is needed.*" Jesus spoke to her in love, but addressed the issue very clearly. He knew her heart and knew that she was worried and upset. Jesus pointed out to her that Mary had chosen the best option, which was to listen to Him. This gave her rest and peace in her soul.

Jesus was not angry with Martha, but He did show her what her priorities in life should be. You and I should ensure that we regularly sit at the feet of Jesus rather than simply rushing around in His name.

June 4

What remains?

"But only one thing is needed. Mary has chosen what is better, and it will not be taken away from her."

༄ LUKE 10:42 ༄

When Jesus visited the house of Martha, Mary, and Lazarus in Bethany, He spoke to Martha about her frustration when Mary spent more time listening to Him than helping her prepare the meal. Jesus helped her see that she should not be upset and worried about such matters. He helped her get her priorities straight.

Of course, we do have to pay attention to earthly matters. If we do not eat then we won't live very long! So preparing food and drink is important for our survival. But there is a right time and place to focus on them. If, however, we focus on them too much, we will begin to neglect our spiritual relationship with the Lord. We consist of spirit, soul, and body. And each of these three aspects needs to be healthy. It seems that Martha paid more attention to the physical aspect than to spiritual matters.

According to Jesus, Mary chose the best part. He said, *"It will not be taken away from her."* Earthly things, no matter how important, are of a temporary nature. We enjoy the food we eat today, but by tomorrow we will have forgotten it. Our bodies use it up and so we need more food in order to carry on living. But the words of God never return void. They remain in our spirits for all eternity. They will never be taken from us if we accept them in faith, into the good soil of our hearts, as described by Jesus in His parable. They will continue to bear more and more fruit for the glory of God.

We do not need to neglect earthly things, but let's get our priorities straight. We should eat of the words of God that can never be taken from us. May the Lord help us to achieve the right balance in life and to make the right decisions.

Martha, Martha

"Martha, Martha," the Lord answered, "you are worried and upset about many things."

LUKE 10:41

We might be tempted to see Martha in a negative light when we read Jesus' words that Mary had chosen what was better by sitting at His feet. It almost seems as if she did not have a spiritual relationship with Him and did not have deep spiritual insight.

But this conclusion is not altogether correct. We know that she loved Him very much and that she showed her love in practical ways, such as her desire to care for His needs. Perhaps Jesus' words about what was best – busyness and concern about looking after someone or sitting quietly and listening to His words – gave her a new perspective on her life. Later, when her brother, Lazarus, died, and Jesus went to their house, John tells us, *"When Martha heard that Jesus was coming, she went out to meet him, but Mary stayed at home"* (11:20). Then we see that Martha, not Mary, gave spiritual insight into the situation when she said, *"Lord, if you had been here, my brother would not have died. But I know that even now God will give you whatever you ask"* (11:21-22). Her brother had been in the grave for four days already and yet she spoke these words of faith in the power of Jesus and in His ability to change the situation.

Martha was the practical one, but she had a deep faith. Listen to what she said, *"Yes, Lord, I believe that you are the Christ, the Son of God, who was to come into the world"* (11:27). And then she went to Mary and very gently, without reproach and with much love, said, *"The Teacher is here, and is asking for you"* (11:28).

June 6

Please, Daddy!

"Which of you fathers, if your son asks for a fish, will give him a snake instead?"

ஐ Luke 11:11 ଓ

When the disciples asked Jesus to teach them to pray, He gave them the model we call The Lord's Prayer. Then He told them a parable about a man who was already in bed one night and yet he got up to help a friend who came to ask for food. Jesus ends the section by referring to the example of earthly fathers.

The question Jesus asks is whether there is any father who would give his son a snake when he had asked for a fish. If the child asked for an egg, would he give him a scorpion instead? The answer is obvious: of course not! Good fathers do not treat their children with such meanness. Sometimes dads will not give their children certain things because they know they would not be good for their children to have. Sometimes it is best to say no to a child's request. But if the child truly needs something, as in the examples Jesus used, then a father has no greater joy than giving his child what he or she has asked for. He would definitely give his child a fish or an egg if it was at all possible for him to do so.

Jesus then says, *"If you then, though you are evil, know how to give good gifts to your children, how much more will your Father in heaven give the Holy Spirit to those who ask him!"* (v. 13). Yes, God will give us everything that we have need of. He gives us good things, including the gift of the Holy Spirit. Someone once said that the Holy Spirit is like the executor of God's estate. He issues the promises of the New Testament to us – promises made by the Father and given to you and me through Jesus Christ. He knows what we need and gives us what God wants to give us.

Ask God freely today to give you what you need.

The finger of God

"But if I drive out demons by the finger of God, then the kingdom of God has come to you."

☙ Luke 11:20 ❧

On more than one occasion Jesus cast demons out of people. Once, when He cast a demon out of a man who could not speak, the people were amazed. But some were skeptical and said that He had done so with the help of Beelzebub whose name means the commander of flies. But Jesus answered that he had cast the demon out of the man by the finger of God, and that this was a sign that the kingdom of God was truly among them.

The finger of God? What does this expression mean? It would seem that references to the finger of God refer to His power. Some interpreters say that it is the working of the Holy Spirit. However we understand it, it does remind us of when Moses stood before Pharaoh and instructed Aaron to swing his rod and hit the floor with it. As he did so, people and animals were suddenly plagued by millions of gnats. Every grain of dust in Egypt seemed to turn into a gnat, the Bible tells us. The magicians of Egypt tried to do what Aaron had done, but they could not. The magicians then said to Pharaoh, *"This is the finger of God"* (Ex. 8:19).

May the finger of God be visible in your life today as God reveals His power in every situation in which you call on Him and trust in Him. His power is indescribably great.

June 8

For or Against

"He who is not with me is against me, and he who does not gather with me scatters."

∞ MATTHEW 12:30 ∞

There is a universal battle in progress between light and darkness. It is not possible to remain neutral in the fight between Christ and Satan. People that are not on the side of Christ are quite simply against Him.

There is no place for compromise in the kingdom of God. Mixed seed cannot be sown in the fields of God's work. Only pure seed can be used. No one can serve both light and darkness. The truth of Christ can never be presented by means of a lie. You are either for Him or against Him.

The Bible has many examples of compromises that ended in disaster. Think about what happened when Saul made an offering to God but was not obedient to the instructions God had given him. God did not accept his offering (cf. 1 Sam. 15:1-23). When Peter wanted to compromise and keep people happy by bending the pure message of salvation through grace to include acts of legalism, Paul confronted him (cf. Gal. 2:11-21). Paul admonished him to both speak and live according to the truth. When the "sons of God" married the "daughters of men" it resulted in such a chaotic mess that God had to send the flood to wipe it all out (cf. Gen. 6:1-2, 13). That is why the true leaders and prophets of God call people to make a clear choice. Joshua said that the people of Israel were to leave their foreign gods and choose God (cf. Josh. 24:15). Elijah spoke to the nation and asked, *"How long will you falter between two opinions? If the Lord is God, follow him; but if Baal, follow him"* (1 Kgs. 18:21).

The Lord is calling us to make a definite choice for Him today. Are you prepared to make that choice?

Sensational news

As the crowds increased, Jesus said, "This is a wicked generation. It asks for a miraculous sign, but none will be given it except the sign of Jonah."

ᘓ LUKE 11:29 ᘐ

People love to hear sensational news. Gossip columns divulging people's weaknesses, scandals and rifts in families – particularly of celebrities – ensure that newspapers and glossy magazines sell like hot cakes. Everything that is corrupt in our society attracts the attention of sensation seekers. What a shame this is. All the beautiful things that happen are overshadowed by the evil that flourishes all around.

Matthew mentions that some of the Scribes and Pharisees came to Jesus and said, *"Teacher, we want to see a miraculous sign from you"* (12:38). It is pretty clear that their intentions were not pure. They wanted to discredit Jesus before the people who followed Him. In a sly and cunning way they confronted Jesus, pretending to want Him to perform spectacular miracles so that they would really believe in Him.

The first question that springs to mind is, What more did they want to see than what Jesus had already done? Had they not seen the miraculous healings, the way people had been freed from disastrous circumstances, the multiplying of the bread and fish, and all the other miraculous signs? They said this wasn't enough. They wanted a miracle straight from heaven, something bigger, something more sensational. But Jesus saw right through their plan and that is why He called them a wicked generation.

Beware of the booby traps of sensationalism! Sensational things only stoke unholy fires in the hearts of people. Hold fast to the simplicity of the gospel and worship God in spirit and in truth.

June 10

The sign of Jonah

"This is a wicked generation. It asks for a miraculous sign, but none will be given it except the sign of Jonah."

℘ LUKE 11:29 ℘

When the crowds, spurred on by the Pharisees, began to call out for a spectacular miracle and challenged Jesus to do it, our Savior simply refused to comply. After all, He knew what was in their hearts and knew what their intentions were. They did not have a hunger for a real relationship with God. But because of their corrupt hearts they wanted to pressurize Him into stimulating their fleshly desires for sensation.

Jesus told them that there would be a sign, but it would be very different from what they expected. They would be given the sign of Jonah. Like Jonah who spent three days in the belly of a fish, so Jesus would be swallowed by the earth in death. And just as Jonah escaped from his sea-creature prison, so would Jesus escape the prison of death. Jonah was saved but Jesus is the risen Savior

Through this comparison Jesus was saying that the greatest miracle of all time would happen during their lifetime. He would triumph over death and would rise as a victor from the grave. What greater miracle can there be than someone rising from the grave to live forever? Jesus is the one who overcame death.

These days there are people, including theologians, who question the veracity of Jonah in the fish. So it is interesting to note that Jesus uses this Old Testament incident to make the point about the greatest miracle ever. Jonah was an example of His own life.

Jesus rose from the dead for you and for me. His resurrection was the greatest demonstration of His power. Rejoice and be glad because your spiritual eyes were opened to the greatest miracle of all time. Even though you may be surrounded by many mockers and scorners who, like their counterparts of old, are asking for a miracle before they will believe, you can simply say that you believe in Him, the Risen Lord.

Nineveh will rise!

"The men of Nineveh will stand up at the judgment with this generation and condemn it; for they repented at the preaching of Jonah, and now one greater than Jonah is here."

℘ LUKE 11:32 ℘

Jesus said that on the great Judgment Day the people of Nineveh will rise and bear testimony against unbelievers. They will testify about what happened in their city and their testimony will count against the Scribes and Pharisees and people who thronged around Jesus but refused to believe. Instead of acknowledging Him as Messiah, they challenged Him to perform miracles.

The testimony and example of the Ninevites will be overwhelming. They will tell of how a prophet named Jonah came to them and warned them to repent before God and they did. But the Scribes and the Pharisees had the Son of God in their midst. And over and over again He spoke to them about the Kingdom of God and called them to repentance (cf. Mt. 4:17). Jonah was foolish and sinful, but Jesus Christ was completely without sin, filled with the Holy Spirit, with love and with great wisdom.

Jonah warned the people of Nineveh that if they did not repent their city would be completely destroyed. The message Jesus brought was one of grace, forgiveness and salvation that no person could earn or deserve. Jonah performed no miracles, but the ministry of Jesus teemed with the miraculous. And this is why the testimony against those who heard Jesus but did not believe will be so forceful. They will have no excuse on the Day of Judgment when the people of Nineveh will rise and testify.

Dear friend, don't insist that the Lord should show you miracles. Simply believe Him with childlike faith. Read His Word, listen to what He says and see all that He did. Accept the words of Jesus and respond to them with enthusiasm. Follow Him and serve Him. Then Nineveh will not be able to bear witness against you on the Day of Judgment.

June 12

The queen bears witness

"The Queen of the South will rise at the judgment with the men of this generation and condemn them; for she came from the ends of the earth to listen to Solomon's wisdom, and now one greater than Solomon is here."

ꝏ LUKE 11:31 ꝏ

After speaking about the sign of Jonah and the Ninevites, Jesus goes on to speak about the Queen of the South, the Queen of Sheba, who will rise on the Day of Judgment together with the people of His day, and she will testify against them. She came from the far reaches of the earth to listen to the wisdom of Solomon. But Jesus is greater and more important than Solomon!

- In 1 Kings 10 and in 2 Chronicles 9 we are told about how far she traveled so that she could visit King Solomon's realm. The Scribes and Pharisees and others like them did not go to any great lengths to get near to Jesus. They did not realize that He was Immanuel, God with them.
- The Queen of Sheba gave many wonderful and expensive treasures and gifts to Solomon, but the indifferent crowds around Jesus gave Him nothing. In fact they decided to take His life from Him! They hated Him.
- The Queen of Sheba made her long journey because she had heard rumors about the riches and wisdom of Solomon but the people around Jesus heard His truth from His own mouth.
- It doesn't seem as if she received an invitation from Solomon to visit him. And yet Jesus issued many invitations to the people around Him – invitations to accept His wisdom and truth and to be included in His kingdom.

Will the Queen of Sheba testify against us on the Judgment Day? We can make sure that won't happen if we listen to His wisdom and accept what He says to us.

A clean eye

"Your eye is the lamp of your body. When your eyes are good, your whole body also is full of light. But when they are bad, your body also is full of darkness."

Luke 11:34

Recently I spoke to an elderly lady who, after years of not being able to see clearly, underwent a small operation. The doctors removed the cataracts that had been growing over her eyes. Her whole face shone as she told me how she can once again see clearly and how well she can once again read. With a playful grin on her face, she said that the weeds that had been growing in her eyes had been pulled out and everything was once again clean.

Jesus used a simple image in this passage. If your eyes are clean and bright and wide open then you can see clearly. Your body will be able to gauge exactly what needs to be done. Your hands will take hold of things easily and your feet will walk without tripping and stumbling. On the other hand, if your eyes have been affected by cataracts or some kind of disease they cannot function accurately and you struggle to move around freely. The worst extreme of this is complete blindness, a permanent darkness.

When your inner vision has been set right, washed by the blood of Jesus and made holy by the presence of the Holy Spirit, your entire character is enlightened. Suddenly you have a clear and definite insight into the things of God. The glory of God becomes very real. Your new spiritual eyes help you to see things of God that you had never noticed before. But if your heart is not right with God you are living in a sad state in which you stumble around in moral and spiritual darkness.

Let us ask the Lord to make our spiritual eyes clear and clean so that we can see what is unclear to us now!

June 14

Completely lit up

"Therefore, if your whole body is full of light, and no part of it dark, it will be completely lighted, as when the light of a lamp shines on you."

ꙮ LUKE 11:36 ꙮ

The Gospel of Jesus Christ is often compared to light. The darkness is the sinful world. The prince of darkness rules over people who live in the darkness. But Jesus is the Light of the world and He came to bring light to people.

In today's text Jesus says that our whole body must be lit up and all the dark places brought into His light. Then we will be filled with light, which is what God wants for you and me. He wants us to shine brightly for Him. The emphasis here is that we should be *"completely lighted, as when the light of a lamp shines on you."* No particle of our being should be in darkness. If this is true then the quality of the light that will shine through us will be so clear and bright that it will be exceptional. In other words, Jesus is saying that if your whole being is flooded with His spiritual light – that is His wisdom, His holiness, His joy – then you will be truly enlightened. You will be as sharp and brilliant as the brightest light.

All Christians are engaged in a battle to allow God's light to shine in us, and as we do so we will find that certain areas of our lives are brightly lit. But there are still areas where darkness has not been removed. We don't really allow God's light to shine in these dark places. We still cosset certain sins, we refuse to let go of certain passions, we do not move out of the prison of certain things that bind us. And so we are not completely in the light.

Let us ask the Lord to shine His light on every aspect of our lives. Make a point of identifying your dark spots, and switch His light on.

Practices

But the Pharisee, noticing that Jesus did not first wash before the meal, was surprised.

LUKE 11:38

One day a Pharisee invited Jesus to have dinner at his house. The Pharisee also invited many of his colleagues. He might very well have had a sincere desire to find some clarity about Jesus. On the other hand he could have wanted to debate with Jesus, which is something the Pharisees did a lot of in those days.

When Jesus was reclining at the table the Pharisee noticed that He had not performed the ceremonial washing of His hands, which was essential to the Pharisee's interpretation of the law. He was amazed at this, although he said nothing. But Jesus knew what was going on in his heart.

The Scribes and Pharisees had a long, complicated list of practices that they had to fulfill in every detail of their lives. These were ceremonial acts that they performed because they believed that through them they would gain God's favor. Mark informs us that the Pharisees, and Jews in general, did not usually eat until they had thoroughly washed their hands. There were masses of other traditions that had been passed down, such as the right way to wash cups, jugs, bowls, and chairs (cf. Mk. 7:4). These things had little to do with proper hygiene or with a good relationship with God. For the Pharisees they were religious rituals that they had learned and that they very narrowly followed. Jesus was clean. But according to the Pharisees, after Jesus had touched a heathen He would not be clean in the eyes of God and that is why He should wash His hands. It was not about clean hands, but about spiritual purity.

Beware of spiritual practices and customs that we carry out without thinking about what we are doing. Are our spiritual practices manmade, or are they truly the will of God?

June 16

"Yes, you Pharisees!"

Then the Lord said to him, "Now then, you Pharisees clean the outside of the cup and dish, but inside you are full of greed and wickedness."

෴ LUKE 11:39 ෴

Jesus began to address the Pharisees very strongly. They had a façade of righteousness but they had no power to live a godly life. They focused on appearing outwardly good, but their hearts were sinful. The Pharisee who invited Jesus to dinner was astounded that He did not wash His hands according to the accepted rituals and traditions. He wasn't concerned about germs, but about religious regulations.

What does it help, Jesus asked them, if a person's body is clean on the outside but his heart is mean and filthy? God, who made our bodies, also created our spirits and He is more concerned with what goes on in our hearts than what can be seen on the outside.

The issue here is hypocrisy. Jesus is not opposed to spiritual traditions as long as they are not used to disguise the truth. As long as they do not lead people away from the central focus of the message of the Kingdom. There are many places in the Old Testament where ceremonial laws seemed to conflict with spiritual obedience (cf. example Is. 1:10-17; Amos 5:21-24; Mic. 6:6-8).

What is important is that our hearts are right with God. Let us examine our hearts. Do we tend to focus more on outward expressions of worship? Are we often tempted to try to impress people with our "spirituality"? What's really important is what is in our hearts. Make sure that yours is clean and pure. A good churchly demeanor is worth little if our hearts are not pure. Let us make sure that we are not like the Pharisees.

Love and herbs

"Woe to you Pharisees, because you give God a tenth of your mint, rue and all other kinds of garden herbs, but you neglect justice and the love of God. You should have practiced the latter without leaving the former undone."

∞ LUKE 11:42 ∞

Jesus entered an open battle with the Pharisees. He stripped them of their masks of hypocrisy. It was as if Jesus had tolerated the sanctimoniousness of the Pharisees long enough. He talked to them about their lives, about the things they did and the condition of their hearts. He was very direct with them, but as we read His words we can see that He was upset about how they so foolishly wandered far from the truth of God's Word. He dearly longed to help these religious leaders develop a different attitude.

These religious men followed the regulations on tithing laid out in Leviticus 27:30-33 and Deuteronomy 14:22-29 to the smallest detail. They went even further than what was required, and ended up going to extremes. They had decided that it was necessary to measure a tenth of even the smallest herb that grew in their gardens, and they instructed their followers to do the same. But there was nothing in the law of Moses that required such a thing. Imagine trying to determine how many of your mint leaves should be given to the temple as part of your tithe! The Pharisees also went too far in the matter of fasting, washing of hands, and keeping the Sabbath. Today they would say you cannot even switch on a light on the Sabbath, because that would be work.

Jesus wanted to show them that the law was not about keeping petty rules, but about the love and righteousness of God. Of course we must obey what God commands us to, but we must do so out of a heart of love for Him.

June 18

Places of honor

"Woe to you Pharisees, because you love the most important seats in the synagogues and greetings in the marketplaces."

LUKE 11:43

Jesus continued to point out the hypocrisy of the Pharisees and the inconsistency of their actions. They were seen as the religious leaders of Israel, but in fact they confused people with all their regulations and ridiculous observing of manmade traditions. They were very conscious of performing outward actions properly, but the condition of their hearts was ignored.

Jesus said that wretchedness awaited them. He said that misery would come upon them because they loved to be given the places of honor in the synagogues and they felt great when people greeted them with honor and respect in the streets. They were arrogant leaders who jostled for position and really wanted other people to look up to them and honor them. They dressed fastidiously and elaborately, with false piety, and acted in ways that would attract the attention of other people. They wanted people to feel as if they should bow before them and greet them with formality and respect. The most important places in the synagogue were right at the front, and people who sat there faced the rest of the congregation. If you sat there you would be near to the person who was leading the service, but you could also see everyone else. And what's more, they could see you! These seats were considered important places for people who were honored.

Beloved, you and I have been called to be servants. We should not want to have special and important seats in church. We should not chase after positions of honor. We must not seek honor from other people. We must simply serve and love. Remember, the one who is first will be last.

Unmarked graves

> *"Woe to you, because you are like unmarked graves, which men walk over without knowing it."*
>
> LUKE 11:44

Jesus spoke directly to the Pharisees in an attempt to expose their hypocrisy. They put all their effort into maintaining a good image in the eyes of people.

Jesus said that they were like unmarked graves over which people walked unwittingly. Before the Jewish pilgrims set out for the Passover feast in Jerusalem, the graves alongside the roads were whitewashed so that they would be clearly visible. This practice ensured that no one would become ceremonially unclean by walking over dead men's bones. Jews were not allowed to participate in the important feasts if they were ceremonially unclean, and they believed that walking over places where bodies were buried would make them unclean. Unfortunately, in the process of marking the graves, some were overlooked and not painted white. Jesus was saying that people, without knowing it, could be ceremonially unclean because they did not know that they had walked over graves.

He said that the Pharisees were like those unmarked graves. Their lifestyle and teachings were full of dead men's bones and those who figuratively "walked" over them by obeying what they taught would actually become spiritually impure. This must have been a difficult thing for the Pharisees to hear. After all, they thought that they were the best, the super-spirituals! They looked down on everybody else (Lk. 18:9).

Let us make sure that what we teach brings the life of Jesus into people's lives.

June 20

The key has vanished

"Woe to you experts in the law, because you have taken away the key to knowledge. You yourselves have not entered, and you have hindered those who were entering."

℘ Luke 11:52 ℘

Once Jesus had given the Pharisees a thorough going over about their hypocrisy and arrogant attitudes that lacked spiritual depth, He began to focus on the experts in the law. They had studied law and were attorneys and advocates, but they belonged to the same party as the Pharisees. That is why one of them said to Jesus, *"Teacher, when you say these things, you insult us also"* (v. 45).

Jesus did not want to humiliate them. He only wanted to admonish them and point them in the right direction. They had been living a lie under the banner of the truth. That is why He told them that woes awaited them too because they overloaded people with burdens too heavy to carry, but would not lift a finger to try to help them lift the load.

They built monuments and shrines to the prophets, but it was their forefathers who had murdered them. Jesus said that the blood of the prophets would be on their hands because their actions agreed with what their forefathers had done. Hard words! Wretchedness waited for them because they, who were supposed to unlock the door to true wisdom and knowledge of God, had lost the key. They did not even walk in the wisdom they pretended to know about. And they prevented those people who wanted to enter the place of wisdom from going in.

The true key to the knowledge of God lies in repentance, in coming to Jesus to find peace, and being born again from above. They did not understand any of these things that Jesus tried to teach them. But you and I can make sure that we carry the true key that will unlock the door that will allow people to come to God.

Yeast

Be on your guard against the yeast of the Pharisees, which is hypocrisy.

LUKE 12:1

When Jesus spoke to the crowds about the Pharisees and the lawyers, He warned them of the hypocrisy and inconsistency of the Pharisees.

Duplicity and hypocrisy are metaphors drawn from the theater and acting. They describe a person who keeps his real self hidden behind a mask. Such behavior is false, dishonest, and misleading. It has nothing to do with truth and sincerity.

The influence of the Pharisees and lawyers was like yeast that works itself through a lump of dough. Yeast is mixed into bread dough so that it will rise. The Pharisees worked quietly in the background so that you could not see exactly what influence they were having. But their influence was enormous. The sins of the Pharisees affected the whole community negatively. Paul, in 1 Corinthians 5:6, says that a little yeast causes the whole batch to rise. He then admonished the Corinthians to get rid of the old yeast so that they could celebrate the Passover feast properly with the unleavened bread of purity and truth. The old yeast, their previous sinfulness, could have no part in the feast.

Through this image Jesus stated that the blind spiritual leaders had actually become channels of sin. They spread their yeast wherever they went. But before we begin pointing fingers at anyone else (Jesus was at liberty to do so because He was without sin) we must examine our own hearts and see if we have fought the yeast of sin in our own lives. If there is any hypocrisy or falseness about us when we act in the Name of the Lord, then we are no better than the Pharisees.

June 22

See all, hear all

"There is nothing concealed that will not be disclosed, or hidden that will not be made known. What you have said in the dark will be heard in the daylight, and what you have whispered in the ear in the inner rooms will be proclaimed from the roofs."

Luke 12:2-3

When Jesus spoke about the Scribes and the Pharisees, He pointed out their falseness and hypocrisy. He said that there is nothing that is hidden that will not be revealed. And that there are no secrets that will not be made known to everyone. Everything that people say in the dark will be heard in the daylight. Things whispered to others behind closed doors will be shouted from the rooftops.

Not only are hypocrisy and falseness dishonest, but they are also foolishness. The Bible reminds us on almost every page that the truth will be victorious, if not in this life, then definitely on the day on which the Last Judgment will take place (cf. Mt. 10:26, Rom. 2:16, Ecc. 12:14). On that day the books that record every detail of every person's life will be opened (cf. Rev. 20:12).

God Himself will reveal the secrets of each person (cf. Rom. 2:16). On that day everything will abruptly be laid bare for everyone to hear and see.

It is, therefore, foolish to live under the illusion that things can be kept secret and hidden and that we can live day by day behind a façade. Jesus calls people to live openly and honestly before Him, to be honest about their sins and truly repent of them rather than to live behind a mask in the foolish hope that no one will ever notice. When we do something wrong we can, thank God, turn to the Lord Jesus who paid the penalty for our sins on the cross and who is prepared to wipe out the record of our guilt and sin. Christians do not have to live in fear of the secrets that will be made known on that day. We have been set free by His blood.

Of whom are you afraid?

"I tell you, my friends, do not be afraid of those who kill the body and after that can do no more."

℘ LUKE 12:4 ℘

It is an unfortunate fact of life that people are not always good to one another but can hurt each other and sometimes even kill. Murder has become an everyday occurrence in our society. People do not place a high value on human life. Some people have even been killed for a few cents.

And yet Jesus told His disciples that they should not fear people who could kill their bodies and could do nothing more to harm them. We consist of more than our bodies. We are actually spiritual beings and long after we have left our earthly bodies behind, our spirits will continue to exist. Jesus wanted to help His disciples and us to keep things in perspective. Our bodies are just temporary homes. Paul compares them to a tent that will be dismantled (2 Cor. 5:1). Paul lived with the knowledge that any day could be his last, and yet he did not fear other people. And today there are many Christians who have good reason to fear others, for they are persecuted just because they are disciples of Jesus.

It is important to remember that people can only harm your body, but they cannot touch your spirit. It was this idea that led Victor Frankl to develop his life's philosophy and formulate the foundation for his psychotherapy. When he was incarcerated in a Nazi concentration camp, he noticed that even though his body deteriorated, no one could break his spirit. What a victorious perspective to have!

Jesus said that we should rather fear God. This does not mean that we should be frightened of Him but that we should honor and respect Him. He remains the high, exalted, holy Lord. Bow before Him and worship Him. Serve Him with honor. If you remain in right standing with Him you will live no matter how much your physical body is threatened.

June 24

Your hair

> *"Indeed, the very hairs of your head are all numbered. Don't be afraid; you are worth more than many sparrows."*
>
> ꕤ LUKE 12:7 ꕤ

Some of us have a thick mop of hair while others lose hair every day. Men who are balding apply all kinds of remedies to try to prevent further hair loss. But, says Jesus, God knows about every strand of hair that you have. He has counted each hair on our heads, therefore we have no need to fear. The Lord pays attention to the tiniest details in the lives of each of His children.

Jesus then went on to say how we are worth more than many sparrows. There were thousands in the areas where He preached, and even though they are tiny birds, He said that God has His eye on each one. People used to catch the sparrows, kill them and pluck their feathers. Then they would grill them and eat them. They were regarded as delicacies, and still are in some regions of the world. People often used to sell the sparrows, and Jesus refers to this when He says that two are sold for a penny. The original Greek text says that two were sold for an *as* or *assarion* (Mt. 10:29). The sparrows were very cheaply bought in the market places and yet Jesus assured His disciples that not one of them is lost to God's sight. Even when they fall they are under His loving care.

Jesus wanted to assure us that all people, and particularly His children, are very precious to Him. That is why we do not have to be afraid of anything and can trust Him wholeheartedly. We are worth far more than a flock of sparrows, more than a hundred sparrows, more than an infinite number of sparrows. Christian, take heart! God's loving care will never let you down, not even in your hour of death (cf. Rom. 8:31-39).

Gehenna

"But I will show you whom you should fear: Fear him who, after the killing of the body, has power to throw you into hell. Yes, I tell you, fear him."

ꕤ LUKE 12:5 ꕤ

Hell does exist. Jesus often referred to it and warned people about it. In today's verse Jesus encourages His children to live in respect of God and to fear Him because He has the power and authority to banish people to hell after their deaths.

The English word, *hell*, is *Gehenna* in the original Greek. This word is derived from Ge-Hinnom which means the land belonging to Hinnom. This stretch of ground was a narrow valley that originally belonged to a man named Hinnom. It is found on the outskirts of Jerusalem, just south of the city in a westerly direction. At first it would have been a very pretty valley. Those of you who have visited Jerusalem will know that it is a beautiful city situated on some hills with beautiful valleys stretching from it in all directions. But unfortunately this valley did not remain beautiful. An altar to an idol was built there. Later on it was renamed Topheth, which means "the burning place".

This beautiful valley changed into a dreadful place. It was here that the evil kings Ahaz and Manasseh offered their children to the dreadful god Molech (2 Chr. 28:3, 1 Kgs. 11:7). In the minds of the people the valley became associated with the place where God would deal with unbelieving and evil people. It would be the valley of slaughter (Jer. 7:31-34). They were relieved when King Hosea declared that all the places used for worshiping idols were to be destroyed. And so the valley became the refuse dump where garbage was burned. Flames could be seen rising from the valley on a regular basis, and the place stank. Thus it became a symbol for hell.

Those who are in a right relationship with God need not fear Gehenna.

June 26

No forgiveness

"And everyone who speaks a word against the Son of Man will be forgiven, but anyone who blasphemes against the Holy Spirit will not be forgiven."

ꕤ LUKE 12:10 ꕤ

In this verse Jesus was talking about the blasphemy against the Holy Spirit.

The Bible is full of examples of people who sinned against God, people who wandered off the right road and deliberately opposed God's will. And yet the Bible tells us that each one of these people was forgiven if they repented and confessed their sins to God. Think of David who committed the sins of adultery, duplicity, and murder. His sins against the Father were forgiven. Think of Simon Peter who denied Jesus three times. Jesus forgave him and restored him. Think of Paul who massacred Christians, but who was completely forgiven and then appointed by Jesus to serve in His Kingdom.

There is only one kind of person who cannot be forgiven. Jesus said those who blasphemed His Holy Spirit could not be forgiven. He was talking about people like the Pharisees who were bitter opponents of Jesus. They attributed the things Christ did to the devil while it was actually the Holy Spirit who was responsible for revealing the power of God to people. And they never retracted these foolish statements. There was no sorrow in their hearts and no desire to repent. They brought judgment upon themselves by their own hardness of heart. Their sin could not be forgiven because they were unwilling to walk the humble road of repentance. There is hope for a thief or a murderer who shows regret and remorse, but there is no hope for one who will not repent.

Friend, if you desire to live in purity and righteousness before God, then you do not have a hard heart. For you forgiveness, redemption and a new beginning are a glorious reality.

You will know

"When you are brought before synagogues, rulers and authorities, do not worry about how you will defend yourselves or what you will say."

Luke 12:11

People were often brought before the synagogue to be tried for their sinful behavior. This was a dreadful experience for the ordinary man on the street. The disciples realized that Jesus was in trouble with the Pharisees and Scribes and that they wanted Him dead. This placed their lives at risk too. They must have been wondering what they would say in their defense if they had to stand accused before a tribunal of Scribes and Pharisees. At the very least the possibility of having to defend themselves filled them with dread.

Yet Jesus told His disciples not to be afraid. Something wonderful would happen to them when they were brought before the men who had studied the law all their lives. The Holy Spirit would teach them what to say. At the exact moment you need to know what to say, the Holy Spirit will work in you in a miraculous way. He will work in your understanding to give you the insight that is needed to be able to say exactly what needs to be said in that situation.

What a wonderful promise this is. We see that these words were fulfilled when first Peter, and then later Peter and John, were brought before the council in Acts 4:8-12, 19-20. We see a similar thing with Paul in Acts 21:39-22:1 and in other places. Many more modern Christians have also testified how the Lord, through the Holy Spirit, gave them the right words at the right time so that they declared the truth in the way needed in their situation. This is one of the most wonderful privileges given to the children of God. The Holy Spirit helps and teaches us in all kinds of situations. Let us rejoice in this!

June 28

"Don't worry, be happy!"

Then Jesus said to his disciples: "Therefore I tell you, do not worry about your life, what you will eat; or about your body, what you will wear."

LUKE 12:22

One of the most beautiful parts of the Bible is where Jesus promises that He will look after His children. He emphatically tells us that we do not need to worry about anything that will happen to us tomorrow, or even about today. He said that we should not worry about what we will eat or what clothes we will wear.

Jesus declares that He will care for us, but He also gives us a command. Think about how often you have disobeyed this command of His. How often have you worried about things like your income, having enough money to pay accounts, your physical needs, and so on? As Christians we know that our lives, and that includes our bodies, are under God's constant care. God alone is able to extend our lives by a single hour, or day, or year. If He has given us life as a gift and if He has made our bodies, can He not also take care of the small details? Food and clothes are not hard for Him to provide for us. And to illustrate His point, Jesus points to the birds of the air. He specifically talks about ravens. They know nothing about farming or about how to gather food into barns. And yet God looks after them. Furthermore, the Bible lists ravens among the "unclean" birds (Lev. 11:13-19). But God still cares for them. The implication is very clear: why, then, should we be anxious? Are you not worth far more than the birds?

Make a definite decision that today, and for each day of the rest of your life, you will trust God more and more and be less and less anxious. Just as the song says, "Don't worry, be happy!"

Life and lilies

"Who of you by worrying can add a single hour to his life?"

ꕤ Luke 12:25 ꕤ

Let's spend a little more time looking at the important lesson that Jesus wants us to learn in Luke 12. We should not worry about anything but trust Him to care for us. Stress only brings problems into our lives. That is why we must cultivate the good habit of handing our worries to Him in faith. Faith is trusting God on the basis of the promises He has made to us. A person who walks in faith cannot, at the same time, be worried. The one excludes the other. Faith is surrendering to God's loving care.

Jesus rhetorically asked if you or I could lengthen our lives through continually worrying over earthly matters. Of course not. We might end up worrying ourselves to death, but not to life! Anxiety shortens a person's life, never lengthens it.

Look carefully and see how the lilies grow, says Jesus. We cannot know for sure what kind of lily Jesus had in mind. He was probably referring to wild flowers in general. Look and see how beautifully and freely and easily wild flowers grow. They don't go shopping in boutiques; they don't wander around malls looking for fancy clothes to wear. And yet Solomon in all his glory was never dressed as wonderfully as the lilies of the field. Wild flowers do not live for very long, but soon there will be new flowers that God will care for.

Once again we find the wonderful message: the Lord God undertakes to care for His children and so we should learn to relax in His care. Why do we lie awake at night, tossing and turning worrying about all kinds of things? Let's break that bad habit today.

June 30

Different

"For the pagan world runs after all such things, and your Father knows that you need them."

LUKE 12:30

People who live without faith in God very definitely have a problem. They have to provide for themselves. They have to figure out ways of making ends meet at the end of each month. They have to find ways of getting by on their annual budgets. They lie awake at night devising ways to survive their old age, when they grow too old to work. Jesus says, *"For the pagan world runs after such things."* This is how people in the world react. This is how they live. This is their nature and their way of approaching life.

Jesus goes on to emphasize that the children of God, those who believe in Him and trust Him, live with a completely different attitude. *"Your Father knows that you need these things."* Christians have a different way of thinking, a different way of speaking, a different way of behaving. There is a difference between them and unbelievers. Christians differ in their innermost desires and they set their hearts on different things. They are governed by different values. They are motivated by a different kind of love. Not a love of self or possessions, but the love of God and His Kingdom.

If the church does not look different from the world, if we do not dance to a different tune, if we do not respond differently to disappointments, if we do not celebrate in different ways, if we do not think differently about money, then there is something very, very wrong.

Christians are not concerned about material things, but are focused on a God who will provide.

July

What a promise!

"But seek his kingdom, and these things will be given to you as well."

ঌ LUKE 12:31 ଓ

Christians are not supposed to worry about their lives. They are also not supposed to set their hearts on material possessions or to worry about what they will eat or drink. If they are not supposed to worry about these things, then what are they expected to do?

Christians have a different goal. They do not focus on earthly possessions, but on a heavenly kingdom. The kingdom of God has become more important in their lives than anything else. The king of the kingdom rules and reigns in their hearts and their lives belong to Him. That is why Jesus said that we must seek the kingdom of God and then everything that we need to live will be given to us as a gift from the hand of God.

Followers of Christ are thus advised to make sure that God's rule is more and more evident in their lives and also in the lives of others and the community in which they live. They desire to establish God's kingdom in their work, the sports they play, in their social life, in their children's schools. That means that they give of their best at all times and do all they can to establish God's kingdom wherever they go.

The heavenly Father sees what they do and as a reward of grace He makes sure that not only do they have an abundance of spiritual blessings, but also the daily care they need in terms of food, clothing, and shelter. God will provide for them in their daily needs. What a promise! Let us live as citizens of the kingdom of Heaven.

Commit and receive

"Do not be afraid, little flock, for your Father has been pleased to give you the kingdom."

ꕤ LUKE 12:32 ꕤ

Jesus, in verse 31, told His disciples that they needed to commit themselves to the kingdom of God. If they do so then He will give them everything they need day by day.

Then He followed with these wonderful words, *"Do not fear, little flock."* This is the only place in the New Testament that this term is used. He is the heavenly Shepherd and we are His little flock. And He has undertaken to care for us. Then He adds that the Father wants to give us the kingdom. First we must commit ourselves to the kingdom then we will receive the kingdom. Is this not a contradiction?

Not at all, because Jesus came to establish His kingdom on earth. He invites people to be part of it and gives it to them as a gift. But as soon as they receive it, a new kingdom law begins to operate in their lives. They become active in the kingdom. They begin to live in a way that reflects kingdom principles. They receive their strength to live from the Holy Spirit. They work out their own salvation with fear and trembling, but can only do so because God is at work in them. *"For it is God who works in you both to will and to do for His good purpose"* (cf. Phil. 2:12-13). As they live out the principles of the kingdom, the kingdom increases in their lives. And God delights to give His children their heritage in the kingdom.

Let us commit ourselves to the kingdom of God and as we do so we will see His kingdom expand in our lives.

July 3

Sell your possessions?

"Sell your possessions and give to the poor. Provide purses for yourselves that will not wear out, a treasure in heaven that will not be exhausted, where no thief comes near and no moth destroys."

Luke 12:33

When Jesus says that we should sell our possessions and give the proceeds to the poor, it could lend itself to much misunderstanding. We must understand this instruction in its context. In the previous portion of Scripture, Jesus had told the parable of the rich fool (vv. 16-21). This man kept all he had for himself. He was selfish, and Jesus now addresses this kind of attitude. Christians should not hold on to their possessions, but should be prepared to share what they have with others.

Must they sell everything they have? No. Jesus did not tell all His followers to sell all they had and give the proceeds to the poor. If this were so, Christians would become a burden to society. Remember that the first church community in Acts sold what they had and shared it among themselves. And very soon they became a needy congregation! Paul had to collect money from other congregations to keep them going. We are supposed to be generous but we are not supposed to be irresponsible by giving everything away and then having to be dependent on others for charity.

The Bible gives us clear guidelines about how we should manage our money. Consider passages such as 1 Corinthians 16:2-3 and 2 Corinthians 8:1-9, as well as Galatians 6:10. The Lord gives us possessions and property and He makes us self-sufficient in every way so that we can have enough to give to others. There are so many poor and needy people around us. Let us help them any way we can.

Treasure in Heaven

"Sell your possessions and give to the poor. Provide purses for yourselves that will not wear out, a treasure in heaven that will not be exhausted, where no thief comes near and no moth destroys."

ꟷ LUKE 12:33 ꟷ

As Christians, we focus on a treasure that is stored up in heaven. And that is why our resources will never run dry. We have an incomparable treasure in heaven that no thief can touch and that no moths can destroy.

Everything that we do on earth in the name of the Lord is an investment in His kingdom. And in heaven there are no thieves, no moths, and no rust. Our riches consist of far more than money. We have a treasure chest of God's faithfulness, a life that will never end, a spring of living water that will never cease to flow. It is gift that will never be lost, a love from which we can never be separated, a calling on our lives that will never be withdrawn, promises from God that are "yes" and "amen" in Jesus Christ. His treasure is a secure foundation that will never give way beneath us and an inheritance that will never be lost. We are truly rich in Christ!

We are no longer foolish enough to make the things of this world our goal. We are no longer driven by a need to accumulate more and more money, or popularity, or prestige, or power, or status. We see beyond the here and now. In humble gratitude before God we now serve His kingdom, and the Lord Himself becomes our greatest treasure. And so our hearts are focused on Him. A person's heart cannot be in two places at the same time. Either your heart is focused on earthly treasure or it looks to the riches of heaven. Where is your heart?

Stand ready

"It will be good for those servants whose master finds them watching when he comes. I tell you the truth, he will dress himself to serve, will have them recline at the table and will come and wait on them."

LUKE 12:37

The slaves had been laboring all day and by now were exhausted. It was almost midnight but they did not know when their master was expected home. And he had instructed them to wait until he returned. He had been to a wedding. And, as is sometimes the case with weddings, things could go on for much longer than anticipated. He might not even get home before the rooster began to crow at dawn. But they were slaves, and this was part of their work. They had to wait for the owner of the house to return.

And so they did not even loosen the girdles that tied up their robes. Their robes were drawn up into their waistbands and they were ready for action. They had lighted all the lamps in the house, as if the owner of the house was about to arrive any minute now. They were ready to serve him the second they heard his knock on the door.

Jesus told this parable to remind us that we should always be ready for His Second Coming. He explained, *"It will be good for those servants whose master finds them watching when he comes"* (v. 37). And then He gave a wonderful promise that would never apply to slaves on earth. *"I tell you the truth, he will dress himself to serve, will have them recline at the table and will come and wait on them"* (v. 37). This is an amazing promise that when He returns, He will serve us just because we were wide awake and ready for His return. When Jesus was on earth His nature was to serve. Remember how He washed His disciples feet. He said that He was among His disciples as one who serves (cf. Lk. 22:27).

Let us make sure that we are blessed children of the Lord, ready and prepared for His return. We do not know when He will come, but let us make sure that we are ready. Perhaps it will be today!

The faithful and the unfaithful servant

"That servant who knows his master's will and does not get ready or does not do what his master wants will be beaten with many blows."

Luke 12:47

A man was ready to begin a long journey. Before he left he appointed his senior slave to take care of his business in his absence. That meant he also had to be responsible for the other slaves.

It is good for a wise and faithful manager when his master returns and finds that he has fulfilled his responsibilities. He will then put him in charge of everything he owns.

There is a second possibility. The manager who is appointed to take care of his master's goods could make a different decision. He might think to himself that his master will be away for a very long time, and so he beats the slaves that he is supposed to be looking after. He throws his weight around and makes life very unpleasant for them. And at the same time he eats all he can find, drinks his master's wine and gets drunk, and altogether develops a dissipated lifestyle.

But then suddenly, without warning, his master returns. He is deeply disappointed and immensely angry with the slave he put in charge. He punishes him severely, and casts him out. The slave knew what his master expected, but decided not to carry out the wishes of the one who owned him.

This was only a story, but it conveys a powerful and important message. Because we know that we have been called to live for our Lord, and because we know that He will return one day to take us to our eternal home, we need to be ready and faithful. We must decide to fulfill the duty that He has appointed for us.

Carpe Diem

"But the one who does not know and does things deserving punishment will be beaten with few blows. From everyone who has been given much, much will be demanded; and from the one who has been entrusted with much, much more will be asked."

∞ Luke 12:48 ∞

Jesus ended the parable of the faithful and unfaithful servants by saying that much will be expected from those who have received much. Much more will be expected from the person who has been entrusted with much. This makes it clear that the gifts and talents that the Lord has given us must be used for His glory. We should not be lazy in carrying out the responsibilities that God gives us. God gives us gifts, and He gives us the responsibility to develop and use those gifts for Him.

As with the slave in the parable who was given certain responsibilities, the Lord gives each of us certain responsibilities that we need to fulfill. We can choose whether we do so well, or badly. But if we approach the things God has given us to do in the wrong way, we will have problems on the Day of Judgment. If we are responsible about the things God has called us to do, and honor Him in the way we do His work, then we will receive our reward on that Day (cf. 2 Cor. 5:10).

What has God given to you? What gifts and talents have you received from Him? What are the things that you like to do? What can you do that will help other people? Do not be lazy with these things because you will be expected to give an account of everything that has been given to you. God expects you to use the gifts and talents and abilities that He has given you in practical ways. Use them to bless others. *Carpe Diem* – seize the day.

Make the most of every opportunity and redeem the time, we are admonished in Colossians 4:5. Make full use of everything God has put in your hands.

Fire must burn

"I have come to bring fire on the earth, and how I wish it were already kindled!"

LUKE 12:49

Jesus made an interesting statement when He remarked that He came to bring fire to the earth, and He wished that the fire had already been ignited!

We often find a connection between fire and judgment in the Bible. In many places we read that the judgment of God is likened to a burning flame. Isaiah says, *"For with fire and with his sword the Lord will execute judgment upon all men"* (66:16). When Amos describes God's coming judgment he says, *"I will send fire upon the walls of Gaza that will consume her fortresses"* (1:7). God, speaking through the prophet Joel says, *"I will show wonders in the heavens and on the earth, blood and fire and billows of smoke"* (2:30).

Paul, too, when talking about Christ's return and the judgment that will follow, says, *"This will happen when the Lord Jesus is revealed from heaven in blazing fire with his powerful angels. He will punish those who do not know God and do not obey the gospel of our Lord Jesus"* (2 Thes. 1:7-8).

So when Jesus says that He came to start a fire on earth then it is likely that He was talking about the Judgment of God that would be carried out against the sins of the people. The Lord had to settle the debt of sin. The judgment of sin took place on Golgotha. Jesus was the sin offering that was offered on the cross. And there He fulfilled the righteous requirements of God's judgment. And as He was offered in our place, our sins were consumed in the fire of God's judgment that burned against Him.

Jesus said that He wished the fire had already been kindled. It wasn't that He was looking forward to the pain and suffering, but He knew that if He did not suffer then the people He loved would never be set free. Our salvation depended on His pain, His suffering, the fire that He went through.

July 9

Baptism of fire

"But I have a baptism to undergo, and how distressed I am until it is completed!"

ꟷ LUKE 12:50 ꟷ

It is extremely painful to accidentally put your hand into boiling water. Your instinctive response would be to pull your hand out as quickly as possible.

The Greek word that has been transliterated as our English word "baptism" refers to something that has been completely submerged in water. Jesus had been baptized by John the Baptist, but here He refers to a different baptism that He would have to go through. This one is a baptism of fire, a baptism of pain. He mentioned how even the thought of it distressed Him, and how the distress would not diminish until the baptism was over. Jesus was referring to the immensity of the pain and suffering that lay ahead of Him. He would be thrown into the furnace of a horrific experience. Psalm 42 gives us a glimpse of what Jesus had to go through, *"My soul is downcast within me; therefore I will remember you from the land of the Jordan, the heights of Hermon – from Mount Mizar. Deep calls to deep in the roar of your waterfalls; all your waves and breakers have swept over me"* (vv. 6-7).

When James and John asked the Lord if they could have positions of honor in His kingdom, Jesus said to them, *"You don't know what you are asking. Can you drink the cup I drink or be baptized with the baptism I am baptized with?"* (Mk. 10:38).

When Jesus prayed in the Garden of Gethsemane, He pleaded for a way for the pain and agony that were overwhelming Him to be taken away. We cannot begin to imagine the agony that Jesus endured. He was completely submerged in pain. We can only thank Him for what He did for us. He was baptized in pain.

The Prince of Peace brings unrest?

"From now on there will be five in one family divided against each other, three against two and two against three."

ꕥ LUKE 12:52 ꕥ

When we read this portion of Scripture, we might think that Jesus is contradicting Himself. After all, doesn't the Bible call Him the Prince of Peace? Doesn't Isaiah 9:6 prophesy that He would bring peace to the earth? And didn't He Himself say that His followers should be peacemakers? The Bible is full of statements that declare that Jesus came to bring peace on earth. How could it then be possible that Jesus said that He did not come to bring peace to the earth – but division?

There is a technique in Jewish literature, called a *maschal*, that was used to elicit a specific response from those who read or heard it. It is a statement that seems to contradict itself, a paradox. When it is stated, one part seems to be untrue. It shocks the one who hears it into considering the statement carefully, and was used to drive a particular point home. What Jesus was therefore actually saying was not that He would not bring peace into the world, but that as a result of His kingdom being established, there would be divisions among people and in situations. Of course He is the Prince of Peace who came to give us His peace and who desires that people live in peace with one another. But those who accept His offer of peace and live according to it often come into conflict with those who reject His peace.

In one very real sense Jesus is actually the Great Divider. He brings people to the point where they have to make a choice. On the one side are the people who have chosen Him on the other side are those who reject Him. Those who desire His peace versus those who reject His peace. The tragic reality is that members of families could be divided against each other just because some of them have asked Christ into the home, and others don't want Him there.

July 11

How does the wind blow?

"Hypocrites! You know how to interpret the appearance of the earth and the sky. How is it that you don't know how to interpret this present time?"

Luke 12:56

Every day we watch weather forecasts on TV or read them in the newspapers to see what the weather will be like. When Jesus was on earth there were also many people who spent much time watching the sky to see what kind of weather to expect.

There are two main kinds of winds in Israel. The west wind blows in from the Mediterranean Sea and brings the moist sea air over the land that brings rain with it. But there is also another wind that comes from the south or the east. This wind blows across the hot southerly desert regions and it brings with it the high desert temperatures. This results in excessively hot weather and no rain. This is called the Sirocco wind. The Israelites all knew that when a southerly wind blew the weather would be hot and dry.

Jesus pointed out that people were clever enough to interpret the signs of the weather, but that they were unable to interpret God's spiritual winds. Jesus' presence on earth was like a new wind that blew across earth from heaven, and yet most people did not interpret the signs correctly. His time on earth was the most important event in the history of mankind. The Son of God came to earth to live and die, and take upon Himself the judgment of God. He was about to be crucified for their sins and yet most people understood nothing of what was happening.

And still today there are many people who do not even begin to feel the winds of God that blow. They are spiritually blind and know much more about share prices and cars and politics than about spiritual matters. We, as Christians, need to be sensitive and become finely tuned for the things God is doing. We must not be spiritual ignoramuses. Be sensitive to the things of God!

Think a little!

"Why don't you judge for yourselves what is right?"

LUKE 12:57

It is amazing how many people allow themselves to be caught up in the flow of public opinion. They think that if the majority accepts something then it is valid, and they act accordingly. Others are manipulated by people with strong personalities, a husband, or wife, or friend, and allow themselves to be influenced into making decisions without thinking them through.

Jesus emphasized that His disciples should decide for themselves about the right things to do. They should go and find a place to sit quietly and think through the pros and cons of a situation and come to their own conclusion. They should use their common sense. But more than that, Jesus said that they should test everything against the Word of God, which is right and true and acceptable, and do what the Scriptures proclaim as right. They need to be responsible in drawing the right conclusions, rather than allowing other people, like the Scribes and the Pharisees, to think for them. They also need to follow what they know in their heart is right.

Each one of us will have to account to God one day for everything that we think, say, and do. We will not be able to hide behind anyone else, particularly on Judgment Day. We will give account of ourselves before God individually, one by one. That is why we need to discern what is important in making every decision. We must not let other people think for us. We must draw our own conclusions. As Christians, we have the Person of the Holy Spirit and the Word of God that is like a lamp to our feet and that lights our way. This makes it easier for us to make life-changing decisions that will honor God. But the answers will not just fall out of the sky and into our laps. We must seek them prayerfully and weigh the options before us in the light of God's Word.

July 13

It is better to agree

"As you are going with your adversary to the magistrate, try hard to be reconciled to him on the way, or he may drag you off to the judge, and the judge turn you over to the officer, and the officer throw you into prison."

Luke 12:58

Newspapers often report stories of people who drag each other to court to settle their disputes. The case is registered in court, but before it can be presented before a judge for a ruling, it is settled out of court. The two parties came to some sort of agreement, and so it was not necessary for the judge to decide the matter.

Jesus uses this image to explain how important it is for us to settle our case with the Great Judge, God, before His judgment falls. All through Luke 12 He talks about the One we need to fear. And He illustrates this through the parables of the rich fool who made the wrong choice, and of the slave who kept watch for his master's return, as well as of the faithful and the unfaithful stewards. He also mentioned that we need to read the spiritual signs correctly. The whole chapter refers to the end times and the Judgment of God that will fall. And now Jesus pleads with His hearers to settle their case with God so that they will not be dragged before the Judge.

It is just as well that we are still living in a time of grace. We still have time to make right before God, the things that are wrong in our lives. We can approach Him and settle our accounts with Him so that we will not one day have to stand in the place of judgment.

Jesus fulfilled all the righteous requirements of the law. He stood in the place of Judgment on behalf of you and me. If we call on the One who died in our place, then we are no longer guilty. Make sure that you have settled your case with God.

Repent

"I tell you, no! But unless you repent, you too will all perish."

꧁ LUKE 13:3 ꧂

Many of the Jews in Jesus' day believed that dreadful things would happen to them because of their sin. They often attributed disasters that came upon themselves, or others, to the fact that they must have done something to displease God. And we still find people who have similar ideas today. There are times when the things that happen to us are a result of the discipline of God (cf. Heb. 12:5-11), but often the pain and suffering that people experience are a result of the brokenness of the world, or of the poor decisions that they made.

Jesus used a particular incident to encourage people to repent. Of course, He frequently called people to repent, to turn aside from following their own way and to walk with God. But this incident illustrated His point clearly. People came to Jesus and told Him about a group of people from Galilee who were preparing to offer some animals in sacrifice. They had gone to Jerusalem to present their sacrifices to God when suddenly Pilate (who, according to Josephus and Philo, was a very unstable, stubborn, and violent procurator) ordered his soldiers to kill them. So much blood was spilled that human blood was mixed in with the blood of the sacrifices. We do not really know why Pilate had them killed, but some people have suggested that they were members of a Jewish resistance movement – a fanatical, political-religious group.

Jesus used the opportunity to remind people that if they did not repent and make things right with God, then such things, and worse, would come upon them. Make right with God! That is Jesus' message. A horrendous future waits for those who will have to stand in the place of judgment without the blood of Christ to cover them.

July 15

Repent

"I tell you, no! But unless you repent, you too will all perish."

ꙮ Luke 13:5 ꙮ

Personal catastrophes are not always the result of personal sins, even though the Jews thought they were. Jesus tried to set their thinking on this matter right, but at the same time emphasized that without sincere repentance no one can be saved. We would all run aground. And so He used another example to help them understand.

The tower of Siloam had been built in the southeastern section of the walls of Jerusalem. It had been erected near the Pool of Siloam, where the waters sometimes had healing properties. The water came from the spring at Gihon and was carried into the city to the pool at Siloam.

An accident occurred at the tower of Siloam. The tower collapsed and crushed eighteen people. Jesus told His listeners that these people were not guilty and were not judged because of their sin. They were no more sinful than any other people in Jerusalem. And yet disaster had come upon them.

Each one of us needs to examine our own lives, our own hearts, and our own attitude and ask if our lives are right with God. Jesus said that if people do not repent, similar things will happen to them. The emphasis is not on what happened to the eighteen people, but on the responsibility that each of us has to be ready to meet God every second of our lives. Jesus said we must repent then we will escape eternal damnation. Let us make sure that we are ready to die.

Where are the figs?

"For three years now I've been coming to look for fruit on this fig tree and haven't found any. Cut it down!"

ꟿ Luke 13:7 ꟿ

Fig trees grow prolifically in the regions around the Mediterranean Sea, including in Israel. These leafy green trees do not only yield a rich harvest of fruit but they also provide wonderful and much-needed shade. In Bible times many poor people gathered figs off the trees in order to keep from starving.

Jesus told a parable about a man who planted a fig tree in his vineyard. This was not an odd thing to do, because fig trees would be very well cared for in vineyards. After a while the man went to the tree hoping to pick some fruit. It would have been in May or June when the trees are supposed to bear their fruit, but he found nothing on its branches. He was very upset and told the gardener who cared for the vineyard, *"For three years now I've been coming to look for fruit on this fig tree and haven't found any. Cut it down! Why should it use up the soil?"*

Even though he was extremely disappointed, the gardener begged him not to chop the tree down. He had obviously spent much time and attention on this tree and so he asked permission to keep the tree for another year, to give it another chance to bear fruit. He promised that if it still did not produce any figs after that, he would cut it down.

It is always a good idea to look for the main thing that Jesus wanted to emphasize in His parables. And the central message of this parable is that the time of grace will come to an end. People should not put off bearing fruit for God's kingdom. God's grace and His patience are wonderful, but if you and I keep delaying then we might miss His time of grace. We must bear fruit in keeping with repentance today.

July 17

Crippled

"Then should not this woman, a daughter of Abraham, whom Satan has kept bound for eighteen long years, be set free on the Sabbath day from what bound her?"

༄ LUKE 13:16 ༄

It was the Sabbath and Jesus was busy teaching people in the synagogue. Suddenly His eye caught sight of a woman who was crippled and shriveled like an old tree. For eighteen long years she had suffered under the influence of an evil spirit who had weakened her completely. She had walked through life literally bent double as if the burden of the world rested on her shoulders. She was so crippled that she was unable to stand up straight.

Jesus immediately knew what was troubling her. That is why He called her forward and said to her, *"Woman, you are set free from your infirmity"* (v. 12). Then He placed is hands on her crooked shoulders and immediately an amazing miracle took place. She stood up straight and began to praise God. The burden had been lifted from her shoulders. She had been healed.

But because this incident occurred on the Sabbath day, the Scribes and the Pharisees were highly indignant. The ruler of the synagogue was exceedingly angry and upset because Jesus could even think of healing someone on the Sabbath. He claimed that He should have used one of the other six days in the week to minister to this woman.

Jesus called him a hypocrite, saying that according to the Jewish law it was permissible to give an animal water on the Sabbath day. If the needs of animals could be taken care of how much more should this woman receive what she needed after more than eighteen years in bondage to the devil? Where was the ruler's love and compassion for people?

What about us? Do we really care for the needs of those around us?

The tree

"It is like a mustard seed, which a man took and planted in his garden. It grew and became a tree, and the birds of the air perched in its branches."

ꙮ Luke 13:19 ꙮ

Jesus came to proclaim the kingdom of God on earth. This was the central theme of His ministry, as recorded in the four Gospels. The term the *Kingdom of God* had its origins in the Jewish expectations that God would radically change the future of their nation. They believed that He would change the lives of His people for the better by freeing them from the power of their enemies. They were anticipating the arrival of the Messiah who would show the way to a new kingdom of God. And now Jesus had arrived. But most of the Jews did not recognize Him as the Messiah who came to usher in the kingdom of God.

Jesus taught that the kingdom of God has its own, unique, inherent power. To illustrate this He told a short parable in which He said that the kingdom of God is like a mustard seed that someone planted in a garden. It grows, spreads, and its branches become wider and wider. Mustard trees can grow to about four meters in height. Many birds can build their nests in its branches and its leaves provide much shade.

In the same way, the kingdom of God becomes a place of refuge and a home for many people from many nations. The tree of the kingdom has gathered birds in its branches from cultures in every corner of the world. It reminds us of the cedar tree described in Ezekiel 17. The Lord says of it, *"I myself will take a shoot from the very top of a cedar and plant it ... on a high and lofty mountain. It will produce branches and bear fruit and become a splendid cedar. Birds of every kind will nest in it; they will find shelter in the shade of its branches"* (Ezek. 17:22-23).

The kingdom grows and grows, and nothing will stop it.

July 19

Yeast and dough

"It is like yeast that a woman took and mixed into a large amount of flour until it worked all through the dough."

ꕥ LUKE 13:21 ꕥ

The kingdom of God was established when Jesus came to earth. God's kingdom was the central theme of all that Jesus taught.

Jesus said that the kingdom of God was like a yeast that a woman took and mixed into a large measure of flour – approximately 10 pounds of it! – until the yeast affected every particle of it. That's a massive lump of dough.

Jesus was saying that He understood that the world is a very big place and that there are many people who need to be reached. The kingdom is like yeast that needs to be worked into the dough so that it has the desired effect. The whole lump of dough, not just a part of it, needs to be influenced by the yeast. Jesus was saying that those people who receive the kingdom of God in their hearts will have a great impact in the community in which they live.

God's rule and reign comes from outside of us and enters into our hearts where it changes who we are as people. It penetrates into the very depths of your being and transforms you from within. And now you can touch other people's lives with its influence. Every aspect of life is improved in this way.

Christians are not saved only so that they can go to heaven. We are those whom God uses to bring His influence to others on earth. That means that we stand on the side of truth when it comes to social and humanitarian issues such as child abuse, rape, corruption in government, famine, and AIDS. We need to make our influence felt concerning unnecessary wars, abortions, and the abuse of power. We must also stand up for honesty and integrity in business, commerce, and industry. And all of this should be the result of our heart's desire to reach the nations with the gospel of Jesus Christ.

Let us work as the yeast of God that changes the world.

How many will be saved?

Someone asked him, "Lord, are only a few people going to be saved?"

LUKE 13:23

Someone asked Jesus if only a few people would actually be saved. Jesus' answer confirmed the man's suspicions that only some people will enter the kingdom of God. And that the group would be relatively small.

The old Jewish writings show that the Jews clearly believed that every Israelite would be saved. They thought God's salvation was a national issue rather than a personal one. But Jesus came to declare something new. Each person will have to give account of him or herself individually to God. Each person needs to take responsibility for his or her faith relationship with God. This teaching contradicted what the other rabbis taught. And today there are still teachers who confuse people with a gospel message not based on the truth.

One of the major pressures in society today is to conform, even if it means compromising, so that no one will be upset. There are Christian leaders who join protest marches together with Muslims, Hindus, and New Agers, and they identify themselves with a new kind of world order. Such actions imply that all religions are equal, and that Christianity is not exclusive. They suggest that all people on earth actually worship the same God, and that everyone is His child. Such arguments confuse people and lull them into a false sense of security.

When Jesus said that people needed to make an effort to enter through the narrow door, He was also saying that many would try to get in but would not go about it in the right way. Whether we like it or not, only a few will be saved.

Let us hold fast to the words of Jesus. Those who in humility depend on Jesus' reconciliatory death on the cross, and in faith accept what He did for us will be saved.

July 21

In the ring

"Make every effort to enter through the narrow door, because many, I tell you, will try to enter and will not be able to."

℘ LUKE 13:24 ℘

When Jesus answered the man who asked if only a few people would be saved, He said, *"Make every effort to enter."* The original Greek word used here is *agonuzo*, and it refers to a fight.

Jesus does not indicate how many people will be saved but He does say that you and I need to make every effort to ensure that we will enter through the narrow gate. The image He uses comes from a boxing or wrestling match. There is a fight in the ring. A battle is taking place. You are confronted by one or more opponents. And you need to use every ounce of energy that you have to withstand their attacks. Every muscle must be used to maximum effect in an effort to win. Our opponents are Satan, sin, our self – our human nature – and also the fallen world.

When Jesus uses this image, admonishing us to make an effort to enter by the narrow gate because there are many who will not find the way through, He does not mean that we have to work for our salvation. We cannot get into heaven through our own works. Jesus' words do not refer to getting into heaven based on our own merit or our own strength. Jesus alone is the door through which we enter eternity. But you and I must make an effort to come to the point where He will give us eternal life. We must accept what He says, we must believe, we must hold fast to Him, we must surrender ourselves to Him.

Jesus did not want to frighten God's children, making them think that they will not make the grade. He is not saying that we must be completely without sin. But we must persevere in the fight against sin. We must take up our cross daily and follow Him. No matter what happens we must obey Him and follow Him (cf. Phil. 2:12-13).

The desperate knock

"Once the owner of the house gets up and closes the door, you will stand outside knocking and pleading, 'Sir, open the door for us.'"

ꕤ LUKE 13:25 ꕤ

People who have been saved and are accepted into the kingdom of God have knocked on the door while there was still time. They knock, they seek, they pray, they deny themselves. The door is opened to them and they find, they receive, and their prayers are answered.

Jesus told His listeners that the door to eternity will one day be closed and locked and then people will stand outside desperately knocking and calling out for the door to be opened. But it will be too late. They delayed for too long, they slept after the alarm sounded. The door will be closed forever. Then they will testify that they ate and drank with Him and that He taught people on the streets of their towns. But Jesus will say that He never knew them. Just because they lived in close proximity to Him does not mean that they served and followed Him.

The fact that He taught where they lived does not mean that they accepted what He said. Nothing in their lives indicated that they knew Him, for they did not do what is right. And so they will be turned away at the door.

Once again we hear the same message from Jesus' mouth. It is not what we see or hear that affects our lives, but what we actually do. If we follow Jesus, if we listen to Him, if we do what He asks, then our lives will bear testimony that He is our Lord and King. Our hands and feet and mouths will confirm that we have a relationship with Him. Not in theory, but in practice. Not just a theory of faith, but an experience of faith. We hear what God says and then do it.

May we freely receive of the glories of heaven because we have entered through that door and we will live with Him not only in eternity, but here on earth as well.

The grinding of teeth

"There will be weeping there, and gnashing of teeth, when you see Abraham, Isaac and Jacob and all the prophets in the kingdom of God, but you yourselves thrown out."

LUKE 13:28

The words of Jesus are not always easy on the ears. Jesus is not a smooth-talker. He doesn't just offer pretty sounding clichés that comfort people. He shows us the reality of our lives and hearts. We saw His love for us when He died on the cross so that we can live. But His love is a mature love. His love is frank, His love is honest. You can trust His love. And when His words sound somewhat uncomfortable, we can be sure that it is to our benefit. As the proverb says, "Sometimes you must be cruel to be kind." Wouldn't it be better for someone to tell you outright that you had cancer, rather than saying that everything was fine, and then leaving you to die? Such a person does you no favors.

So when Jesus talks about the Final Judgment and the pain and suffering that awaits those who are eternally lost, He does it to warn people. He says that people will weep and wail and gnash their teeth when they see all the believers and the prophets in the kingdom of God, while they will be banished to outer darkness. They will mourn. This grieving will not be over remorse for their sins or because they did not honor God in their lives. They will also not mourn because they have been separated from their loved ones or because they are seeking sympathy. Their tears will fall because they cannot be comforted. They will never again be free from the most intense misery possible. They will weep because of an utter, unfathomable, and eternal sense of hopelessness. As they weep they will grind their teeth together because of the intensity of the horrendous pain they will endure. And the worst is that this will never come to an end.

It isn't very popular to talk about hell these days, but beloved, we must listen to what Jesus said. Hell is a dreadful place.

A heavenly banquet

"Indeed there are those who are last who will be first, and first who will be last."

ഌ Luke 13:30 ഌ

Although it is difficult for us to imagine it with our limited human minds, we do know that there will be millions of people from all backgrounds and cultures who will come together in heaven to be part of the bridal feast of the Lamb. I'm sure we will all be fascinated by what happens there. Our mouths will probably hang open when we see the people from every nation, tribe, and tongue who will be seated at God's table. Jesus Himself said that there would be people from the east and from the west, from the north and from the south. They will all celebrate at the feast because they are all part of the kingdom of God. Are you excited that your name has been included on the guest list for this celebration?

Jesus wants us to remember: the last shall be first and the first shall be last. Our human ideas about who is most important will probably be completely turned around when we get to heaven. It could mean that some of the people who were the first to hear the gospel message did not accept it and yet those who heard it later accepted it immediately. It could also refer to the fact that the Jews largely rejected the message of salvation and so the heathens were actually the first to make the message of the kingdom their own.

Many people who were honored on earth and who held prestigious positions might not be given positions of honor in heaven. We might just find that people that were regarded as unimportant and insignificant on earth might very well have the most prominent positions in heaven.

Whatever the case, we can look forward with excitement to the feast that will take place in heaven.

July 25

The calf in the ditch

Then he asked them, "If one of you has a son or an ox that falls into a well on the Sabbath day, will you not immediately pull him out?"

℘ LUKE 14:5 ℘

A distinguished Pharisee invited Jesus to dine at his house. He was an important man, and this dinner was not just an everyday supper. It was the weekly Sabbath meal. And Jesus was now reclining at his table. Of course, the question we would love to ask is, why did such a distinguished and prominent Pharisee invite Jesus for dinner? And we find the answer in the words, *"he was being carefully watched"* (v. 1). They wanted to see what He would do. This important Pharisee and his sly friends wanted to find a reason to accuse Him before the Sanhedrin.

A man with a severe problem stood before Jesus. He suffered from dropsy. His kidneys, liver, blood, and heart were affected by this serious illness. Had the Pharisee planted him there? After all, they knew that Jesus' heart was always compassionate toward sick people, and He had previously healed many people.

But Jesus knew their hearts and instinctively knew that they were challenging Him about healing on the Sabbath. So He took the initiative and preempted them by asking if it was lawful to heal on the Sabbath. It seems that the Pharisees and Sadducees were of the opinion that healing was only permissible on the Sabbath if it seemed that the person would not survive until the next day. But they gave no answer to Jesus' question.

And so He healed the man.

And then Jesus posed a question for them. If a calf or a cow, or even one of their sons were to fall into a deep ditch on the Sabbath day, would they not immediately get them out, even on the Sabbath? And again they had no answer to give because they knew they did not really have a case. The love of Jesus triumphed over their hard hearts.

The least

"For everyone who exalts himself will be humbled, and he who humbles himself will be exalted."

℘ Luke 14:11 ℘

A Pharisee invited Jesus to eat the Sabbath meal at his house. He wanted to keep an eye on Him to see if he could trap Him into doing something that would stand up in the Sanhedrin. While Jesus was there, He was very aware that the other invited guests pushed past each other in an attempt to get the best seats for themselves. They elbowed their way forward to see who could get the most important places first. Jesus was struck by their arrogance and presumption. Their lack of humility was very obvious.

And then Jesus told a short parable to all who were there. He told of a wedding feast and of all the people who were invited. They had all been allocated seats but someone came in and sat in the most important place, which had actually been reserved for someone else. The host asked him to move somewhere else – to the least important seat (the only one left) because someone more important than him needed his seat. The man had to drag his feet all the way to the back of the hall and he had to sit in the least important place. And then Jesus explained that when we are invited to a function we should rather go and sit in the least important places. And then perhaps when the host comes he will see us there and ask us to move forward to the better seats. Jesus ended by saying that those who are proud will be humiliated but that those who humble themselves will be treated with honor.

The Bible is full of examples of people who held onto their pride but were humiliated before God and other people. But there are also many examples of people who humbled themselves before others but were promoted by God. We should be careful not to think of ourselves more highly than is proper. We should regard ourselves as less important than the people around us. We are, after all, servants of God and our fellowmen.

July 27

Back scratching

"But when you give a banquet, invite the poor, the crippled, the lame, the blind, and you will be blessed."

℘ Luke 14:13-14 ℘

Scratch my back and I'll scratch yours. Do me a favor and I'll owe you one. Sometimes we help other people simply because we think that they will in their turn be able to do something for us. But that is a very selfish way to live.

We know that it is natural for like to seek like, for birds of a feather to flock together. People who have the same interests and lifestyle usually end up in the same social circle. Jesus is not opposed to our normal social life, but He does warn against the tendency for people who have been privileged to spend all their time with other privileged people. If all the wealthy people only help other rich people, or educated people only speak to others with similar educational backgrounds, and influential people only deal with other influential people, what will happen to all those who are not so rich, not as intelligent, not so influential?

The strength of the gospel of Jesus Christ is in doing what we can for people outside of our own little circle. And so Jesus says we should not only have dinner parties for people who are on our A-list. We are called to be hospitable to those who least expect it – to love them and let them share in the abundance of what we have been given. We should be especially kind to those who are in desperate situations. When did we last invite someone really poor to have a wonderful meal at our house? Is this not what Jesus would do?

We should try to give more of ourselves, of our time and possessions to those who have nothing. If we give away more of ourselves in order to bless others our life will be filled with great joy. There is an unexpected joy in sharing things with others without expecting anything in return.

The feast of the hobos

"The servant came back and reported this to his master. Then the owner of the house became angry and ordered his servant, 'Go out quickly into the streets and alleys of the town and bring in the poor, the crippled, the blind and the lame.'"

Luke 14:21

Jesus told a parable about a man who organized a great feast and sent out invitations to all those he wanted to invite. But before the day of the appointed feast, everyone came up with excuses why they couldn't attend. Their excuses were blatantly silly. What they were really saying was that even though they had initially accepted the invitations they really didn't want to go.

And so the man who had organized the feast sent invitations to people who had not expected to be included on the guest list. He invited people in off the streets, people who lived in the back alleys of the city, people who were poor and crippled and blind and lame. The outcasts of society heard the invitation and came to the feast. But there was still room in the banqueting hall. The man who had arranged the feast was big-hearted and generous and hospitable. He really wanted to share all his riches with other people, so he sent invitations to people outside the city – to those on the highways and byways of life. And they also came and they all enjoyed the feast together.

Through this parable Jesus wanted to show us that God has issued a wonderful invitation to people. He wants people to celebrate the saving grace that He has given us though Jesus Christ and our faith in Him. But people come up with all kinds of odd excuses for not accepting this invitation. But, fortunately for us, God sent His invitation to all people in every part of the world, asking everyone to partake in His great feast. And so the heathens, including you and me, were included on the guest list for this feast. Rejoice that you have been invited to this hobo-feast. If you are still standing out in the cold, you can accept God's invitation right now.

July 29

It will cost something

"If anyone comes to me and does not hate his father and mother, his wife and children, his brothers and sisters – yes, even his own life – he cannot be my disciple."

ꕤ Luke 14:26 ꕤ

Large crowds of people followed Jesus. One day He turned to them and said that it would definitely cost them something if they wanted to follow Him properly. He meant that people who really want to be His disciples need to be prepared to make sacrifices and to show their absolute surrender to God through the way they live.

Jesus said anyone could be one of His disciples if they forsake their mothers and fathers, brothers and sisters, and even their own lives. This sounds like a very hard command! Does Jesus really expect us to deny our own families and loved ones? As in many cases, Jesus was using hyperbole to make a point clearly. What He said sounded very drastic in isolation, but His full intention must be understood. And yet, the spiritual truth that He wanted to convey – that commitment to Him means that His kingdom must be our first priority and passion – is very real. If it ever came to a choice between our relatives and God, then we would have to choose God.

Jesus was talking about being completely committed to God. He wants us to serve Him with a loyalty that is so real and so sincere that it is better and higher and greater than any other loyalty or tie we have with anyone else. Even our own lives need to be subjected to the loyalty that we have to God. To serve Christ half-heartedly is far less than what the Lord deserves from us. Let us serve Him with our whole heart and all of our soul and all of our strength.

First count the cost

"Suppose one of you wants to build a tower. Will he not first sit down and estimate the cost to see if he has enough money to complete it?"

☙ Luke 14:28 ❧

This is a short parable that Jesus told about a man who embarked on a building project, but first sat down and calculated how much it would cost. He approached the project in a responsible way. Did he have enough money to pay for the bricks and cement? Would he be able to complete the building, put on the roof and the finishing touches? If he had not done this, he would probably have started building, got halfway through and then suddenly discovered that he hadn't enough money left to continue building. And then other people would laugh at him and mock him. They would say that he started well but he couldn't finish.

Jesus wanted to teach us to follow Him wholeheartedly, and this means that we should first calculate the costs. It isn't always easy being a Christian. There are certain things that it requires of us. Jesus often mentioned in His sermons that following Him isn't some kind of a game. It costs His disciples something. And they should know that before they begin. They will be persecuted as He was persecuted. They might be misunderstood, as He was misunderstood. It is important, when you become a child of God, to make a decision that you will put your shoulder to the wheel and that you will persevere until the end. You must complete what you begin. Think of people like Judas and Demas who fell by the wayside and stopped following and serving Jesus. They turned back on their original commitment and decision to follow Him.

Let us decide that we will follow Him to the end. Count the cost, and pay in full!

July 31

The wise king

"Suppose a king is about to go to war against another king. Will he first not sit down and consider whether he is able with ten thousand men to oppose the one coming against him with twenty thousand?"

LUKE 14:31

Jesus expects complete commitment from His followers. Absolute surrender. Wholehearted obedience. Nothing less than this is enough for the King of kings who sacrificed His life to rescue us from death and give us life.

To illustrate His point, Jesus told the story of a king who got involved in a war. He had ten thousand men, but the enemy who had come against him had double the number – twenty thousand. The king had to sit down and figure out if he was able to oppose this mighty army. He had to plan carefully, to calculate the costs, and then make a decision. And Jesus suggested that the best decision might be to first send a delegation to his enemy to try to settle their differences peacefully.

There is a definite lesson to be learned here. We have an enemy who wants to launch a fierce attack against us. His strength is awesome. And so, like the king, sinners also have to make a decision. It is not possible to remain neutral in spiritual matters. What is the sinner to do? The answer is clear. Be reconciled to God. That is the wise and responsible course of action. Make things right with God, then you will avoid trouble. Make peace with God and so avoid His judgment. If you are not for Him, then you are against Him. Paul also says, "*We implore you on Christ's behalf: Be reconciled to God*" (2 Cor. 5:20).

Sit down and calculate the cost. Think carefully about your life. Will you be able to remain standing in the battle between life and death? Accept your God! Accept His reconciliation today. To receive the peace of God, we must, Jesus said, be prepared to give up everything we have.

August

August 1

Pour out your heart

"What are you discussing together as you walk along?" "What things?" he asked. "About Jesus of Nazareth," they replied. "He was a prophet, powerful in word and deed before God and all the people."

ည LUKE 24:17, 19 ဇ

It was late Sunday afternoon. It had been an unbelievable few days and they needed to talk about all that had happened.

Suddenly there was a man walking alongside them. They couldn't quite see where He had come from. He greeted them amiably and asked, "What are you discussing together as you walk along?" Was this man a stranger in Jerusalem? They asked him how it was possible that he did not know *"the things that have happened in these days"* (v. 18).

"What things?" He wanted to know. Their doubt and heartbreak bubbled over their lips as they talked about Jesus of Nazareth who was mighty in word and deed not only before God but in the eyes of all people. But He had been arrested by the Chief Priest and had been given over to the Roman council to be crucified. They had so hoped that He was truly the One who would liberate Israel. But now He was dead, and even worse – His body had disappeared. One of the women had told them that an angel had told her that He was alive! They didn't know what to think.

When Jesus asked, "What things?" of course He already knew the answer. He already knew about their frustration. And yet He urged them to share their confusion, to talk about everything that had happened and unburden themselves. If things have upset and troubled your heart, then Jesus is probably standing next to you in Spirit right now, and asking you to tell Him all about it.

Find a place where you can sit and pour out your heart to Him. Talk until you have nothing left to say, and then let Him fill you with His peace.

Heart-warming news

He said to them, "How foolish you are, and how slow of heart to believe all that the prophets have spoken!"

℘ LUKE 24:25 ℘

When Jesus invited the two men to tell Him what was in their hearts, they unburdened everything. All their doubt. All their hurt. All their questions. Jesus answered by saying, *"How foolish you are, and how slow of heart to believe all that the prophets have spoken! Did not the Christ have to suffer these things and then enter his glory?"* (v. 25). They could have felt that He was treating them too harshly, and taken offense.

But Jesus forced them out of the chaos of their souls and on to the level ground of spirit and truth. What did God say? What did the Word say? What had Jesus Himself said about it all? Your spirit is heavy because you do not yet believe. You wallow in your emotions, until even your soul has become bitter. Go back to the Word! Think! Understanding, insight – that's what is needed! *"And beginning with Moses and all the Prophets, he explained to them what was said in all the Scriptures concerning himself"* (v. 27).

And as He spoke to them their cold hearts warmed – more than that – the Bible says they became like a burning fire within them. Where there had been doubt, a new certainty was established. Despair bowed out and confidence took its place. Depression fled before an unsurpassed joy. Suddenly their heavy, dragging feet found new strength.

Beloved, our own limited insights often send us on an emotional roller coaster. The more we tread water, spiritually speaking, the worse it gets. At such times we need to take a long hard look at the Rock under our feet. The Word of God and His promises. That which God has said and which no person can change. On this Rock you will once again find security for your life.

August 3

Simply my duty

"So you also, when you have done everything you were told to do, should say, 'We are unworthy servants; we have only done our duty.'"

ꕤ LUKE 17:10 ꕤ

In Bible times many people were sold into slavery. They were dependent on their master as long as they lived. Their master was responsible for their livelihood, and they no longer had any say in their own lives. They belonged to their master, and that was that! The master spoke, and they responded. Even if they had personal desires and needs.

On a hot day in the stifling heat of the Judean sun, a particular slave thought it would be wonderful to lie down and rest for a while. He imagined arriving home, reporting on the day's activities to the master, and then, being able to kick off his sandals, sink into a comfortable chair, and pour himself a long, cool drink.

But the reality was completely different. That's what Jesus said. When this slave actually arrived home, there was a message waiting for him to see the master. The master didn't even ask how he was. He didn't ask if he was tired. No – instead he gave the slave instructions that would keep him busy for at least the next four hours. "Make me something to eat. Then put on your apron and come and serve me while I eat my dinner and enjoy something to drink. After that, you can get something for yourself to eat." Ouch! And he wasn't even thanked for all he did, said Jesus. He was, after all, not doing his master any favors – he was just doing his job.

Jesus told this parable to remind us that we belong to God. We have been bought with a price. We are in His service and need to do what He calls us to do without complaining. It's the least we can do in response to all He has done for us.

Bow before Him and give thanks

"Go, show yourselves to the priests." And as they went, they were cleansed.

Luke 17:14

Just before Jesus was about to enter a village, ten lepers scraped together their courage and from a distance called loudly, *"Jesus, Master, have pity on us!"* Jesus looked at them with empathy and love. He was not afraid, and He did not turn away in horror. Instead He simply said to them, *"Go, show yourselves to the priests."* With that their hope once again disappeared. After all, it was the priests who had declared them lepers and exiled them from the community. How could the lepers return to the priests now?

But they began walking toward the synagogue … half stupefied, half in response to the authority of His word. And then it happened. The man with the crippled foot was the first to shout out, "Look! My sores are disappearing!" Stunned, they gathered round to look at him. And then they looked at their own bodies. The unbelievable had happened. Oh, the joy, the relief, the gradual awareness – we can once again live as normal people. And the lepers began to run toward their homes.

One of them, when he saw he was healed, came back, praising God in a loud voice. He threw himself at Jesus' feet and thanked Him – and he was a Samaritan. Only him. The Samaritan among the Jews.

Jesus could only comment, *"Were not all ten cleansed? Where are the other nine? Was no one found to return and give praise to God except this foreigner?"* (vv. 17-18) Oh, what ingratitude! They had already forgotten who had healed them. They just accepted the miracle as a matter of course.

We have much to be grateful for. Saved. Filled with His Spirit. A new creation. Delivered out of hell, and with heaven in our hearts. Let us also bow before Him and give Him thanks.

August 5

Stumbling blocks

Jesus said to his disciples, "Things that cause people to sin are bound to come, but woe to that person through whom they come."

ꟷ Luke 17:1 ꟷ

We all still make many mistakes. Before we know what's what, we've done or said something that is definitely contrary to God's will. And the consequences are always bad.

When we struggle we often also cause someone else to stumble. When we sin other people are affected too. When someone stumbles he's thrown off balance and almost topples over. And he is embarrassed by his weakness.

Unfortunately, it is all too easy for us to cause others to stumble without really meaning to. Jesus did warn us that it is inevitable that things would happen that would make people stumble.

But when we knowingly and deliberately act in a way that will hurt someone, put them at a disadvantage, or cause them to stumble then we are going against God's will. And yet it happens all too easily. Jesus makes some sobering comments on such actions, *"Things that cause people to sin are bound to come, but woe to that person through whom they come"* (v. 1). He goes on to say that such a person should rather fasten a large stone around his neck and be thrown into the sea, because if he causes one of the least of those who belong to Christ to stumble, he will stand before God to be judged one day.

Listen to this warning! Pray that you will not cause anyone to stumble. If you have already sinned in this area repent and ask forgiveness. Don't repeat your mistake.

It is good to get into the habit of looking back over your day before you go to bed and asking the Lord to forgive you for all your conscious and your unconscious sins. Then you will sleep in peace.

Seventy times seven

> *"If he sins against you seven times in a day, and seven times comes back to you and says, 'I repent,' forgive him."*
>
> LUKE 17:4

Jesus said that we should caution our brother if he does something wrong. He went on to say, *"So watch yourselves. If your brother sins, rebuke him, and if he repents, forgive him. If he sins against you seven times in a day, and seven times comes back to you and says, 'I repent,' forgive him"* (vv. 3-4). To warn and admonish is one thing, but to forgive is more important. In fact, if we are not prepared to forgive, and to do so as soon as someone has offended us, then we cannot even begin to think of admonishing them.

Forgiveness starts with the words, "I'm sorry." Every time. Even if the same thing happens over and over again. But so often our patience wears thin when someone makes the same mistakes over and over. And we put conditions on our forgiveness. But Jesus says we must simply forgive. Open your heart wide, and figuratively take your brother into your arms. Forgive once more and keep praying for the one who has offended you. Don't stop. One day he'll get the breakthrough he needs.

There are unfortunately many people who say that they are sorry, but only to get you off their back. They aren't really sorry. Their words are empty and meaningless. Ask God to give you the discernment to know when someone is truly sorry. But don't play judge. Leave the judgment to God. Instead, forgive, in obedience to the words of Jesus. And then we will learn to forgive even before someone says, "I'm sorry."

Go and warn them

"I have five brothers. Let him warn them, so that they will not also come to this place of torment."

LUKE 16:28

Once there was a rich Jew who lived in a luxurious villa surrounded by exquisite gardens. At his gate lay a beggar named Lazarus who longed to eat the scraps that fell from the rich man's table.

The poor man's sad life finally came to an end and he died. But even though he had lost everything he had had on earth, he still clung firmly to his faith in God. As he opened his eyes a split second after his soul had left his body he was in the arms of the angels. And when they set him down he was in the most glorious place he had ever seen. A trillion times better then the rich man's villa. And Abraham was next to him. Oh, what a special, wonderful place!

Jesus continued the story by saying that the rich man also died and that he was dragged through the valley of the shadow of death. He was in anguish and torment, beset by pain, surrounded by chaos and fire. He was in the place of the dead, where all life and festivity come to an end forever. The stench of burning flesh hung in the air, and the pain, oh the pain!

With all the strength he could muster, he called out to Abraham, who together with the poor man, could be seen from hell. "Send Lazarus," he begged. Just to ease the burning on his tongue with a drop of water. But it couldn't be done. The rich man then begged, "Please! Warn my brothers!"

My friend, hell is real. And if you die without Jesus an eternity of pain and anguish stretches before you. Receive the gospel message of Jesus and you can have the assurance that you will live with Him forever.

It is no secret

"For there is nothing hidden that will not be disclosed, and nothing concealed that will not be known or brought out into the open."

℘ LUKE 8:17 ℘

It would be so much easier for us if we could hide our faults and mistakes, and then no one would know of the stupid things we do. We all have things in our past that make us blush and that we'd rather no one else knew about.

The bad news is that everything we do is recorded. In Revelation we find reference to the book of each person's life, in which all the good and bad things we have done are written down (cf. Rev. 20: 12). Daniel also wrote about the Book that will be opened on the Day of Judgment, and the judgments that have been written against us will be read aloud for all to hear (cf. Dan. 7:10).

Jesus clearly tells us that there is nothing that is hidden that will not be revealed and brought into the light. You might, on that day, wish that the mountains would fall on you and hide your embarrassment and shame, but it won't happen. Even if you, like Jonah, flee across the seas in a ship, you will not escape.

There is, however, good news too. Jesus tells us about absolution from guilt. Of being exonerated. Of being forgiven. And Paul rejoices that in Christ Jesus we no longer stand condemned (Rom. 8:1). When Daniel, in chapter 7, describes the great throne room of God he says he saw someone – someone who has been given the glory, the honor, and the authority to rule as king. That Someone is Jesus! That is why, when my case is presented before the judgment seat of God, I believe that my heavenly Lord and advocate will stand up in my defense and point out that my punishment has already been paid. Jesus took my punishment on the cross.

Bring all your scandals and sins into the light of God's forgiving presence. Confess and repent, appeal to the death of Jesus, because He died on the cross for you. And as you receive His forgiveness, you will be exonerated and forgiven.

August 9

The light shines

"For there is nothing hidden that will not be disclosed, and nothing concealed that will not be known or brought out into the open."

LUKE 8:17

We must bear in mind that life in Bible days was completely different from life today. Electricity had not yet been discovered, and no one had even considered that it can be generated and utilized. There weren't even such things as gas lamps. At dusk the wicks of the oil lamps were ignited so that they could help people see at night. The most common type of lamp was so small that it could be held in your hand like a candle in a candlestick. But there were also larger lamps that gave more light. These lamps were set on stands quite high off the ground so that they could light a room or part of the house from above.

It was this kind of lamp that Jesus had in mind when He said that no one would be foolish enough to light it and then hide it under a bed. It was placed on the stand so everyone who came in would be able to see in the light it gave and would be able to do the things that needed to be done. The light would show up everything that was in the room. Things that were lost could be found. Things that people would otherwise not have noticed could be clearly seen.

In Matthew 5:15, Jesus said that we are like lights that reflect God's glory to the people around us. But His emphasis in Luke was a little different. Everything that we say or do is laid bear and exposed before God who is the eternal light. In His light we can see things as they are. Luke says that everything that is in God's light is visible. Even those things that we had hoped could be hidden. Light exposes all these things to God. That is why we should be careful to live in the light, without shame. To live right. To obey God's Word.

How well do you listen?

"Therefore consider carefully how you listen. Whoever has will be given more; whoever does not have, even what he thinks he has will be taken from him."

Luke 8:18

Earlier in Luke 8, Jesus had called out, *"He who has ears to hear, let him hear!"* (v. 8). When I was still a kid, and I didn't do what my parents asked me to, my mom used to tug my ear playfully and ask, "Have you got ornaments on the side of your head? If these are really ears why don't you listen?" There are many places in the Scriptures where Jesus emphasizes how important it is for us to listen to what God says to us. But before we can hear, we need to want to listen.

What we listen to is important. Don't be too eager to listen to wrong things. As we used to sing at Sunday school, "Be careful little ears what you hear."

The text for today tells us that it is also important *how* we listen. How should we listen? With interest. With attention. With judgment. With discernment. In other words, be prepared to listen, listen to the right things, and listen attentively. Sometimes I find that I read God's Word but don't really listen to what it says. Sometimes I listen to a sermon from God's Word, but my attention wanders. Sometimes I hear dubious spiritual opinions, and accept them without discernment and without testing them against the Word.

We are living in an age that bombards us with words. There are so many concepts, so much knowledge, so much information. We can never take in everything that is said to us. We need discernment to know what to take and what to leave. Decide today that the words of Jesus will not be left out of your life. Without them your days will be filled with problems, the future will be dark, and eternity uncertain. Be careful of what you listen to, and how you listen.

August 11

More or less

"Therefore consider carefully how you listen. Whoever has will be given more; whoever does not have, even what he thinks he has will be taken from him."

Luke 8:18

Spiritual matters require commitment. If God gives you resources to use, then you need to do something with them. There is no place for spiritual sloppiness, as laziness in spiritual matters can lead to an empty heart.

This is what Jesus meant when He said that we need to listen to Him carefully. If we do so, we will be inundated with spiritual blessings. Our lives are enriched and enlarged beyond our wildest imaginings. What we have received from Jesus in our spirits just keeps on snowballing until we have more, and then more and still more. Conscientious obedience to the Lord is the best investment anyone could ever make.

But those who have nothing – they do not have because they have refused to listen to Jesus – discover another law. That which they thought was theirs falls away, and then what do they have left? Less than nothing.

So many people become discontent in their relationship with God. At first they seem eager and on fire about the things of God. But then all the worries and concerns of life pull them in every direction and take their focus away from their relationship with God. They find excuses not to attend Bible study. Family devotions go by the wayside. Watching TV becomes more important than reading the Bible. They become spiritually lazy. And the consequence is that they become spiritually poor. After a while they become so spiritually emaciated that they don't even cast a shadow.

"Use it or lose it" is a spiritual principle. We can only build spiritual muscles through regular application of the Word of God to our lives.

My beloved daughter is dead

"Don't be afraid; just believe, and she will be healed."

Luke 8:50

Jairus's daughter was dying. The doctors had said there was no hope. That is why he was in a hurry to find Jesus. Perhaps He could do something. Perhaps the days of miracles were not actually over …

And so he fell to his knees on the dusty road in front of Jesus. "I beg You, please help us! My only daughter is at death's door. She's only twelve years old. There's nothing more they can do for her. Please, if You can do anything, have compassion on us!" Jesus' heart was moved and He turned to walk with the father to his house while a crowd of people milled around Him.

But then came the dreaded news! It was too late! Your daughter is dead. Forget the Rabbi. He could do nothing now. But Jesus said to him, *"Don't be afraid; just believe, and she will be healed"* (v. 50). With his heart breaking in two Jairus, the ruler of the synagogue, led Jesus to his house. As they got near to the house they could hear the rising crescendo of the mourners. But Jesus said to them, "Stop wailing. She is not dead but asleep." They whispered to each other and they laughed in His face, and scornfully looked down on Him. But Jesus was not deterred. He took the little girl's hand and said, *"My child, get up!"* (v. 54) And she did. Straight away.

Does your situation seem hopeless? You might feel that it is so, but let Jesus have the last word!

August 13

The fox

He replied, "Go tell that fox, 'I will drive out demons and heal people today and tomorrow, and on the third day I will reach my goal.'"

℘ Luke 13:32 ℘

Some Pharisees came to Jesus warning Him that Herod wanted to kill Him. They told Jesus to flee to another country. But Jesus saw right through their attempts to get rid of Him. The death threat did not perturb Him. He knew that He would have to die because of the sin of mankind. That was why He came to earth. It was His calling. To be God's sacrifice for sinners.

He knew that Herod and the Pharisees had formed an alliance against Him (cf. Mk. 3:6, 12:13), although their reasons for wanting to get rid of Him were different. So He sent Herod, and them, a message saying, *"Go tell that fox, 'I will drive out demons and heal people today and tomorrow, and on the third day I will reach my goal.'"*

Jesus called Herod a fox because of his sly political maneuverings. He played the crowds and ignored the truth. He was cunning. And Jesus knew it. But He feared no man. He bowed before only one: His Father.

The message Jesus sent Herod via the Pharisees was carefully worded. He wanted Herod to know that He cast out demons and healed people. He wanted Herod to know that He was no threat to his rulership – He was too busy helping those in need.

Jesus reminded Herod that things would happen according to God's timetable, not the Roman Emperor's. On the third day – the day on which all things pertaining to Him would be fulfilled – God would decide what was to happen when and where. Jesus would accomplish His goal. What a wonderful way to describe His death! He would be successful. He would complete what He had been sent to do.

And He did. Because God is in control. And on schedule. He will never be embarrassed, or caught unawares. And He is still the same today. Still in control. Hallelujah!

A hen and her chickens

"O Jerusalem, Jerusalem, you who kill the prophets and stone those sent to you, how often I have longed to gather your children together, as a hen gathers her chicks under her wings, but you were not willing!"

꧁ LUKE 13:34 ꧂

When Jesus saw Jerusalem, the aching of His heart came pouring out. He was probably standing and looking down on the beautiful city from one of the hills that rise up around Jerusalem. The city of God. Zion. The capital city of the nation of Israel, God's covenant people. It symbolized the spirit and ethos of the whole nation.

Jesus' heart was broken because of the evil that had fermented in this city. Evil that opposed Him and the message of the Kingdom that He had come to proclaim. He had received death threats and knew that rejection, pain, and death awaited Him. And it was the leaders in Jerusalem who would persecute Him, even though His intentions were good and noble, and the works that He had done bore witness to this. So many people had been healed, and helped, and set free, and drawn closer to God because of His love. And yet they wanted to kill Him.

Jesus ended His passionate speech with a beautiful image. That of a hen who eagerly hides her chickens safely under her wings. Perhaps because a fox or other animal wanted to prey on them. Perhaps because a hailstorm threatened to break over them. Jesus said that He wanted to gather Jerusalem to Himself in the same way, so that they would be protected, helped, comforted, embraced. But they turned away from Him.

And He longs to do the same for you today. His heart breaks when you turn away from Him because He knows what lies ahead of us … the fox, the storm. Come, let us find shelter under His wings.

August 15

Rich in the Lord

"This is how it will be with anyone who stores up things for himself but is not rich toward God."

ꕥ LUKE 12:21 ꕥ

They named him Farmer of the Year. His barns were full, and they hadn't even finished bringing in the harvest. He didn't have place to store all the grain his lands had yielded. One night, as he lay awake grappling with this rather pleasant problem, he came up with the perfect solution. He would demolish his existing barns and build bigger, better ones. A barn like no one had ever seen before. It would be like a monument to himself. And every time he looked at it, he would feel confident about all the years to follow. And he would say to himself, *"You have plenty of good things laid up for many years. Take life easy; eat, drink and be merry"* (v. 19). Travel overseas, retire at the coast. Do nothing. Just live, and live well. You've got everything you'll ever need. You have it made!"

But, according to Jesus, God called this man a fool *"You fool! This very night your life will be demanded from you. Then who will get what you have prepared for yourself? This is how it will be with anyone who stores up things for himself but is not rich toward God"* (vv. 20-21).

Wealth might bring comfort, but riches can be dangerous. They can cause us to think that we do not need to depend on God. They can give us a false sense of security. They can lull us to death. Of course, riches can be a blessing, if you do not forget that everything you have actually belongs to God and that He has simply given you these things to manage for Him.

True wealth is when your barns are filled with spiritual treasures – treasures from heaven. Things such as faith, trust in God, the fruit of the Spirit, God's spiritual gifts, and His Word. These things bring satisfaction far beyond any pleasure that earthly riches bring. And heavenly treasures remain in and with you – for eternity!

Wanted: Joy

"I have told you this so that my joy may be in you and that your joy may be complete."

JOHN 15:11

How we try to fill our lives with things that we think will make us happy! We have parties, go on interesting outings, invite people over for a good meal, plan dream vacations, and do heaps of other similar things just for a little enjoyment and pleasure. Because we want to be happy.

On more than one occasion Jesus said that He would give His disciples joy. Jesus seemed to understand how scarce happiness is in most people's lives. Milton wrote a famous epic poem entitled *Paradise Lost*. As the result of sin, man lost his place in Paradise, and happiness became a sought-after commodity. Jesus came to restore joy to the lives of people on earth. That is why the Bible is often called The Good News. If we truly want to find the secret to joy in our lives, then we should listen to Jesus.

The joy Jesus offers is vastly different from the happiness offered by the world. His joy is of a deep inner nature. It is like an underground spring that bubbles up continuously. It is found nestled in your heart. It is a unique kind of joy. A joy with integrity. A joy that is not dependent on circumstances. Basically, as Paul says, it is a fruit of the Holy Spirit who dwells in us (cf. Gal. 5:22)

The joy Jesus offers us is always linked to His words, *"I have told you this so that ... "* We need to do what He expects of us. He wants us to follow in His footsteps. To say *yes* when He issues a command. This is what unlocks the treasure houses of true joy. And, Jesus says, this joy is perfect.

Listen to what Jesus says to you today, obey Him and you will be filled with joy!

August 17

Love that lasts

"As the Father has loved me, so have I loved you. Now remain in my love."

ꕥ John 15:9 ꕥ

One thing that Jesus never doubted was the Father's love for Him. The Bible tells us that God is love. John writes that God so loved the world that He gave His only Son so that anyone who believes in Him will not perish but have eternal life. This was the motivation for Christ's ministry on earth. The love of God, His Father. And His own love for people.

And then Jesus gives this wonderful assurance, *"As the Father has loved me, so have I loved you"* (v. 9). Do you really understand what this actually means? The love that is the essential nature of the God of love is the exact same love that Jesus has for you and me personally! If you are anything like me, your immediate reaction is probably to say, "But I'm not worth such love." It's good to know that being loved like this does not depend on whether or not we are worthy to be loved. Jesus simply states that He loves us. With the Father's love. If you doubt that He loves you, then you will not be able to achieve the fullness of your purpose in life. You will live instead with the wind of rejection buffeting you. And you will not successfully achieve your destiny. You must accept God's unconditional love for you and hold onto it with all your might.

Jesus goes on to say that we need to abide in His love. We should always be conscious of His love for us. This love should be the driving force in our lives. Its momentum will carry us through our difficult times. Stay in His love. Remind yourself every minute of the day that He loves you. Jesus could also have been encouraging us to stay in His love so that we do not disobey God and so limit His loving presence in our lives. We must not quench Him. We must not grieve Him. We must do as He says, and then the flame of His love will always burn brightly in our hearts.

Abide and obey

"If you obey my commands, you will remain in my love, just as I have obeyed my Father's commands and remain in his love."

JOHN 15:10

Jesus describes His love for us in this wonderful passage of Scripture. He loves us with the same love that the Father has for Him, and for us. One of the greatest miracles possible will always be the fact that God, who is love, loved us so much that He decided to rescue us from eternal death. It is miraculous that He did not give up on us. That He chose not to turn His back on us. To have done that would have been to deny the very essence of His nature. His love compelled Him to the most wonderful action of all time – the giving of His only Son, Jesus Christ, to die in our place so that we could live forever. What indescribable love!

And here Jesus calls us to abide in His love. To live in the atmosphere of His love in everything we do. To be aware each day of His loving arms enfolding us and of His loving words encouraging us. We must remain in His love. He goes on to explain very clearly what we need to do to experience the fullness of His love. *"If you obey my commands, you will remain in my love ... "* There is only one way to truly experience God's love for us; we have to conscientiously obey the things God tells us through His Word. The words of Jesus are the beacons by which we can confidently plot our way forward. As we walk the road through life we discover that this is the way of love – carrying out the commands of Jesus.

Jesus Himself set an example for us to follow. He obeyed every command of His Father and so remained in His Father's love. He speaks to us out of His own experience. The instructions that He had to follow were probably the most difficult that anyone, anywhere at any time has had to accomplish. He was sent to be crucified on a cross for the sins of mankind. And He did it. And so the love of the Father was a living and vital experience for Jesus. Let us carry out His commands so that we can abide in His love.

August 19

Chosen to bear fruit

"You did not choose me, but I chose you and appointed you to go and bear fruit – fruit that will last. Then the Father will give you whatever you ask in my name."

JOHN 15:16

We did not have to fill in an application form when we began to serve God. In fact, we weren't even involved in the process. Instead, He simply chose us. And once He had chosen us we became aware of the fact that we had a wonderful job to do. Jesus worked in the same way with His disciples. While He walked along the shores of the Sea of Galilee, His Father showed Him which men to choose to follow Him. And when He came to the office of Matthew the Levite, the businessman with a reputation as a tough dealer, He simply appointed him as His disciple. And Matthew left everything and followed Him.

When Jesus chooses people to minister for Him, it isn't just so that they can have a good time. It isn't about becoming members of an elitist club. It isn't a status thing. We are chosen with a purpose, and with a function to fulfill.

Apart from the fact that God loves us so much that He wanted to reconcile us to Himself through Jesus Christ, He also gives us a specific job to do. Christians who do not know what their purpose and goal are, do not really understand what life is all about. They do not have a clear idea of who they are. We have been chosen for a reason and purpose. That is why we are alive. Find your purpose in the pages of the Bible and in the still small voice of the Spirit of God that whispers in your heart. Find your place in the kingdom of God and go forth and bear fruit that will last. The fruit of your hands, your words, and your deeds. Fruit that will not cease on the day you die, but that will bring glory to God throughout eternity. Go and begin today. You have been chosen and appointed – go and bear fruit!

Give all you have?

"You did not choose me, but I chose you and appointed you to go and bear fruit – fruit that will last. Then the Father will give you whatever you ask in my name."

ꕥ John 15:16 ꕥ

In an earlier devotion we considered the wonderful fact that God has a calling on our lives. That Jesus chose us (before we were even aware of it), to live the great adventure of fulfilling His purpose for us. Yes, we have been appointed to bear fruit that is not for this life only but that will have significance for all eternity.

When Jesus gave this commandment to us, a wonderful promise accompanied it, *"Then the Father will give you whatever you ask in my name"* (v. 16). Often we read this verse in isolation. It is such a beautiful promise that we can't help getting excited when we read it. But if it is read out of context then it sounds as though the Father will just give us everything that we ask for. We know, however, that that is simply not true. There are many things that you and I have asked the Father which He just has not given to us. If He had answered our short-sighted and selfish prayers, then we would have been in much trouble today. No, the Father does not give us everything we ask for. He loves us too much for that!

Then what does this promise mean? We need to read it in context with the first part of verse 16. The promise relates to our commission to bear fruit. Jesus is actually saying that if we want to bear fruit for the Lord, and if we carry out the vision that He has for us, then He will give us all the resources that we need to be able to do what He has asked of us. The Father will then give us all that we ask for in His name so that we can bear fruit for Him. After more than thirty years of ministry I can only say that I have found this to be absolutely true. God gives us all that we need so we can fulfill His commission.

August 21

What a Friend

"I no longer call you servants, because a servant does not know his master's business. Instead, I have called you friends, for everything that I learned from my Father I have made known to you."

ꕤ John 15:15 ꕤ

Friends are the most wonderful part of every person's life. True friendship is often rare to find. A person who has a special friend knows how much that friendship means to him or her.

In John 15, where Jesus explains that He chose His disciples to bear fruit for Him, He also explains the implications of such a relationship. He does not want His disciples to be servants or slaves. Instead He calls them His friends. If they do what He asks of them then they are more than just slaves. They become His intimate friends. A level of trust had already developed. He had discussed certain intimate issues with them, and had taken them into His confidence regarding everything that was about to happen. He had told them about His kingdom and of the special mission the Father had sent Him on. He had taught them about the smaller details of His will and what was expected of them. Between Jesus and His disciples there was a measure of mutual love, respect, and trust. All that Jesus had heard from His Father He had passed on to them.

You have probably sung that beautiful old hymn *What a Friend We Have in Jesus* many times. It is a lovely hymn, but it has little meaning if you have not experienced the friendship of God in your life. Pause your reading for a moment and ask yourself the question, "Am I a friend of God?" Jesus said, "You are my friends." Therefore, be a friend of and for the Lord. Remain in a relationship of intimate trust with Him. Talk to Him. Tell Him how much you appreciate Him. Let Him know that you love Him. The Lord isn't satisfied for us to simply carry out His instructions as slaves would. Our obedience needs to be an expression of our love for Him.

A command to love

"This is my command: Love each other."

℘ John 15:17 ℘

In the text for today, Jesus declared His love for His disciples and encouraged them not only to love Him in return, but to remain in His love always. He said that they would demonstrate their love for Him as they carried out His wishes and commands. And this continued obedience would fill them with continuous joy. As soon as Jesus had said these things, He gave them a new commandment, *"Love each other as I have loved you"* (v. 12). And He continued, *"Greater love has no one than this, that he lay down his life for his friends"* (v. 13). Then He concluded the discussion with the admonishment, *"This is my command: Love each other"* (v. 17).

Most people don't really like being told what to do. One reason for this is that most instructions we receive are given by people who are themselves imperfect and apt to make mistakes. But when God gives us a command we can relax in the knowledge that it will always bring about a glorious result in our lives.

Jesus looked deep into the hearts of His disciples and issued a significant commandment. They were to love one another. And He reminded them that the best kind of friend is one who is prepared to lay down his life for the sake of others. Jesus did this for us – He laid down His life in a demonstration of His love. And this is how we should love one other. True love has nothing to do with romantic ideas of moonlight and roses. It doesn't even ask if you actually like the other person. You simply love others because it is the right thing to do. As Don Francisco reminded us in one of his songs, "Love is not a feeling, it's a choice of the will." So let us do what Jesus asked us to do – it is after all a commandment that He gave us! Let us love one another as Jesus loves us.

August 23

Unavoidable

"If the world hates you, keep in mind that it hated me first."

ꕥ John 15:18 ꕥ

If the gospel of Jesus Christ that we present appeals only to popular and pleasant ideas of what Christianity should be like, then we are not preaching the full truth. In today's passage Jesus very clearly explains that His disciples will not escape persecution. If the world hates Him, they will definitely also hate His disciples. That is the reality of Christianity. There is often a price that has to be paid for following Christ. But, in spite of this, Christians definitely agree that following Jesus is worth far more than any difficulties that might be faced. That is why so many people, including His original disciples, were prepared to die for Him.

Take Dietrich Bonhoeffer for example. He wrote a powerful, gripping book called *The Cost of Discipleship*. About seven years after the book was released the Gestapo in Flossenburg sentenced Bonhoeffer to death and executed him for his faith in Christ. Bonhoeffer stood up against the Nazi rulers, declaring that they were opposing the will of God. He was hated for this, persecuted, and martyred.

There is a price to pay for taking the words of Jesus to heart. You might not be as popular with people as you once were. You might lose your status in your social circle. You might even lose your job. Jesus does not try to hide the hard truth. He told His disciples very clearly that following Him would cost them something. Perhaps even their lives.

Why He said so

"All this I have told you so that you will not go astray."

JOHN 16:1

In the last part of John 15, Jesus warned His disciples that the world would hate them because He chose them to come out of the world, and they therefore no longer belonged to the world. He explained that a slave is not more important than his owner and if the world persecuted Him, they would definitely persecute those who serve Him. And the reason that the disciples would be persecuted was that the world would not accept the teachings of Jesus. Christians would be hated without reason and falsely accused. *"They hated me without reason"* (Jn. 15:25).

Jesus told His disciples that He was teaching them about these less than pleasant things so that they would not be caught unawares. Could this be why there are so many backslidden Christians these days? Have they fallen away from following Jesus because they have not heard and understood the full and true gospel?

Perhaps we as the church are guilty of being overly anxious to attract people to our congregations, or we are so eager that those who are lost should make a decision for Christ that we are not completely honest with them. We serve them a double thick chocolate milkshake version of the gospel, without telling them what it will cost.

We should be sure that we tell people the whole truth, not just the attractive parts. Let us challenge people to follow Jesus whatever the cost. Let's tell them how wonderful it is to serve Him even though it isn't always easy to live as His disciple among unsaved people.

August 25

The Spirit bears witness

"When the Counselor comes, whom I will send to you from the Father, the Spirit of truth who goes out from the Father, he will testify about me."

JOHN 15:26

While Jesus was talking to His disciples about the opposition that they would face because of their decision to follow Him, He inserts a surprising comment, *"When the Counselor comes, whom I will send to you from the Father, the Spirit of truth who goes out from the Father, he will testify about me."* Why did Jesus mention the role of the Holy Spirit here?

Jesus had told them of the venomous accusations that people would throw at them. They would experience exactly what He was going through right then. People rejected Him and hated Him without reason. But God was still in control. Through Jesus He was bringing the plans He had made to build His Kingdom to pass. And that is why the Holy Spirit would also be sent to the church.

It is interesting to note that Jesus said when He had returned to the Father He would Himself send the Holy Spirit to us. He is the Spirit of Truth, and He testifies of Jesus. In spite of all the opposition that Jesus was facing, and that His disciples would continue to face once He had returned to heaven, the Holy Spirit would carry on the work of Jesus on earth. He would witness to the hearts of people. And they would be convicted of the truth. The work Jesus begun will be completed in spite of opposition.

So, when we follow Jesus and are persecuted, we know that it is not in vain. Through it all the Holy Spirit is busy with His work of conviction in men's hearts. And we bear witness together with Him that we are the children of God.

The presence of the Holy Spirit

"But I tell you the truth: It is for your good that I am going away. Unless I go away, the Counselor will not come to you; but if I go, I will send him to you."

JOHN 16:7

Have you received the Holy Spirit? Do you experience His indwelling presence at work in your life each day? Was there ever a time in your life when you did not have the Holy Spirit? If so, then you will know how beneficial it is for you that Jesus sent us His Holy Spirit.

The Holy Spirit is a wonderful Person. He is one with the Father and the Son. In a way that is beyond our ability to understand or describe, He is able to take up residence in the spirits of people who were once sinful and work in and through their lives. That is why Paul says that our bodies are temples of the Holy Spirit. What a miracle!

When Jesus lived on earth He was bound by the limitations of His physical body. He could only be in one place at a time. He could not be in Jerusalem and Galilee at a time. He chose to become human, and human beings have limitations. But the Holy Spirit can be everywhere at the same time. He can live in millions of people simultaneously, from China, to Germany, to South Africa.

Wherever He is across the earth He can, in every person who has received Him, teach and explain the words of Jesus. What a benefit! He is with you right where you are at this moment.

August 27

What will He do?

"When he comes, he will convict the world of guilt in regard to sin and righteousness and judgment."

JOHN 16:8

Jesus was preparing His disciples for all that lay ahead of them. It wouldn't be long before He would be arrested and crucified. And so He spoke to them of the work of the Holy Spirit. His words bring comfort to us as well.

Jesus had already said that it was to our advantage that He went back to His Father in heaven so that the Holy Spirit could come to us. And now He explains that the Holy Spirit comes, like Jesus, has a mission to accomplish. He has a special task that He has come to carry out. His work is related to, but different from the work that Jesus did on earth.

One of His functions is to show the world that they are guilty of sin. Isn't it odd how many people live extremely sinful lives and yet don't even realize that they are sinning? It is almost as if they have a blindfold over their eyes. We shouldn't really be surprised because, after all, it is the nature of sinful people to sin! They are used to their sin. And have been since birth. Which is why they often don't know what sin is.

And so it is one of the functions of the Holy Spirit to convict such a person of their sinfulness. It is not up to us to try to convince people that they are sinners. Simply share the good news with them, and leave the work of conviction to the Holy Spirit. That is His work. Pray that it will be so. Do not stress when it seems that the person you are speaking to has not been convicted of his or her sins.

It is right

"When he comes, he will convict the world of guilt in regard to sin and righteousness and judgment."

JOHN 16:8

The work of the Holy Spirit is to bring about conviction. He convicts the world of sinfulness. And this conviction will either bring people to their knees in repentance, or make them harden their hearts. Not all those who become aware of their sinfulness respond positively. But the Holy Spirit helps us to be effective instruments in the work of convicting people of their need for a relationship with God.

Jesus tells us that the Holy Spirit not only convicts people of sinfulness, but also of righteousness. The Holy Spirit points to Jesus as the truth. He reveals that Jesus is the only one who can fulfill the requirements of God's righteousness. That He alone is right. And if we follow Jesus then we too will come into a right relationship with God.

Jesus allowed Himself to be offered as a sacrifice on the cross, and so fulfilled the righteous requirements of God's law. If we accept the sacrifice that He made for us, then, through it, we are brought into right standing with God. We are righteous because of Christ's act of redemption. That is why Paul could say that Christ is our righteousness (cf. Rom. 10:4).

You too are in right standing with God because of Jesus Christ. The Holy Spirit confirms that in your heart.

August 29

Judgment and the Spirit

"When he comes, he will convict the world of guilt in regard to sin and righteousness and judgment."

JOHN 16:8

When Jesus taught His disciples about the Holy Spirit who was to be sent to them, He explained that He would have various functions to fulfill. He was to testify of Jesus and convict the world of sin. He would also bear witness to the righteousness of Jesus Christ. It is only Jesus who can bring people into right standing with God. Only Jesus can make things right between God and man. Outside of Him, any relationship that people try to establish with God is wrong. Jesus is the only way to the Father. There is no other name in heaven or on earth by which people can be saved.

Jesus also taught that the Holy Spirit will convict the world of judgment. Verse 11 says, *"and in regard to judgment, because the prince of this world now stands condemned."* There is truly an eternal judgment to come, in which each person who has ever lived will stand before God, the Great Judge. But the Holy Spirit wants to show people that the devil, who is the prince of the dead, has already been unmasked by Jesus Christ and that his judgment has already taken place. He has been allowed to remain on earth and to harass people and try to win them to his side, but he has actually already been fully and completely judged.

What comfort this is for every Christian – to know that the devil has already received the death penalty. Although he is still in his cell on death row, waiting for that fateful day when he will be finally crushed under the feet of Jesus.

Jesus is the victor! He lives and will rule for all eternity! The devil, our enemy, has already been judged.

Do you hear what He says?

"But when he, the Spirit of truth, comes, he will guide you into all truth. He will not speak on his own; he will speak only what he hears, and he will tell you what is yet to come."

JOHN 16:13

Jesus' time on earth was coming to an end. In the relatively short space of three years Jesus had started His earthly ministry, selected His disciples, begun to teach and perform miracles. One of His most important functions on earth was to give His disciples a course on the kingdom of God. When He returned to His Father, they would become His ambassadors, His agents on earth. That is why it was important for them to understand what was going on. And there was so much that He wanted to teach them.

That is why He said, *"I have much more to say to you, more than you can now bear"* (v. 12). This highlighted the other problem He was facing. His disciples were not yet in a position where they could understand everything that He had to say to them. Too many things had happened to them in a short space of time. They just couldn't take in any more. But the Holy Spirit would come. And when He – who is also known as the Spirit of Truth – came, He would lead them into all truth. And what He told them would not come from Himself. His greatest task would be to bring glory to Jesus on earth.

There are many times when our minds just can't seem to fathom the deep things of God. It is impossible for us to learn all we need to know in a week, or even in a year. But the Holy Spirit is an infinitely patient teacher.

Do you sometimes feel that you know very little about the Lord? Do not be impatient with the learning plan that the Lord has established for you. Be committed and diligent, but don't be impatient. Trust Him to teach you step by step.

August 31

Just a little while longer

> *"In a little while you will see me no more, and then after a little while you will see me."*
>
> JOHN 16:16

Jesus told His disciples that He would be with them for only a little while longer. But He comforted them by saying that they would soon see Him once again, and then they would be very glad. They would be filled with joy because they would see the glory of God. And no one would ever be able to take that joy away from them.

What did Jesus mean by all of this? He compared the time of waiting for these events to happen to a pregnant woman anticipating the birth of her baby. The first signs of the birth are the beginning of the labor pains, and the birth process is not very easy or pleasant. But there is only a short time of pain and suffering, and afterwards there is joy unspeakable! She sees her baby, holds him in her arms and suddenly all the pain is forgotten.

Jesus used this image to refer to the fact that He would be taken away from them to be crucified. And that would bring them much heartache. But He would soon come to them again and change their sorrow into joy.

When the disciples saw Him in His glorified body after the resurrection they realized that He truly is the glorified Son of God. They had believed that it was so, but now they knew for sure. And the Holy Spirit also came and reassured them. He confirmed this glorious truth in their hearts. Then their questions were all settled because they knew that He is truly God. Then they would bow in worship and then rise up to serve Him forever. The Holy Spirit would open their eyes so they could see Him every day.

September

September 1

An improbable group

As he walked along, he saw Levi son of Alphaeus sitting at the tax collector's booth. "Follow me," Jesus told him, and Levi got up and followed him.

℘ MARK 2:14 ℘

Has it ever struck you what an interesting group of people Jesus chose to be part of His inner circle of disciples? It is really an improbable group of people. When we look at their backgrounds and personalities, we find it hard to understand exactly why Jesus chose them to be His disciples. Fishermen, John and James (the Sons of Thunder), Thomas the doubter, and then Simon the Zealot – a member of the militant Jewish resistance movement. This looks like a recipe for disaster to us. But it wasn't. Jesus knew what He was doing.

The Gospels make it clear that Jesus spent a night in prayer before He appointed them. He wanted to know which of them the Father had especially chosen to be His disciples. Something that stands out is the ease with which Jesus chooses the disciples. Time and again Jesus simply came and stood in front of someone, asked him to follow Him, and then, the Gospels record, those people simply got up, left everything, and followed Him. Amazing!

Think about Levi, the tax collector. He had his own business. Most ordinary people would never even think of simply locking the office door and just walking away from everything they had built up over so many years. And yet the Bible tells us that's exactly what he did. And so it was with all the others too. Each one left his job and earthly calling to follow Jesus. Just because He had invited them. Only God can prepare people's hearts so that when the invitation comes, they leave everything and follow Him.

The mere fact that you and I believe today is proof that the team He chose was successful.

Give

"Give, and it will be given to you. A good measure, pressed down, shaken together and running over, will be poured into your lap. For with the measure you use, it will be measured to you."

ℬ Luke 6:38 ☙

All of us have been given things ever since we were little. When we were needy babies and toddlers we had one goal in mind – to be given what we needed so that we could live and grow.

But a day came when we had to learn to give. And that was not an easy time. We were so used to just receiving! Suddenly there were play pals who entered our lives and wanted to share our toys. What a shock! Suddenly life didn't seem to be such fun anymore. We had to begin to give things to others. The process of learning to share is never without tears. And the worst is that sharing remains a challenge for us no matter how old we get.

One of the first things that Jesus wanted His disciples to learn was how to give. And that is why He so often talked about giving.

Giving doesn't mean that you are always on the losing end. You give, and then suddenly you find that you are receiving all kinds of things. And Jesus went on to promise them that what they received would be a good measure, pressed down, shaken together, and running over.

The symbol He used was drawn from grain markets in the region, but the same principle is found all over the world. Anyone who knows anything about the buying and selling of grain knows that a container or bag that is loosely filled contains far less than one in which the grain has been pushed down, shaken together and has had more added to it, until it runs over. Jesus uses this image to tell us that if we give abundantly we will receive abundantly. And He ends by saying, *"For with the measure you use, it will be measured to you"* (v. 38).

Let us learn from Him and give with open hands and open hearts. Just because it feels so good to give.

September 3

In the ditch

"He also told them this parable: 'Can a blind man lead a blind man? Will they not both fall into a pit?'"

ꕤ Luke 6:39 ꕤ

The teachings of Jesus were like a fresh breeze that blew across Jerusalem, the surrounding villages and all over Galilee and Judea. That is why people flocked in the thousands to hear Him. How different His preaching was from the usual sermonizing of the Pharisees. Their ministry was lifeless, a sickly, warmed-up concoction that nauseated their listeners and gave no nourishment to their souls.

Jesus brought fresh, new insights. He taught that the poor are blessed, that the rich needed to be cautious, that we should all love our enemies, that we should lend to others and expect nothing in return, and many more such ideas. These uncommon ideas challenged His listeners and caused them to think deeply. He gave them real food for the soul. Matthew 7:28, says that He taught as one with authority *"and not as their teachers of the law."*

This short parable focused on the differences between Jesus and the Pharisees. He said that they were like blind men. They could not show others the light, because, when all was said and done, they were not able to see the light or bring honor to it. They were like blind guides trying to lead a blind man along a path, but soon both end up in a ditch. A blind person needs someone who can see to guide him. And those who are spiritually blind also need guides who can lead them on the right road spiritually. Jesus is the perfect guide.

If we yearn for greater spiritual insight then we must make sure that the person who guides us in the name of Jesus truly has the Light in his heart. Otherwise you will find yourself lost in a maze.

Student = Teacher

"A student is not above his teacher, but everyone who is fully trained will be like his teacher."

℘ Luke 6:40 ℘

Jesus' disciples were shocked and surprised when He told them that the Pharisees were like blind people trying to lead the blind. How could they tell when someone was blind – spiritually blind? They were after all, for the most part, simple fishermen. They did not have a fancy education. The Pharisees would have considered them ignorant and uneducated. If Jesus said that the Pharisees were blind, what hope did they have?

But Jesus assured them that they had nothing to worry about. Jesus, with all His wisdom and insight, was streets ahead of the Pharisees in His spiritual understanding. And therefore, He had far more understanding than the disciples too. He would teach them about His kingdom and they would begin to grasp something of the truth of His teachings. They would learn from Him not only by what He said, but also by watching Him and doing what He did. In this way they would develop spiritual insight.

Of course they could never attain the levels of insight that Jesus had, but His nature would begin to rub off on them, and they would begin to act like Him. What He taught them is all that they needed to help them live victoriously in this broken world. The people that they told about Jesus would begin to say that they could see that they were disciples of Jesus. As it was in Acts 4:13: *"When they saw the courage of Peter and John and realized that they were unschooled, ordinary men, they were astonished and they took note that these men had been with Jesus."*

If Jesus has opened your eyes to the truth, then you will be able to lead other people on the right road. Your teacher, Jesus, will fill you with the right knowledge.

September 5

Splinter problems

"Why do you look at the speck of sawdust in your brother's eye and pay no attention to the plank in your own eye?"

℘ LUKE 6:41 ℘

A beam is a heavy piece of wood that is used to support the roof of a building. A splinter, on the other hand, is a tiny piece of wood that has broken off the beam. Jesus uses this image to tell the story of someone who sees a minute splinter in his brother's eye, and asks if he can remove it, while all the time he has a massive beam in his own eye.

The question is, who are these opticians who offer to remove splinters from other people's eyes? Jesus called them hypocrites, a word He frequently used to describe the Scribes and Pharisees of His day.

These were the men who thought that they had a monopoly on spiritual wisdom and understanding. These were the people who thought that they lived close to God and that everyone else was far from God. They were the ones who patted themselves on the back about their own self-righteousness before God, and then looked down on everyone who was not as religious as they were.

Yes, it is possible for someone to look good in his own eyes but if he is not humble, God sees a huge beam in his eye. The beam of self-righteousness. He first needs to get his attitude right, humbly acknowledge his own faults, perhaps weep in repentance at the feet of Jesus, and then he might be able to help the man with a splinter in his eye. Pride needs to give way to humility. Self-righteousness needs to make way for an awareness of one's own imperfections and brokenness.

We need to be aware of our own faults, acknowledge them, and then in humility we will be able to offer to help others.

Lord, Lord

"Why do you call me, 'Lord, Lord,' and do not do what I say?"

LUKE 6:46

The word *Lord* was commonly used in New Testament times. The Greek word for Lord is *kurios*, and it means a person who has power and who is clothed with authority. It refers to the lord or master or kingly ruler who has the power to rule. And this is the word that we use when we speak of the Lord Jesus Christ.

It is interesting to note that long before Jesus was crowned Lord of all in heaven after His ascension, (cf. Phil. 2:9-11), He was already called Lord here on earth. The authority and power with which He went about His business caused people to instinctively bow before Him in spirit.

But Jesus was not interested in titles or status. He came to serve. It wasn't about position for Him, but about the work that He was called to do. That is why He asked, *"Why do you call me, 'Lord, Lord,' and do not do what I say?"* Such behavior is a blatant contradiction. If you address someone as lord, king, master, then it is because you are under that person's authority and you acknowledge their right to govern you. And that means that you are under obligation to carry out his commands. You must do what he says.

Let us acknowledge Jesus as our Lord. And then let us demonstrate our commitment by being obedient to what He asks us to do.

September 7

Storms and foundations

"I will show you what he is like who comes to me and hears my words and puts them into practice."

Luke 6:47

You probably know the Sunday school chorus that children love to sing: "The wise man built his house upon the rock ... and the rains came tumbling down. And the rains fell down and the floods came up ... and the house on the rock stood firm!" But there is also the verse about the foolish man who built his house on the sand, and when the rains came the house on the sand fell flat.

This is one of the best-known parables that Jesus told, and His purpose was to illustrate a very important life-principle. Each one of us is in some way or another a builder. The mere fact that we are alive means that we are building something. In this parable Jesus draws attention to the building project of every person who hears the gospel.

There are two types of builders. The one, according to Jesus, is a wise builder, while the other is a foolish one. The wise builder has the necessary insight and understanding and so builds his house – in other words, his life – on Christ who is the Rock (cf. 1 Pet. 2:6, Rom. 9:33, 1 Cor. 3:11, 10:4). Even the Old Testament describes God as our Rock (cf. Deut. 32:15, 18, Ps. 18:1, Is. 17:10).

You should make sure, therefore, that you are building your house on the Word of Christ. With zeal and prayer adjust your life so that it is built according to the design that Jesus laid out in the Word. Then the storms of life can come against us and we will stand firm.

Jesus amazed

When Jesus heard this, he was amazed at him, and turning to the crowd following him, he said, "I tell you, I have not found such great faith even in Israel."

ꕤ LUKE 7:9 ꕤ

The centurion's trusted slave, who was worth much to him, was very ill. And so he sent some of the elders of the Jews to Jesus to ask if He could please heal his slave. When they came to Jesus, they poured out this wonderful testimony to Him, *"This man deserves to have you do this, because he loves our nation and has built our Synagogue"* (vv. 4-5).

This did not really impress Jesus, but He decided to go along with the Jewish elders. When they got near to the Roman officer's house, some of his friends came to meet Jesus with this message,

> *"Lord, don't trouble yourself, for I do not deserve to have you come under my roof. That is why I did not even consider myself worthy to come to you. But say the word, and my servant will be healed. For I myself am a man under authority, with soldiers under me. I tell this one, 'Go,' and he goes; and that one, 'Come,' and he comes. I say to my servant, 'Do this,' and he does it"* (vv. 6-8).

Jesus was amazed. Now this impressed Him. What amazing faith! And that from a Roman heathen! He eagerly shared His amazement with those who were with Him. *"I tell you, I have not found such great faith even in Israel"* (v. 9). Jesus did not enter the Roman's house. He had already spoken the words and because of the faith of the officer, his slave was healed.

Oh, if we only had as much faith in the words of Jesus! Then we could ask Jesus to speak one word – just one word – into our situation. If we just had faith like the Roman's ...

September 9

Coincidence?

He said, "Young man, I say to you, get up!"

℘ LUKE 7:14 ℘

When Jesus, His disciples, and a crowd of followers walked into the town, they found most of the inhabitants on their way out. At the center of the crowd was a woman in mourning.

The woman's husband had died some years before this, but she was fortunate to have a son who could look after her. Her only son. But a second blow had now hit her hard. Her son had also died! She was left all alone with no one to care for her. Her pain was deep, her future uncertain. They were carrying the corpse to the cemetery where they would bury it.

She walked out through the town gate and as she passed Jesus, He looked at her. That's what the Greek text says – He just looked at her. And a meeting took place. A heavenly meeting. Heaven bent down and touched the hills around Nain. Glory reached out to comfort one who was suffering. As Jesus looked at her His heart was overwhelmed with compassion for her. Immediately He went up to her and reached out to touch the bier. The pall bearers came to a standstill and then Jesus spoke, "Young man, I say to you, get up!" Oh, listen to the authority in His voice, see the compassion in His eyes!

Was it coincidence that Jesus was in the right place at the right time? If He had arrived in Nain about 50 minutes later, the young man would have been buried! Was it coincidence that the ram was caught in the bush just as Abraham was about to sacrifice Isaac (cf. Gen. 22:13)? When Abraham's servant had to find a wife for Isaac and just as he arrived in a far, strange country, Rebecca just happened to be drawing water for her camels (cf. Gen. 24:15)?

No. God does not play some kind of heavenly lotto with our lives. There are no coincidences. He planned all these things. And He has a unique plan just for your life too.

See His authority

He said, "Young man, I say to you, get up!" They were all filled with awe and praised God. "A great prophet has appeared among us," they said. "God has come to help his people."

ꟷ LUKE 7:14, 16 ꟷ

It must have been fascinating to see how Jesus went about doing the things He did on earth. He was still a young teacher in terms of the Middle-eastern culture of His time. Men were not allowed to begin teaching until they had reached the age of 30, and they had to teach for many years before they were really considered to have any authority. Jesus was still young, just over thirty, and yet He taught and acted with great authority. It was as if He had been teaching for many years.

In the passage that records how Jesus raised the young man from the dead, there are a few things that stand out. In the first instance we see how wonderfully God organizes and controls events. It was part of His great, all-encompassing plan that Jesus should enter the town gates of Nain just as the funeral procession was leaving.

Jesus spoke to the widow and in His words and tone of voice she could sense His deep compassion, His unsurpassed wisdom, His unlimited authority, and His incredible power. All of this was evident when He raised her son from the dead.

The same Jesus who raised that boy from the dead is on the throne in heaven today. That does not mean that He has distanced Himself from the problems that you and I face. Just the opposite! We know that through His Word and His Holy Spirit that He is still our Emmanuel, God with us. He has the same compassion and sympathy for you that He had for the widow of Nain. He is near us and He still speaks His wonderful life-giving words into our lives. And we are filled with awe and a song of praise is on our lips, just like the crowd that witnessed this miracle.

September 11

Dance

"They are like children sitting in the market place and calling out to each other: 'We played the flute for you, and you did not dance; we sang a dirge, and you did not cry.'"

ꕤ Luke 7:32 ꕤ

Childishness belongs to children. Adults should be more mature. And yet we so often find childishness in the Body of Christ that causes relationships to be strained and the atmosphere of worship to be soured.

In Luke 7 Jesus speaks out against the childishness of the spiritual leaders of His time. And in doing so He makes use of a lovely image – that of children playing in the market place. On the days that were not market days, the market squares were wonderful open areas where children could come together and play freely. At first the children would play happily with each other, but after a while they would begin to quarrel.

One of the children had a flute that he would play. And some of the children wanted him to play his flute and they would all dance and pretend that they were at a big wedding feast. But they had no sooner begun to play this game when one of the children sat down and said he was tired of playing at weddings, and he wanted to do something else. He thought it would be a better game to pretend that they were at a funeral. And some of the others agreed with him.

Pretty soon all the kids would be screaming at each other, pointing fingers and pulling tongues. One group wanted to dance, while the others wanted to cry.

This is how it so often is in the church too. We are just like children. One person suggests one thing, and somebody else has a different idea. We should rather ask the Lord to play the flute for us and follow His lead.

A glutton

"For John the Baptist came neither eating bread nor drinking wine, and you say, 'He has a demon.' The Son of Man came eating and drinking, and you say, 'Here is a glutton and a drunkard.'

ꟷ LUKE 7:33-34 ꟷ

It's quite interesting to watch how people so often sing someone's praises, but then soon afterwards point out all their faults. Perhaps they deliberately look for that person's faults because they cannot handle seeing only good in someone. Someone once said that society creates heroes for itself, and as soon as they have erected statues in honor of their heroes they see how quickly they can break them down.

John the Baptist and Jesus found the same thing in their lives. John had an unusual calling and ministry and was completely committed to the work God had given him to do. John the Baptist did not eat bread nor did he drink wine. He did not follow the patterns of living that so many other people do. His lifestyle was admirable, and yet some people said that he was demon-possessed.

And they did the same thing to Jesus. He, who is the Son of God, behaved differently yet again. He did eat bread and drink wine. And people were amazed at how approachable He was. He lived among the ordinary people in the towns and villages of Judea and Galilee. He visited people in their homes and gave of Himself and of His love to people around Him. But the critics weren't happy with Him either. They said of Him, *"'Here is a glutton and a drunkard, a friend of tax collectors and "sinners"'"* (v. 34).

But Jesus answered that God is wise and His actions prove it. The Lord knows how He wants to use each person. Do you do what God has called you to do, even if other people do not understand it?

September 13

All kinds of people

> *"To what, then, can I compare the people of this generation? What are they like?"*
>
> ꕤ Luke 7:31 ꕤ

When Jesus came to earth He ministered to many different kinds of people. There was nothing exclusive or elitist in His ministry. He served all kinds of people from all kinds of backgrounds. He saw every person He came across who had a need or whose situation was desperate as someone He could minister to.

We are, however, often exclusive in the way we treat people. Of course there are some people that we like better than others, but we have been called by the Lord to minister His love to others. He touched our lives and He wants us to be His instruments of peace in this broken world. This puts our relationships with other people into a different light.

Jesus was no respecter of persons. He loved everyone. He was at home with all kinds of people. He was comfortable talking to anyone, no matter who they were. As we read the Gospels we see that one minute He was with rough, down-and-out fishermen and laborers, then with people like tax collectors and prostitutes. The next we see He was having dinner at a Pharisee's house (cf. Lk. 7:36). No sooner had He left the synagogue where He had been among godly people, when He was found sitting at a well with a Samaritan woman. He could converse with the learned Nicodemus, but He just as easily chatted to children, and blessed them. He ministered to Roman officers and to Jewish widows. That's how Jesus is: available to everyone in all circumstances.

Let us learn from Jesus. When we truly love people and want to serve Him, then we overcome our fear of people. Then we are no longer motivated by whether or not they accept us, or whether we like them. They become the object of God's love in us. Then we can look them in the eyes, spend time with them, and truly love them.

A precious offering of tears

Then he turned toward the woman and said to Simon, "Do you see this woman? I came into your house. You did not give me any water for my feet, but she wet my feet with her tears and wiped them with her hair."

ꕤ LUKE 7:44 ꕤ

Her life was a mess. She was a wild one, a rebel of sorts who challenged the norms and conventions of her day. She often did just as she pleased, even though she got quite a few raised eyebrows. The people of her town knew her … and they warned their wives and daughters to be wary of her. She was a *femme fatale* – a dangerous woman. A sinner. But had any of them noticed the emptiness in her heart? Did they look past her wildness and rebellion and see the hunger for a life of meaning and purpose in her eyes?

One day she had stood quietly among the crowd that was listening to Jesus. And suddenly something happened in her spirit. She was mesmerized by what He was saying. An indescribable realization that she could have a new beginning in life began to awaken in her. And so, all in a moment, she found God, and wept because of her sinful rebellion. And a peace such as she had not known was possible came to rest in her heart. And days later it was still there.

And so she decided to thank Him – in her own way. She went and bought an expensive alabaster jar of perfume, found out where Jesus would be that evening, and entered the room. Her heart was full of thanks and adoration. She went and stood behind Jesus who was reclining at the table, and broke the delicate, white neck of the alabaster jar. And she poured the aromatic oil on His feet. As she did so she began to sob uncontrollably – tears of gladness and gratitude drenched His feet. This was the perfume of her heart. And then she used her hair to wipe the tears and perfume from His feet. A wonderful scent filled the room – the aroma of her worship.

What will you and I give to say thank You for what He has done for us?

September 15

A difficult situation

"Therefore, I tell you, her many sins have been forgiven – for she loved much. But he who has been forgiven little loves little."

LUKE 7:47

When Jesus, at the invitation of Simon the Pharisee, was dining at his house, something happened that upset the distinguished Pharisee very much. A woman with a bad reputation walked up to Him. The audacity! Everyone in the village knew that she led a sinful life. She was definitely not a regular visitor in the Pharisee's house, nor was she welcome there. Simon was immensely angry with her, and muttered to himself, *"If this man were a prophet, he would know who is touching him and what kind of woman she is – that she is a sinner"* (v. 39).

Jesus knew what Simon was thinking and told him a parable of two men who had both borrowed money from the same person. The first one owed $5,000 and the other $5. But neither of them had the money with which to repay the loans. Eventually the man who had lent them money wrote the debts off. And then Jesus asked Simon a question: which one did he think would be the most grateful? "Well," Simon answered, "most likely the one who had owed the most money." Of course! That was why this woman of ill repute was so grateful. She had the most for which to be thankful.

There are times when we can be just as callous as Simon the Pharisee. Recently a tramp entered a church in the middle of the service. He walked right to the front and there he fell to his knees. All those present looked at each other in shock and horror. Then the head deacon got up and walked purposefully and angrily toward the tramp. He grabbed his arm and tried to hustle him out of the church as quickly as he could. But the pastor stopped him and then talked quietly to the man and prayed with him.

Reputation, position and honor are not important. It is a person's heart that is important.

You are forgiven

Then Jesus said to her, "Your sins are forgiven."

ℰ LUKE 7:48 ℛ

One thing Jesus is really eager to do is to reconcile people with God. He is the only one who can bring about this reconciliation. Only He, as the Son of God, who sees into the hearts of people and knows what is within us, can pronounce forgiveness on those who recognize their guilt before God and are truly sorry for their sin.

It is interesting that even before Jesus died on the cross He extended forgiveness to people. Of course we understand that even in the Old Testament people who lived righteously before God and established a relationship with Him according to His Word, were justified through Christ's later death on the cross.

Jesus turned to the woman and once again said, *"Your sins are forgiven."* (v. 48). And that got the people who were seated nearby at the dinner table talking. "Who is this man that He can even forgive sins?" they wondered. But Jesus simply looked at the woman and said, *"Your faith has saved you; go in peace"* (v. 50). Jesus forgave her on the basis of her faith in Him, who, as the Son of God is also the Savior of the world. She had probably listened to Jesus preach, and come to a deep realization of her sinfulness and then made a decision to turn away from her old life and begin a new one. The change that occurred within her heart was so dramatic and far-reaching that she just had to go and thank Him.

The Lord wants you and me to live in the consciousness of the forgiveness of our sins. If you have turned your life around and laid your life at His feet and have a desire to do what He asks you to, then you know that you belong to Him and that He has forgiven you the guilt of your sin.

September 17

Go in peace

Jesus said to the woman, "Your faith has saved you; go in peace."
ꟷ LUKE 7:50 ꟷ

Oh, what storms rage in the heart of a person who does not have the assurance that God has set him free. Augustine said that each person has a restlessness in his heart until he finds his rest in God.

There are so many things that bring unrest in our lives. But they all spring from an unsettled relationship with God. When we have been reconciled with Him and have placed ourselves into His mighty hand, then we can sincerely sing the words of the old song, "It is well, it is well with my soul!" If things do not feel well with our souls, then either we do not truly believe or we are not yet in a right relationship with God.

The Bible tells us that often when Jesus ministered to people He said to them, "Go in peace!" It was as if Jesus spoke to the storms and chaos in people's hearts. Because of His great love for the precious people who came to Him, He wanted to send them away with a new peace and tranquility – a peace such as they had never known before. As Paul later said, *"And the peace of God, which transcends all understanding, will guard your hearts and your minds in Christ Jesus"* (Phil. 4:7). Our God is a God of peace and He does a work of peace in the hearts of people who turn to Him.

Lay your worries at Jesus' feet today. Pour your heart out to God. Let Him address the storms in your heart, speak to the waves, oppose the turbulence that threatens to overwhelm you. Allow the work of Christ on the cross and His resurrection to bring new meaning into your life. Hear Him say, "Go in peace." You can walk with confidence into a turbulent world, and as you go His peace will enfold you.

Women who care

Joanna the wife of Cuza, the manager of Herod's household; Susanna; and many others. These women were helping to support them out of their own means.

ꟹ Luke 8:3 ꟹ

In New Testament times, women did not have much social standing in their communities. They were not allowed to take part in government nor could they function in any leadership positions in their communities. They were mainly expected to support the men.

But Jesus saw women differently. He treated them with dignity and did not consider them to be inferior or second-class citizens. Whenever He had dealings with a woman He spoke to her just as He would to a man in that position. The Gospels tell us of many occasions when Jesus engaged in conversation with women of bad repute because He wanted to turn their lives around. We also read about how some of these women dedicated themselves to following Him because He had forgiven them.

In the first half of Luke 8 we read that a number of women followed Him and His disciples as He traveled from place to place ministering to people. Some of these women had been set free from demonic possession or sicknesses. One of these was Mary Magdalene out of whom Jesus had cast seven demons. There was also Joanna the wife of Cuza who was one of Herod's senior officials. Luke ends this section by saying, *"These women were helping to support them out of their own means"* (Lk. 8:3).

These women served Jesus and His disciples. These women ministered to Him and His disciples with dedication and commitment so that they could continue with the work of ministry. Thank God for the women in the kingdom of God who give wings to the work of Jesus!

September 19

Hear

"If anyone has ears to hear, let him hear."

ꕤ MARK 4:23 ꕤ

There were many people who came to listen to Jesus preach. The words He spoke were very meaningful. They were words that touched their hearts, that addressed their lives. And more than once Jesus said, *"He who has ears to hear, let him hear."*

One of the most important lessons that we have to learn in life is what to listen to. Someone once said, "What you harvest in your mind, you will manifest in your life." What we harvest in our thoughts can be seen in our lives. Our thoughts are usually formed by outside opinions. That is why we need to be very selective about what we listen to.

There are some things that are not good to listen to. For example, a conversation during which negative remarks are made about a person and his reputation is harmed, while he is not there to defend himself. It is wrong to listen to gossip. Next time you find yourself in the company of gossipers, consider saying, "Please excuse me, but I really do not want to hear the negative things you have to say about Joe, or Mary."

If someone starts to tell a joke and you realize it's going to take a dirty turn, then it would be better to get up and calmly excuse yourself.

Or, if you are alone with the one telling the joke, perhaps you could say, "Sorry, but I really do not want to hear dirty jokes." Say this with humility, with love, but firmly. Remember that what you listen to affects your life.

Refuse to listen to chitchat that is smutty or negative or that is full of complaints and that undermines your faith. Rather listen to words that will build you up.

The Word is seed

"This is the meaning of the parable: The seed is the word of God."

Luke 8:11

The emblem of the Bible Society of South Africa is a sower carrying a bag of seed. This logo was developed with Luke 8:11 in mind – the parable Jesus told about the farmer sowing seed. Jesus went on to explain that the seed is the Word of God.

This is a lovely image that aptly describes what the Word of God is and what it does. In times past, sowers would walk across a field and throw seed on the prepared soil so that the seed could germinate. The sower sowed in faith, knowing that every seed had the potential to grow. It was possible for every single seed to produce a stalk of corn, which in turn contained hundreds of seeds.

The seed that was sown looked dead but the sower knew that there was life inside each kernel, life that would begin to grow as soon as the seed fell to the ground.

This is exactly how it is with the Word of God. The writer of Hebrews says, *"For the word of God is living and active"* (Heb. 4:12). Therefore if we sow the seed of the Word into the soil of people's hearts through what we say then it is likely that something wonderful will happen. It might fall into good soil and begin to germinate.

There are countless examples of people who made a comment based on the Word of God without realizing that they had said something extremely significant. Much later someone testifies how the word that you cannot even remember saying changed his whole life. That is how God's Word works. It is like a seed that grows and brings forth fruit in people's lives.

Sow the seed. God will cause it to grow in His time.

September 21

Trampled seed

"A farmer went out to sow his seed. As he was scattering the seed, some fell along the path; it was trampled on, and the birds of the air ate it up."

LUKE 8:5

Seed only germinates if the conditions are favorable. First, it must fall into the right soil. The seed might be good, but if the ground is not, nothing will happen.

In the parable of the seed and the sower Jesus started by saying that the sower goes out to sow his seed. But while he was sowing some of the seed fell on the road, and it was trampled on and the birds came and ate it. This scenario was well-known to sowers in Jesus' time. All seeds, whether oats or corn, were sown by hand. And as the farmer sowed his seed, he couldn't avoid dropping some on the paths that surrounded his field. People's feet hardened the paths and it was impossible for the seed to burrow under the soil. That seed really had no chance at all. It was trampled and couldn't penetrate the soil. And then the birds, in their search for food, came and perched on the hardened clods and pecked up the seed with their tiny beaks.

Both these images – that of the hard ground and the birds that ate the seed – Jesus applied to the devil. The devil is cunning in the way that he works and he will do everything he can to ensure that the seed of God's Word does not take root in someone's heart. He has a bag full of sly tricks. He lures people's attention away from the Word, he distorts the message, he confuses people's thoughts, and he undermines the power of the Word by suggesting it has limits. He will even lull someone to sleep so that he doesn't really hear what is said.

Let us pray that God will prepare the ground before we sow the seed.

Rocky ground

"Some fell on rock, and when it came up, the plants withered because they had no moisture."

ꕥ LUKE 8:6 ꕥ

Seed can produce wonderful fruit, but it needs good soil in which to grow. Jesus said that when the sower sows his seed, some of it falls on rocky ground. The seed cannot grow properly here because there is not enough moisture. The seed will wither and die.

Many places in Palestine (modern day Israel) and the surrounding area have arable land that is found above banks of rocks. The soil hides the rocks from view, but often the underlying rock is so near the surface that the ground above it has no depth. Seed will germinate and begin to grow in this soil, but it can only grow upward. It shoots up but the roots find no place to go down into the ground and so the young plants soon shrivel and die.

Jesus says that the seed that falls on rocky ground is like people who hear the Word of God and receive it gladly. They are excited about the Word, but the Word doesn't really take root in their hearts. Their faith does not last very long. As soon as the heat of the sun touches them then they give up. As soon as they are tested they find that their faith has no substance.

We could call them impulsive believers. They often respond emotionally to what they hear, but they do not have the perseverance to continue when things go wrong. They make all the right choices about faith, but they do not carry them through to their actions. They are largely superficial Christians.

Let us make sure that our spiritual roots are sunk deep into the Word of God so that we can be strong and continue to grow.

September 23

The weed of stress

"Other seed fell among thorns, which grew up with it and choked the plants."

ℰ𝒟 Luke 8:7 ℭℛ

The sower sows the seed, but as he does so some of the seed falls among weeds. And then the weeds grow with the young plants and choke them. Every patch of ground can sustain only a certain amount of plant life. Since the Fall, the bad has always grown more quickly than the good, and this is especially true of weeds. Weeds quickly overtake the grain that is growing, and begin to slowly suffocate it to death.

The seed that falls among weeds is like people who hear the Word but because of the stress and cares of everyday life the seeds cannot grow. Worries and anxieties are like a blight. They eat away at your soul's abundance bit by bit. Stress is one of the worst things that people can suffer from. Try to remove it from your life because it can make you physically and emotionally sick. It breaks down your constitution and eats up your faith.

If we really want God's Word to take root in our lives and to produce an abundance of spiritual fruit that others can see and enjoy, then we need to deal with our worries.

We need to make a decision to unburden ourselves of all our concerns at the throne of God every day. We must learn to let go and let God. We must stop trying to take the full weight of the burdens of life on our own shoulders. We must let the Lord guide us in the paths of life. We must surrender control to Him and allow Him to handle the things that worry us.

Worry and stress will prevent you from experiencing God's abundance.

The weed of riches

"Other seed fell among thorns, which grew up with it and choked the plants."

Luke 8:7

Jesus gave an explanation of the nature of weeds in His parable of the sower and the seed. These weeds choke and push the Word of God out of people's hearts. It isn't only stress and anxiety that does this. It isn't only about lying awake at night tossing and turning because of all the things that make you fearful. Riches can also be like a weed.

The weed that grows in the soil of the wheat fields and prevents us from developing spiritually is the yearning for riches and the insatiable desire to cling to worldly wealth. We do not need to be reminded of the rich young ruler written about in Luke 18:18-24. With sorrow he turned away from Jesus and threw His calling to the wind just because he was too attached to his possessions.

Then there was the rich fool who thought he would be able to enjoy his worldly riches forever (cf. Lk. 12:13-21). And let's not forget about the rich man who cried out from hell to ask Lazarus the beggar to give him a single drop of water (cf. Lk. 16:19-31).

It is not wrong to be rich, but riches and the driving urge to possess more and more of everything that glitters and shines and is pretty or comfortable can be a distinct disadvantage to your spiritual life. The more we focus on things, the less clearly do we see the image of Jesus and recognize His words in our souls. Beware of this weed – the craving to gather more and more material possessions.

September 25

The weed of pleasure

"Other seed fell among thorns, which grew up with it and choked the plants."

ꕤ LUKE 8:7 ꕤ

Jesus said that the seed that falls among this kind of weed is like those who hear the Word but the cares of this world and desire for riches and the pleasures of life suffocate the seed and it can't begin to grow. Let us spend a few minutes thinking about the weed of worldly pleasures.

The ability to enjoy life is a gift from the hand of God. We are reminded of the words of the preacher in Ecclesiastes who said, *"When God gives any man wealth and possessions, and enables him to enjoy them, to accept his lot and be happy in his work – this is a gift of God"* (Ecc. 5:19). Christians should not be opposed to enjoyment and pleasure. God desires that we find pleasure in life. Personally, I believe that only Christians can truly enjoy life to the full, because they don't have to deal with the negative effects of sin. There is, however, a negative side to pleasure. Pleasure seekers who make pleasure their god have no place for the true God in their lives. Jesus refers here to the people who are involved with soul-destroying pleasures. For example, there are people who try to find enjoyment in getting drunk, or in doing drugs, who become addicted to gambling, sexual promiscuity and a host of other such pursuits.

True pleasure is satisfying to spirit, soul and body. So those people who pursue so-called worldly pleasures usually find that they are less satisfied afterward. There is a great emptiness inside that cannot be filled. There are also less obviously dangerous pleasures that can keep us from focusing on our relationship with God. When things like sport, games, parties or other forms of entertainment become more important to us than God, then the Word will not be able to grow to its full strength in our lives. We can only truly enjoy life if God is Number One in our lives.

Good seed, good ground

"Still other seed fell on good soil. It came up and yielded a crop, a hundred times more than was sown." When he said this, he called out, "He who has ears to hear, let him hear."

LUKE 8:8

There is good news at the end of the parable of the sower and the seed. Jesus had explained how so much of the seed that is sown will never grow and will never produce any fruit. And He explained the various reasons for this. By this time His listeners were probably wondering if any of the seed would actually grow.

There is some seed that does fall on good soil. Matthew 13:8 and Mark 4:8 both say that some seed will produce thirty-fold, and some sixty-fold. But there are some grains that will produce one hundred times more.

The seed that falls in good ground represents those who hear the Word of God with open and sincere hearts and protect and nurture it so that it will eventually produce a harvest. These are the people who willingly and gladly receive the Word without preconceived ideas (cf. Acts 17:10-12).

Not only do they hear it, but they hold fast to the Word of God. They share the Word with others through what they say and do. They stand firm and have the ability to persevere in spiritual things. And they continually bear the fruit of the Holy Spirit. Even when they go through hard times.

Is your heart good ground?

September 27

Emotions and decisions

Then he said to them, "My soul is overwhelmed with sorrow to the point of death. Stay here and keep watch with me." Going a little farther, he fell with his face to the ground and prayed, "My Father, if it is possible, may this cup be taken from me. Yet not as I will, but as you will."

ꟸ MATTHEW 26:38-39 ꟸ

It is dangerous to respond to things emotionally. Many people have reacted emotionally to situations, and made decisions based on their feelings, only to find the results are disastrous.

Perhaps you feel like using bad language or shaking your fist when a car cuts in front of you on the highway. But you can decide not to follow your emotions. Perhaps you are romantically attracted to someone, but you are married. And you have to make a decision. Remember David who allowed his feelings for Bathsheba to lead to a wrong decision.

Our emotions can direct our lives. They can govern what we do. They can cause us to make bad decisions. Whenever we feel strongly about something we must first ask ourselves if we are about to do the right thing. Then we need to make a decision. Don't ever side with your emotions over the will of God. Make the right decision.

When Jesus prayed in the Garden of Gethsemane His emotions recoiled from the pain and suffering that He was about to face. But He made the right decision. If He gave into His emotions, He would have turned away and not carried out His Father's will. But He did not make a decision based on emotions. He chose to do God's will. Thank God for that, otherwise you and I would have been lost for all eternity.

September 28

Difficult parables

"The knowledge of the secrets of the kingdom of God has been given to you, but to others I speak in parables, so that, 'though seeing, they may not see; though hearing, they may not understand.'"

LUKE 8:10

Jesus often used parables when He was teaching the people. His parables were spiritual stories that contained deep spiritual meaning. He drew on things that were familiar to His listeners to relate a message straight from the heart of God. And here Jesus makes an interesting comment, *"The knowledge of the secrets of the kingdom of God has been given to you, but to others I speak in parables, so that, 'though seeing, they may not see; though hearing, they may not understand'"* (v. 10).

Jesus explained that those people who listen to Him and accept what He says and so believe that the Father sent Him will understand the secrets of the kingdom of God. The Lord unlocks kingdom issues for them and they gain spiritual insight and understanding. The eyes of their understanding are enlightened just because they believe.

But others, and here Jesus was probably referring to the Pharisees and Sadducees, hear what Jesus says, but they reject Him and His words. Because of their lack of faith it is impossible for them to be able to see anything that pertains to the kingdom. They heard the parables but could not see the spiritual insights that were made. They looked, but they could not see. They heard, but could not understand. They would not open their hearts to the opportunities that God gave them to understand the wonderful secrets of His kingdom. And so God hardened their hearts because they had refused to allow Him to soften them.

It is dangerous to treat the Word of God lightly. Those who do not come to the Lord in faith will always think of His words and parables as foolish. Pretty stories with no real meaning. But God will unlock the secrets of the kingdom for those who come to Him in faith.

September 29

My mother and brothers

He replied, "My mother and brothers are those who hear God's word and put it into practice."

LUKE 8:21

One day, when Jesus was ministering, surrounded by throngs of milling people, a message was sent to Him. The house where He was ministering was packed so full of people that the message must have had to pass from mouth to mouth from the back of the crowd to where He was standing. There were so many people that His family couldn't get near to Him. But the message finally reached His ears. *"Your mother and brothers are standing outside, wanting to see you"* (v. 20). Jesus was, at the time, busy doing what His heavenly Father had instructed Him to do.

His answer was short and to the point. *"My mother and brothers are those who hear God's word and put it into practice"* (v. 21). Wow! That sounded a bit hard. Why did Jesus say something like this?

It is clear from the Bible that Jesus loved His family very much. He had an exceptional relationship with His mother. He loved her dearly and cared deeply for her. We know this from the last words He spoke on the cross – when He asked John to look after her after His crucifixion. But Jesus wanted to bring an important point home. He wanted to emphasize that spiritual ties are more binding than earthly family ties. He did not undermine the importance of physical and family ties, but stressed the importance of spiritual ones.

Jesus wanted to point out that obeying the will of the Father is more important than earthly obligations. The Son of Man had to do what the Father asked Him to do (Jn. 17:4). That is why Jesus did not allow Himself to be distracted from His purposes. It was not an appropriate time to interrupt Him. He was busy doing God's will, and that was the most important thing.

Our family ties should never prevent us from fulfilling God's will in our lives. But we still need to love our families with the love of Christ and to serve them when we spend time with them.

Your home

"Return home and tell how much God has done for you." So the man went away and told all over town how much Jesus had done for him.

ꕤ LUKE 8:39 ꕤ

Next to your relationship with God, your home and family are most important in your life. Blessed is the man or woman, and especially the child, who can, within the security of a loving, caring family, be fully him or herself. Who is accepted as he or she is in the home, and who knows the love of family. Because our families are so close to our hearts, there is usually an atmosphere of mutual trust and understanding among family members. And the Lord wants us to invite Him into our family circle so He can lead us and guide us in His ways.

Often, when Jesus had healed someone or cast evil spirits out of someone, He instructed that person to go back to his home. Here, in Luke 8, the man from Gadarenes whom Jesus had freed from the legion of demons, begged Jesus to let him stay with Him. He wanted to follow Jesus like a puppy follows its master. He never wanted to be apart from Jesus. But the Bible tells us that Jesus sent him away saying, *"Return home and tell how much God has done for you"* (v. 39). Luke records that he did go home and told not only his family, but his whole town what Jesus had done for him.

It is very important that we, in the wisdom and power of God, pay attention to our homes and families. Some people find it very difficult to tell their families of the decision that they made to follow Christ. I can clearly remember how, as a young teen, I was too shy to tell my parents that I had committed my life to God, even though I knew that they would be delighted by my decision. How much more difficult it is for people whose parents or children are not interested in godly things. What do you say to them about Jesus? God promises to help us. Go and live as a follower of Jesus and share the wonderful things that He has done for you with them. That is your privilege. That is your duty.

October

Washing feet

"I have set you an example that you should do as I have done for you."

JOHN 13:15

"We had just returned from Bethany and were really tired after a long hard day. We were all hungry and thirsty and immediately went to recline around the table. The washing bowl and towel were at the side of the table. According to custom we should have washed the dust and dirt from our feet. I don't know why we neglected to do so. Perhaps we were just too tired or too lazy. Besides, somebody usually grabbed the bowl and started the procedure. But not that evening.

"The food was ready, and our feet were still dirty. We were just about to start eating anyway, when Jesus suddenly stood up and quietly walked to the bowl. He poured water into it and removed His outer garment. He took the towel and tied it around His waist just like a slave. And then He began to wash our feet. We were stunned into silence. He took the dirty feet of every single one of us in His hands, washed them, and dried them with the towel.

"Then it was my turn. And suddenly I blurted out that He shouldn't be washing my feet. It wasn't right. But He answered, *"Unless I wash you, you have no part with me"* (v. 8). I felt very uncomfortable with it all but He carried on washing my feet and then dried them completely.

"Then He told us why He had done this and we began to understand. If He, who is the Lord, was prepared to wash our feet then we should be prepared to follow His humble example and wash other people's feet. When He washed our feet He demonstrated yet again that His whole life was a life of service and that He did not seek position or prestige. He only wanted to love and serve people. Later, after He had been crucified and had risen from the dead we began to fully understand what had happened."

October 2

The cock crowed

"Will you really lay down your life for me? I tell you the truth, before the rooster crows, you will disown me three times!"

JOHN 13:38

When the cock crowed, his heart broke. He remembered that Jesus had said that he would deny Him. And he went outside and wept bitter tears. On top of the pain of knowing that they had arrested his Jesus, he had to carry the pain of his own failure. He had desperately tried to prevent them from arresting Jesus but his attempts had been futile.

The servant girl who kept watch at the door recognized him. Her words cut through him like a knife. *"You are not one of his disciples, are you?"* (Jn. 18:17). And before he could gather his thoughts, the words, "No, not me!" came tumbling out of his mouth. He was suddenly gripped by a fear that seemed to crush his chest. He could feel the beating of his heart all the way to his ears. He had tried to keep the conversation going in a different direction when suddenly one of the men asked if he was one of Jesus' disciples. Once again he denied knowing Him. Suddenly everything started to get too much for Peter, and he wanted to get out of there. Then one of the slaves of the high priest, spoke up, *"Didn't I see you with him in the olive grove?"* (v. 26). And then, just as for the third time he denied knowing Jesus and being one of His disciples, the cock crowed. But the worst of all was when Jesus turned around and looked deep into His eyes.

Probably one of the most difficult things for a Christian is when he or she, as a result of fear or personal weakness, is not prepared to stand alongside the cross of Jesus in public. But later on these people feel bad and they realize that they have let their Lord down. Have you had such moments of weakness? It is good to share your heartache over this with God because He does understand everything. And just as He restored Peter, He longs to restore you too.

The rock

"And I tell you that you are Peter, and on this rock I will build my church, and the gates of Hades will not overcome it."

☙ MATTHEW 16:18 ❧

Jesus asked them who they thought He was. And Simon answered that He is the Christ, the Son of the Living God. This was an inspired and amazing answer. Simon had received a supernatural revelation in that moment and was able to truly proclaim who Jesus is.

Jesus was pleased with this answer and said that Simon would be known as Peter from then on. Peter means rock. And He would build His church on this rock. Did this mean that Jesus was making Peter the cornerstone of the church? Of course not. Only Jesus can be the true cornerstone of the church. What Jesus was saying here was that the content of Peter's answer would be foundational to the church. When any person believes in his heart that Peter's revelation is true, that Jesus is the Messiah, the Son of the Living God, and confesses this with his mouth and confirms it with everything that is within him, then that is the substance on which the church will be built. The church consists of those people who have been called out of their sin and have been set free in Christ. Therefore everyone who hears God's call and comes to Him is the church of Jesus Christ. These people know what they believe. They make the same confession that Peter did.

Jesus said that He Himself will build His church on the confessions people make of His deity, and no powers of death will be able to prevail against it. The word Hades refers to the realm of the dead, and the image that is drawn is that of the devil and all his hordes pouring out through the gates of hell in an attempt to attack and destroy the church of Jesus.

We are the church of Jesus. The devil cannot destroy us. With the authority that Jesus gives us, we are more than conquerors. Praise the Lord!

October 4

Three names, one man

Jesus turned and said to Peter, "Get behind me, Satan! You are a stumbling block to me; you do not have in mind the things of God, but the things of men."

℘ MATTHEW 16:23 ℘

Jesus called Peter by three different names.

In the first place, he is called Simon. Simon Bar Jonah, which means Simon son of Jonah. This was the name by which Simon the fisherman who kept a boat on the Sea of Galilee was most commonly known. It seems as though Simon was an open hearted, gregarious, and spontaneous person.

But when he made a spiritual statement that revealed spiritual insight he was given a new name. Jesus no longer called him Simon Bar Jonah, but Peter. The word Peter means rock. Steadfastness. We can imagine that Peter was very pleased with his new name. It was almost like a title of honor.

But just five verses later he was called by another name. And he would not have been very proud of this name. When, in verse 21, Jesus began to tell His disciples that He had to go to Jerusalem and suffer persecution and be killed, and that He would rise from the dead on the third day, Peter took Him aside and began to reprimand Him. The Bible says that he rebuked Him. *"Never, Lord!"* he said. *"This shall never happen to you!"* (v. 22). And then Jesus turned to him and said, *"Get behind me, Satan! You are a stumbling block to me; you do not have in mind the things of God, but the things of men."*

Three names, one man. An ordinary man who became a strong spiritual leader, and was then called Satan. Someone who tried to block what God wanted to do. Oh, how like you and me he was. Sometimes we are strong in the Lord and the next minute we're standing in God's way. That is why we need the Holy Spirit to cultivate more of a Peter in us.

Doubters

When they saw him, they worshiped him; but some doubted.

Matthew 28:17

After Jesus had risen from the dead and before He ascended into heaven, He spoke to His disciples on the slopes of a mountain. When they saw Him they worshiped Him, and yet, the Bible tells us that some doubted.

It's hard for us to believe that disciples of Jesus who had walked with Him and seen Him die and who had seen the wonder of His resurrection and His glorified body could still doubt. But some did. Like Thomas. He was skeptical when the other disciples told him that Jesus had appeared to them. Of course we can sympathize with Thomas, because who would have believed that such things would really happen?

Unless you had had enough faith to take Jesus at His word. He had told His disciples before all these things that He was going to die and that He would rise from the dead. Had they not understood what He had said? Or did they quite simply not believe Him?

Thomas refused to believe that Jesus had risen from the dead. Perhaps he had been so deeply disappointed and hurt by all that had happened that he did not want to build up false hope based on what his friends said. But then, suddenly, Jesus appeared to him and he could not help but believe.

Bible commentators say that those who continued to doubt did not doubt that Jesus had risen from the dead. But they doubted if the man who appeared to them, and who they saw only at a distance, was really Jesus or someone else. That is why verse 18 tells us that Jesus came nearer to them and talked to them. Whatever the case we do know that after this all the disciples followed Jesus with complete faith.

In life there are always some people who are more skeptical than others, even in matters of faith. If Jesus reveals Himself to us in different ways, we should not doubt Him.

October 6

All authority

Then Jesus came to them and said, "All authority in heaven and on earth has been given to me."

℘ MATTHEW 28:18 ℘

Jesus was just about to return to His Father. The ascension was about to take place. And here He gave His last command to His disciples. But before He commanded them to go into all the world and preach the gospel, He assured His disciples that *"All authority in heaven and on earth has been given to me"* (v. 18).

The disciples had no reason to doubt the power and authority of Jesus. For three years they had stood amazed as Jesus had performed all kinds of mighty deeds, from healing people to raising them from the dead. His power and authority had sent demons fleeing. His power had been the source of miracles such as the bread and fish that had multiplied. Through His power and authority the winds and waves had become still. They had seen His power and authority demonstrated in many and various ways.

But when Jesus made this statement He was referring to more than what they had seen and heard for those three years. He said, *"has been given to me."* This sounds as if the Father had specially conferred authority on Him as a result of His obedience in dying on the cross. When He rose from the dead and completed the work of redemption, the Father gave Him an even greater allocation of authority and power. This is confirmed in Philippians 2:9-10, *"Therefore God exalted him to the highest place and gave him the name that is above every name, that at the name of Jesus every knee should bow, in heaven and on earth and under the earth."*

Jesus said that all authority has been given to Him and so His disciples could know that when they went into all the world to proclaim the gospel that His power and authority would be with them every moment of every day. May you be assured of this too.

Teach them

"Teaching them to obey everything I have commanded you. And surely I am with you always, to the very end of the age."

ꕥ MATTHEW 28:20 ꕥ

Jesus commissioned His disciples to go into all the nations and tell them of the wonderful news of Jesus and His Kingdom. He assured them that His presence and authority would be with them and He encouraged them to go.

Then He issued them with a specific command, explaining the nature of the work they were called to do. The original Greek can be literally translated as, "Once you have gone, therefore, teach people to be My students." This has to do with more than just making converts. A convert is someone who chooses to turn away from his or her own ways and to walk with Jesus. But what does this decision really entail? The Greek word for disciple is *mathetes* and it refers to a student, pupil or learner.

When you decide to follow Christ, then you agree to become His disciple, His student. You enroll as a scholar in the school of the Kingdom of God. And this affects every aspect of your life. You give Him your heart and your will, but also your mind. You say, in essence, "Lord, teach me." You learn about your own sinfulness and inability to save yourself. But you learn, too, about God's saving power, of His love, His commandments, and so much more. And what you learn is not merely head knowledge but it drops deep into your heart and remains in you so that you can remain in the truth.

We must be careful that we do not try to force people into the Kingdom of God through some kind of spiritual sausage machine. We must ensure that they learn who they are in Jesus Christ, and what He expects from them.

October 8

Baptize them

"Therefore go and make disciples of all nations, baptizing them in the name of the Father and of the Son and of the Holy Spirit."

℘ MATTHEW 28:19 ☙

There are largely two traditions concerning baptism in the church. On the one hand there is baptism of people who have given their lives to Jesus and have fully committed themselves to Him. On the other hand there is the christening of babies and infants, based on the belief that they are already grafted into the body of Christ because their parents believe in Jesus Christ. There are some churches and congregations that add a baptism celebration as well. This is for people who were baptized as babies but feel the need to celebrate that event when they are grown up. Whatever your view of baptism is, it remains an important commandment that Jesus gave us.

Before we consider what Jesus meant when He said that people who believe in Him should be baptized, it is important for us to accept that because of the differences of opinion regarding baptism, it should never become a point of divisiveness among Christians. The primary focus of Jesus' command was that we go into all nations with the message of salvation. The teaching and baptism are secondary commands. That is why we should never promote baptism as the most important part of this commandment.

Jesus said, *"Baptize them in the name of the Father and of the Son and of the Holy Spirit."* Baptism is the sign that we have been sealed with the righteousness of Christ that is given to us when we accept the gospel message. It is a sign that we belong to Jesus and that we have been reconciled with God. It shows your commitment to dedicate your whole life to God. It points to a life-giving relationship with the Lord God almighty. Let us rejoice that we have been baptized into His body.

Who fasts during a celebration?

Then John's disciples came and asked him, "How is it that we and the Pharisees fast, but your disciples do not fast?"

ꕥ MATTHEW 9:14 ꕥ

The disciples of John came to Jesus with a question. They wanted to know why they, and the Pharisees, often fasted, but the disciples of Jesus never did. Jesus gave an interesting answer.

We know that Jesus spent forty days fasting in the wilderness before He was tempted by the devil. The Bible also has lots of accounts of people who set aside time to fast because they wanted to dedicate themselves more fully to God.

When you fast you choose to put aside the normal issues of life, such as eating, rest and relaxation, and sexual activity, in order to commit yourself to God. It is a time when you surrender to God while you deny your physical needs. People who spend time fasting will tell you that they receive great blessings through doing so. They seem to hear the voice of God more clearly and breakthroughs in their lives seem to be easier during or after a time of fasting.

Jesus was not opposed to fasting. But He answered John's disciples by saying that people do not fast when they are at a wedding supper (cf. v. 15). What did Jesus mean by this? He was so involved with celebrating the coming of the Kingdom of God through His life that He healed people, and edified them, and fed the hungry. There was so much to celebrate that it was not appropriate for His disciples to fast during this time.

Later they would indeed set aside time to fast, but not when they were celebrating the coming of the Kingdom with Him. Jesus was the Bridegroom and they were celebrating the establishing of God's Kingdom on earth with Him. It was not necessary for them to fast then.

Have you ever set aside time to fast?

October 10

Just one thing

Jesus replied: "Love the Lord your God with all your heart and with all your soul and with all your mind."

༄ MATTHEW 22:37 ༄

An expert in the law came to Jesus, hoping to catch Him out with a question he had. He wanted Jesus to tell him what the greatest commandment in the law was. If Jesus were to weigh up each of the laws of the Old Testament against one other, it would probably have been a difficult question to answer. But His answer was brilliant. It cut right through all the rules and regulations and came to the heart of serving God.

Jesus mentioned two things, each of which was concerned with only one issue: love. He said that the first commandment is that God expects us to love Him with all our heart, all our soul, all our mind, and all our strength. Jesus said that this is the most important commandment of all.

It is sad that there are still so many church members who believe that they need to pacify God through doing all the right things. So many people think that if only they give up smoking or drinking or swearing, and if they no longer gossip then they might just be good enough for God. Beloved, this is not what the gospel is all about. It is about relationships. It is about love. Thank God that Jesus came to show us the love that God has for all people. Because He loves us so much, He died on the cross for us and we are now able to love Him in return.

In the second place it has to do with love for people. We need to love our neighbor as ourselves. In fact, we should regard them more highly than we do ourselves. It has everything to do with love. It is important that we love people as God loves them. Every time that we fail to love others, we fall short of God's expectations for us. Let us choose to love God and our fellowman.

Give to the government

"Give to Caesar what is Caesar's, and to God what is God's."

ꕤ MATTHEW 22:21 ꕤ

The Pharisees tried to trap Jesus. They began by complimenting Him. What they said was absolutely true, and we can learn a lesson from their flattering words.

They said, *"Teacher, we know you are a man of integrity and that you teach the way of God in accordance with the truth. You aren't swayed by men, because you pay no attention to who they are"* (v. 16). What a compliment! He gives His opinions honestly, is faithful to the truth, makes God's will known to people, and as He does these things He does not compromise on any issue in order to try to accommodate other people's opinions. He was not concerned by what other people thought of Him. Let us learn of Jesus. We are often so concerned about what people think of us that when we talk to them, we become obsequious and compromise the will and truth of God.

The question the Pharisees asked Him was whether or not it was right to pay taxes to Caesar. Caesar was a heathen ruler. He was an alien ruler over the nation of Israel. Were the Israelites expected to pay taxes to this heathen? He did not serve God and did not know God and so they thought that they should not help him to rule over them. Jesus pointed out that Caesar's head was depicted on the coins that they used every day and so they should pay taxes to him because that was his due. But at the same time they should give God what is due to Him. They should hold nothing back of what they owed either the government or God.

Christians are expected to pay their taxes and fulfill their other obligations to their government and nation, even if you do not agree with the way the government handles certain things. But we must also give God that which belongs to Him – complete surrender and obedience to His Word.

October 12

Childlike praise

"Do you hear what these children are saying?" they asked him. "Yes," replied Jesus, "have you never read, 'From the lips of children and infants you have ordained praise'?"

∞ MATTHEW 21:16 ∞

There was a wonderful atmosphere around Jesus. The life-giving power of the Kingdom of God radiated from Him in all that He did and all that He said. He, who is the Truth and the Life, radiated such life and energy that people fell over their feet to be near Him.

The way people responded to the words and actions of Jesus testified to their excitement and joy. When healings occurred before their eyes, they praised God and magnified His name. And it wasn't only grownups that responded this way. Children did too.

When the leaders of the priests and scribes saw the wonderful things that He did, and heard the children calling out in the temple, *"Hosanna to the Son of David!"* (v. 15) they were indignant. Even though it was children praising Jesus, they wanted them to be silenced. How could they say that Jesus was the Son of David, the Messiah? They were so angry that they asked Him, *"Do you hear what these children are saying?"* Jesus quoted the words of Psalm 8:2, where the psalmist said that children and infants would be the ones to praise God for His great and mighty deeds.

Children are more ready to sing spontaneously than grownups are. Children praise spontaneously out of their spirits. Many congregations expect children to sit quietly because they do not seem to enter into the atmosphere of quiet worship. But when there is life-giving power and joy in the gospel message within a congregation, it will be reflected in the hearts and mouths of the children. And Psalm 8 says that the enemies of the Kingdom are silenced when children praise and worship Jesus.

We too should offer praise to Him in this childlike and joyous way.

On a donkey

"If anyone says anything to you, tell him that the Lord needs them, and he will send them right away."

Matthew 21:3

The celebration of Passover was at hand. Jesus sent two of His disciples ahead of Him to fetch a donkey and her foal. The manner in which the disciples found and got the foal were evidence of the power and majesty of Jesus. God organized all the details from heaven. They simply went into a village and found the donkey at exactly the spot where Jesus said they would be. They untied her and brought her to Jesus.

And so the prophecy of Zechariah was fulfilled. He had said that Jesus would enter Jerusalem riding on a donkey, the foal of a beast of burden. Jesus could just as easily have obtained a beautiful white horse for His entry into Jerusalem. In those days kings and rulers used to ride on magnificent horses. But Jesus chose the foal of a donkey. He made a statement through His choice: He came to serve people. He was humble. He was not concerned with status and position but about the work of redemption He came to do.

Many people see their self-worth and prestige reflected in the vehicles in which they drive. Their cars become a means of showing others what they are worth. The bigger and shinier the car they drive, the happier they feel about themselves. But not Jesus. He was not arrogant and boastful. He came to redeem us, to serve us.

As Jesus entered Jerusalem the people threw their cloaks on the ground in front of Him, along with palm branches that they cut from trees along the route. They shouted, "Hosanna, Lord, save us." They thought that He was about to set Israel free from the tyranny of the Romans. Far from it! He had not come to establish an earthly kingdom, but a heavenly one. The people around Him shouted with loud voices, "Blessed is He who comes in the name of the Lord!" But a few days later those same people shouted out, "Crucify Him!" They did not really understand who Jesus was.

Old and new

"Therefore every teacher of the law who has been instructed about the kingdom of heaven is like the owner of a house who brings out of his storeroom new treasures as well as old."

MATTHEW 13:52

The disciples of Jesus, or His students, according to the original Greek word, are people who acquire knowledge concerning the deep truths of God. This knowledge is like a treasure trove that is unlocked for them, people who previously were spiritually blind and knew nothing about God.

Jesus meant that each of His followers should become a student of His Word. The scribes of Jesus' day spent much time studying the old covenant. They focused on the Scriptures that had been copied and preserved by rabbis and other teachers and were the basis of Jewish culture. Jesus said that if a person who has studied the Word in this way becomes a disciple of His Kingdom, he or she will be spiritually enriched and will develop and expand his or her understanding in ways not even thought possible.

Each of us is called to be Jesus' student, which means we need to get to know the Word thoroughly. We must look at the complete canon of Scripture because God has given all of it to us. There are many riches to be uncovered in the Old Testament concerning the history of the people of Israel. It is such a rich source of knowledge that it would do us good to learn what the old covenant teaches.

But without the knowledge of the Kingdom message of Jesus, the old covenant is simply a legalistic list of commands and events, and cannot be fully understood. It is only through the words of Jesus that we can truly begin to understand the old covenant and it becomes clear to us. If we have the New Testament in our hearts as well as the teachings of the Old Testament, then we will be like the owner of a house who brings forth old and new treasures from his store. The full message of Jesus is insightful and new. It consists of old and new things that bring a sparkle to our lives.

The road of righteousness

"If your brother sins against you, go and show him his fault, just between the two of you. If he listens to you, you have won your brother over."

Matthew 18:15

How should we respond when someone openly makes a mistake and falls in sin? Jesus gives us the way that will help that person to get back on the right road. Whenever anyone opposes the will of God we must make sure that we maintain an attitude of love toward him or her.

It is the responsibility of the person who has been sinned against to take up the matter in love. The first recourse is not to run to someone else for advice. Nor is it to rush to the pastor with your complaints. First, you should go down on your knees and talk to God and only then decide how to handle the situation. Talk to the person with humility, love and compassion, and from the grace of God in your heart. Ask if he would like to examine the truth together with you. If the person listens to what you have to say, the Bible says that you have won your brother or sister back. But the person might not be open to listening to you, and is not prepared to embrace the truth. What do you do then?

Take one or two other Christians with you to speak to the person again. Once again your attitude should be that of love, humility and respect for the person who has wronged you.

If he still does not listen, then the issue needs to be presented before the congregation. The whole congregation must be made aware of what happened and do what they can to make things right between the two of you. If the person still does not listen then he is in fact cutting himself off from the body of Christ and choosing to go his own way.

People in the church of Jesus have many differences of opinion. I pray that you will solve your differences with other Christians in an atmosphere of love and humility.

October 16

A straight path

"But so that we may not offend them, go to the lake and throw out your line. Take the first fish you catch; open its mouth and you will find a four-drachma coin. Take it and give it to them for my tax and yours."

MATTHEW 17:27

The officials who collected the temple tax came to him, perhaps because he was the leader of the disciples. They asked him what their position was regarding the paying of the temple taxes. They were, after all, required to pay it. Peter answered that of course they knew they should pay the temple taxes. But did Jesus?

Every Jewish man over the age of twenty was required by God to pay for the upkeep of the temple (cf. Ex. 30:12-14, 2 Chr. 24:6, 9). That meant Jesus was also required to pay it. When Peter arrived home, Jesus surprised him with a word of knowledge. Before Simon could say a word, He asked him, *"What do you think, Simon? From whom do the kings of the earth collect duty and taxes – from their own sons or from others?"* (v. 25). Peter answered that other people paid the taxes, not their own sons. And Jesus said, *"Then the sons are exempt."* What Jesus meant was that as the Son of God He did not really have to pay taxes to the temple.

But Jesus went on to say that He did not want to offend any person. The Greek word for offend is *skandelon*, which means a trap or a snare or even a stumbling block that causes people to stumble in sin. He paid His temple taxes because God required it, not because people had come up with the idea.

And so He instructed Peter to go and catch a fish with his fishing line. If he opened the first fish he caught, he would find a four-drachma coin inside it. That would be enough to pay the temple tax for both Jesus and Peter. We hardly need to say that that is exactly what happened. Once again we see the majesty and power of Jesus at work! We also realize that money was not an issue for Jesus. Above all, His heart was right before God and He desired, above all else to do God's will. He walked the straight road.

With you

"And surely I am with you always, to the very end of the age."

Matthew 28:20

When Jesus issued His final commandment to His disciples shortly before He returned to heaven, He made it very clear what He expected from them. But He also gave them certain promises. He assured them of His power.

Jesus knew what His disciples were going to go through, and so, even though He was on His way to be glorified in heaven and His disciples would not physically see Him for a long time, He was able to comfort them. He told them that they should not ever forget His promise. They needed to hold fast to the words He had spoken about these things. He said that He would be with them forever.

Sometimes our circumstances or our feelings cause us to forget that the Lord is truly present with us. We forget so quickly! Many people in despair ask where God is in their lives. Everything in them and everything around them seems to indicate that God has deserted them. But this is never true. People reach this conclusion from the incorrect perspective of the problems that they face. God's presence with us is not dependent on what we feel, but on His promises. Jesus promised and emphasized that we must not forget, *"And surely I am with you always, to the very end of the age."*

It is no one less than Jesus Himself who is with you and me every single day. Day in and day out. And night after night too. He assures us that He will never leave us and never forsake us. His grace will always be sufficient for us, every single day. Right until we come to the end of our lives on earth, and then still all through eternity! After all, His name is Immanuel. He is God with us. We have no reason ever to doubt that.

October 18

Dynamite power

"But you will receive power when the Holy Spirit comes on you; and you will be my witnesses in Jerusalem, and in all Judea and Samaria, and to the ends of the earth."

ACTS 1:8

Jesus issued His disciples with a command. They were to go into all the world with the good news of redemption that He made possible for everyone on the cross. They had seen how He had triumphed over death, for they could see the holes the nails had left in His hands and the sword had left in His side. He had been glorified and was ready to return to His Father.

When Jesus commissioned His disciples, He also gave them the assurance that His mighty presence would be with them always. He would support them. He would share the power and authority that He had received as the Risen Lord with them. But how would this happen? The answer is clear – through the Holy Spirit who would come on them.

There is nothing as sad as Christians who have no power. There is such an important work for us to do. We need to reach every nation and people in the world with the gospel message. We need supernatural strength and power to do this. And Jesus provided that strength for us through the presence of the Holy Spirit in us. He is the Spirit of power. The Greek word for this Holy Spirit power is *dunamis*. It is from this word that we derive the English word dynamite. And we know what dynamite is capable of doing. The dynamite power of the Holy Spirit has been made available to you and to me so that we can carry out God's command.

That is why we need to open our spirits and let the Spirit rule in us. We must not be satisfied to remain children in the faith. We must receive the fullness of His equipping in us. Powerless Christians are those who grieve or quench or limit the Holy Spirit.

Be filled with the Holy Spirit and His power today (cf. Eph. 5:18).

We remember her

"I tell you the truth, wherever this gospel is preached throughout the world, what she has done will also be told, in memory of her."

☙ MATTHEW 26:13 ❧

Jesus had been invited to eat at the house of Simon the leper. Simon would be eternally grateful to Jesus because He had healed him from a dreaded and debilitating disease. Martha was also there (cf. Jn. 12:2), with her sister, Mary. Lazarus was at the table with Jesus.

Suddenly a woman came into the room carrying an alabaster jar of expensive and precious aromatic oil. This woman was known as Mary of Bethany (cf. Jn. 12:3). (This was not the same woman described in Luke 7.) She walked up to Jesus, and poured the oil out over Jesus' head. John says she poured it over His feet, and both Matthew and Mark mention that it ran over His whole body. Remember that in Psalm 23:5 David said, *"You prepare a table before me in the presence of my enemies. You anoint my head with oil; my cup overflows."*

John, in chapter 12 of his gospel, reported that Judas was very negative about what this woman did. He was the treasurer of the group of disciples and had very quickly realized the value of this gift of hers. It was worth about 300 denarii, a large sum of money that he said could rather have been given to the poor. It seems that the responses of the other disciples were also negative.

But Jesus silenced them saying that they should stop making things difficult for her. She had done a good deed for Him and had actually prepared Him for His burial. He then promised that wherever the good news of the gospel was preached in the world, the story of what she had done would be told as well. It would be a remembrance of her love for Jesus.

And still today we remember this woman's act of love and worship for her Savior. When last have you poured out a precious fragrant offering to Jesus simply because you love Him?

October 20

What do we learn?

"Teaching them to obey everything I have commanded you. And surely I am with you always, to the very end of the age."

Matthew 28:20

When Jesus issued His final command to His disciples, He said that they were to make other people disciples, or in other words students, of His. That means that people have to come to a knowledge of Jesus. This knowledge will set them free and bring them into a relationship with God, the Heavenly Father.

Jesus said that people from all nations need to be taught to do all the things that He commanded His disciples to do. That seems like an awful lot. It is impossible to mention in this short space everything that Jesus commanded, but that is why we have the Word of God, the Holy Scriptures, that contains the words of Jesus and His commands. That is why it is important for us to spend time in the Word of God. It is only by doing so that we will remind ourselves daily of the things Jesus commanded us to do, and can then make sure that we go and do them.

In general, we could say that everything Jesus said is brought together in the wonderful conversations He had with His disciples as recorded for us in the gospels. Think of all His parables containing so many insights that can help us to establish a right relationship with Him. Think too of all the statements He made about love, self-denial, and the influence we can have in the earth by being salt and light, and so much more. Think about all He said about living a truly fulfilled life and the provision He made for us to live with meaning and purpose from day to day. And think of all the lessons He taught about hypocrisy, prayer, spiritual fruit like humility and trust, and many more.

Before we can teach others, we first need to be students who acquire this knowledge for ourselves.

Hands off!

He said to them: "It is not for you to know the times or dates the Father has set by his own authority."

ꟙ Acts 1:7 ꟙ

There are some things that we will never understand. There are spiritual matters, things of the Kingdom, things that God has determined in His will and has considered in His thoughts that are just simply higher than our thoughts. God does give us certain insights into spiritual matters and we are even privileged enough to have some understanding of things that even the angels don't know, and yet wish that they did (cf. 1 Pet. 1:12).

The disciples asked Jesus when the time would come for Him to establish His Kingdom in Israel. When they asked this question they showed that they did not really yet understand that Jesus' Kingdom had nothing to do with the earthly nation of Israel. His Kingdom encompasses the whole world and includes people from every nation and people. Jesus answered that it was not for them to know the times and circumstances that the Father, in His might and power, has determined for things to take place.

At first glance this seems contradictory because, as Christians, we are supposed to gain insight into the will of God, but here we are told that there are some things that we must rather leave well alone. Modern intellectuals find it hard simply to accept in faith that there are some things that we will never quite understand because we do not have the necessary insight. And yet this is what God expects of us. We have the Word of God and we have the Holy Spirit who will teach us and remind us of all that Jesus said. But there are some issues, such as the time of Christ's Second Coming, that we simply will not know. In spite of this, and even though Jesus Himself said that we will not know the day and time of His return, there are still Christians who regularly predict the date of His Second Coming. There will always be things that we do not clearly understand and that we simply have to accept in faith.

October 22

The wordless Jesus

But Jesus made no reply, not even a single charge – to the great amazement of the governor.

℘ MATTHEW 27:14 ☙

Actions often speak louder than words. More than once Jesus gave no answer or explanation for the situation He was facing, but His attitude, the way He looked at someone or His actions spoke volumes.

One of the most gripping accounts in the Bible is when Peter denied the Lord Jesus and then the cock crowed. At that moment Jesus turned around and looked directly into Peter's eyes. When He looked at him, Peter remembered how arrogant and brash he had been when he said that he would never deny Jesus.

On another occasion, when the accusers of the woman caught in adultery brought her to Jesus, they expected Him to act as Judge. They specifically asked Him if the old covenant regulation was still valid in her situation. If so, she should be stoned to death. But Jesus did not answer them. In fact, He actually ignored the crowd pressing around Him. He simply bent down and began to write with His finger in the dust. We do not know what He wrote, but we do know that those who wanted to judge the woman walked away in shame.

And then there was the time when, during dinner, Jesus took the bowl of water, tied a towel around His waist, and silently began to wash the feet of His disciples. Only after He had completed His deed in humble silence, did He give any explanation of why He had done that.

And then of course the way in which Jesus faced the suffering He went through, spoke volumes. Isaiah 53:7 says, *"He was oppressed and afflicted, yet he did not open his mouth; he was led like a lamb to the slaughter, and as a sheep before her shearers is silent, so he did not open his mouth."* How often the Lord says nothing to you and me, but His loving presence comforts and encourages us.

Stay on the straight and narrow way!

> *"Enter through the narrow gate. For wide is the gate and broad is the road that leads to destruction, and many enter through it. But small is the gate and narrow the road that leads to life, and only a few find it."*
>
> ꕥ MATTHEW 7:13-14 ꕥ

Jesus did not come to present a religion that would be popular and easy. His grace is beyond understanding, but is not to be cheaply had. He never pulled the wool over anyone's eyes about what it costs people to follow Him. What a contrast that is with so many preachers today who present heaven in such a way that it would almost make God embarrassed. Of course there are wonderful benefits and privileges that come with the gift of salvation we receive through Jesus Christ, but the call to follow Jesus is not an invitation to comfort.

Jesus clearly stated that there are only two entrances to eternal life. The one is very narrow, and it leads to a narrow path. And this narrow gate very clearly refers to the obedience that is required of those who follow Jesus. This is not about trying to gain salvation through works, nor does it suggest that we need to do something to earn our way into heaven. But it does refer to the fact that we are to keep the commands of Jesus. We are to do what He tells us in His Word to do. When the believer passes through the narrow gate, he finds himself on a road that looks something like a mountain path between two rocky crevices. There is no place to carry our past sinful baggage on this path. Past habits and old sins must be left behind before we can follow this route. When we are born again we do not automatically leave behind everything that has to do with our old fleshly nature and that is why we struggle to walk along this narrow path. We often need to stop and get rid of sins that are hindering us.

Let us follow the narrow path that we find through the narrow gate, and although only few find this path, let us go forward along it with confidence.

October 24

Broadway

"But small is the gate and narrow the road that leads to life, and only a few find it."

Matthew 7:14

Jesus stated that people who follow Him must be prepared to enter through the narrow gate and walk along the narrow path. With this image He was illustrating that His disciples need to be completely committed to Him and willingly obey the things that He asks them to do. This is the path of the righteous described in Psalm 1. And this is a good choice to make. Those who choose to follow the narrow path have found the way that leads to eternal life.

But there is, unfortunately, another road, one we can call Broadway. This is the path of the dead where people try to bring glory to themselves. This is the path of those who choose not to obey God. It is the path of selfishness and of self-will, and of rebellion toward God.

There are many people on this broad path through life. Masses of people stream through the wide gates, and they look so happy and free, but in actual fact they are chained as slaves of the forces of darkness, the rulers of this world (cf. Eph. 2). They do not have any inner peace and so they can never truly be happy. It just seems that way when we look at the surface of their lives. The path that they follow leads to eternal damnation.

Sometimes we are tempted to think that it is not worthwhile to follow Christ. After all, the path that He calls us to follow is one that requires self-denial. The picture of the broad path filled with people is often a problem for young people and young Christians. But remember the words of Psalm 73:19, *"How suddenly are they destroyed, completely swept away by terrors!"*

The Sabbath is for me

"For the Son of Man is Lord of the Sabbath."

℘ MATTHEW 12:8 ℘

The Lord God had a purpose behind the laws that He gave to people. It was not to restrict them, nor was it to make their lives unpleasant. They were regulations that were designed to help them live better lives and to protect them from wickedness and the things that could harm them.

God set aside one day in the week to give people a chance to rest. The day should be set aside for rest and for focusing on Him. God made the law of the Sabbath for our benefit. But over time the religious leaders made the observing of the Sabbath day something legalistic and bound by regulations so that it became a greater burden than the joy it was meant to be. The Jewish rulers imposed excessively strict laws about what could or could not be done on the Sabbath day. They changed the spirit of the law into something that was simply the dead letter of the law.

So, when the Pharisees complained that Jesus and His disciples walked through the fields and picked some grain to eat on the Sabbath because they were hungry, Jesus pointed out to them that they should not be legalistic about keeping the Sabbath day. He referred to the time when David and his men were hungry after a battle. They went into the temple and ate the show bread that only the priests were supposed to eat. David took and ate the bread, not because he was disrespectful of the law, but because the circumstances he was in justified his actions.

We must not bend the laws of God lightly, just to suit ourselves. But the Lord knows our hearts and He knows our attitude toward Him. He will teach us how to implement His rules and regulations in our lives, even in the twenty-first century. The Sabbath was made for man, not man for the Sabbath. If we love God with our whole heart, obeying His laws will never be a problem for us.

October 26

Unmarried?

"Not everyone can accept this word, but only those to whom it has been given."

MATTHEW 19:11

When Jesus spoke about divorce, and about how important it is for two people to maintain the unity that God has instituted in their lives, His disciples suggested that it would then be better not to get married at all. But Jesus said that it is not possible for everyone to remain unmarried.

Jesus mentions that some people make a decision to remain unmarried for the sake of the Kingdom of God. These people have no desire to marry but want to serve the Kingdom of God with everything that is within them. They thus decide to go through life as singles. Like Paul. He committed his whole love to his heavenly Bridegroom. Peter, on the other hand, chose to take his wife with him when he went on missionary journeys (cf. 1 Cor. 9:5). The one choice is not better than the other. They are simply choices made from a person's free will and as each one is convinced in his or her heart.

There is a lot of pressure placed on young people today to get married. If someone decides to commit his or her life to the Lord and to remain unmarried because they feel they can serve Him better that way, there are many people who do not understand this decision. Whether you are married or not, you must serve the Lord to the best of your ability.

Let us open our hearts to receive the fullness of the message Jesus was teaching through these words.

Relax a little

"Come with me by yourselves to a quiet place and get some rest."

☙ Mark 6:31 ❧

Jesus and His disciples were always very busy. People placed heavy demands on them and from early morning until late at night pressurized them to see to their needs. This depleted their reservoirs of strength and energy. Mark tells us that there were so many people coming and going that Jesus and His disciples didn't even have time to eat. Sometimes we are also so busy trying to meet the demands that people place on us that we don't seem to have enough time to eat or sleep properly. When we become physically drained it is hard to stay spiritually strong.

After the prophet Elijah had achieved a major spiritual victory over the 450 prophets of Baal, he heard that Queen Jezebel wanted to have him killed. He began to fear greatly, became depressed and fled into the desert. There he sat down under a broom tree and wished that he could die. He told God that he had had enough and that it would be best if He just took his life, because he was worthless after all. Where did this turn around come from? From victory to depression? Perhaps he was completely spiritually drained and physically exhausted. In chapter 19 we read that the Lord helped him overcome his depression, and that He provided food for him by sending an angel to minister to him. In this way his strength was renewed and he could continue with the work that God had called him to do.

Jesus told His disciples that they should withdraw to a quiet place. They needed to be alone with Him and to rest. Do you get enough rest? Or do you run around in circles, letting stress rule you? If you want to live wisely, and to be used by God to the fullest extent of your potential, you must set aside sufficient time to rest.

October 28

First to all nations

"And the gospel must first be preached to all nations."

☙ Mark 13:10 ❧

We do not have any real idea of when Jesus will come to take us to heaven, but all the signs seem to indicate that the end is near. Jesus mentioned certain things that would happen to warn us that the last days of earth are at hand. For instance, in Mark 13 He mentions that there would be times of great oppression and that there would be many natural disasters, and that Christians would be persecuted. Leaders will emerge who will mislead people and there will be rumors of wars and actual wars. Earthquakes will increase in number and famine will be widespread.

And yet Jesus also said that before He returns to fetch His Bride, there is one very specific thing that must occur. The gospel must first be preached to all nations. With these words, Jesus set a condition for His return. Worldwide proclamation of the gospel message is a command from God. And so it is the responsibility of the body of Christ to ensure that the gospel is preached in all nations. We must focus our energy, time, money and our planning on evangelizing the world.

If we consider the progress that has been made with missionary work in the last few years, then we can see that we are living in exciting times. There are many organizations today that are mobilizing the body of Christ to pray for the work of preaching the gospel message in previously unreached places. The whole world has become a "global village" through the satellite communication channels, the Internet and so on and it is possible for people to be in contact anywhere in the world in a matter of seconds. It is realistic to think that the gospel will reach every nation in our lifetime.

It remains a great challenge for us to ensure the evangelization of all nations. Only then will Jesus return.

Miracles

"And these signs will accompany those who believe."

Mark 16:17

Jesus commanded His disciples to go out in His name and in the power of the Holy Spirit to exercise His power and authority over the forces of wickedness of this world.

Jesus also promised His disciples that when they laid hands on sick people, they would recover. There are many accounts in the book of Acts of how this happened to the apostles. Still today we can freely come into the presence of the Father and ask Him, in the name of Jesus, to heal people who are suffering from sickness and disease. There are many testimonies of people who have been supernaturally healed. Of course this does not mean that every person who is prayed for will be healed, and neither does this mean that we should not go to medical doctors, for it is often through their knowledge that God heals us.

Mark goes on to say that the disciples would encounter all kinds of dangerous situations but that they would triumph over every single one, whether they ate poisonous food, or whether they picked up venomous snakes, they would be protected from harm. Mark does not mean that Christians are like magicians who play with poisonous snakes and drink poison for dramatic effect. Rather, he means that when they find themselves in situations where such things happen, and if it is God's will, they will not come to any harm.

We have been empowered by an almighty God so that we can accomplish His mission on the earth. We must not be feeble Christians but we should live as people who demonstrate His mighty deeds in this time of brokenness and need.

Do something!

"And if your right hand causes you to sin, cut it off and throw it away. It is better for you to lose one part of your body than for your whole body to go into hell."

ꟾ Matthew 5:30 ꟾ

Isn't it interesting how often we yield to temptations. Sin is such an overwhelming problem for us but we do gain hope when we read that the great apostle Paul also struggled with this problem. In the seventh chapter of Romans he mentions that the good things that he wants to do he doesn't do. But those things that he doesn't want to do, he ends up doing.

This does not mean that we should just lie down and let sin walk all over us. We must not give in and say that there's nothing we can do about it. Jesus calls us to resist sin and He gives us the strength to do so. He also promises that we will never have to face a temptation that is beyond our ability to resist.

Jesus was very serious about dealing with sin. When we read what He said in today's passage, it almost doesn't make sense to us. He exaggerates His message to drive the point home in our hearts. That is why He says that if your right eye causes you to stumble, you should gouge it out and throw it away. It would be better to do that rather than ending up in hell. If your right hand causes you to stumble, you should cut it off because it would be better to go through life with only one hand than to have your whole body burn in the fires of hell.

Jesus did not mean this literally, but what He is very clearly saying is that you and I must deliberately and purposefully take action to get rid of the sin in our lives.

Let us resist sin in our lives. As the writer to the Hebrews says, *"In your struggle against sin, you have not yet resisted to the point of shedding your blood"* (Heb. 12:4).

Swear

"Simply let your 'Yes' be 'Yes,' and your 'No,' 'No'; anything beyond this comes from the evil one."

MATTHEW 5:37

The Bible forbids us from making a false oath (cf. Lev. 19:12). The people of God are expected to keep their word (cf. Num. 30:2). The Bible asks us to be faithful to the truth. People should be able to depend on your word. If you have made a promise, you must do everything possible to keep it. This is what is required of us, because there is nothing false in God at all. Hebrews 6:18 clearly states this.

Jesus says we should not ever swear an oath. We do not need to swear to confirm the truth of our words. Our yes should simply be yes and our no should be no. If we always behave with sincerity and integrity, then if we promise something to others, they will know that we can be trusted, and we will not need to back up our promises with an oath. Jesus does not mean that we should not swear any oath at all, because then Christians would not be able to testify under oath in a courtroom. In fact, Abraham confirmed his promises to the king of Sodom and Abimelech with an oath (cf. Gen. 21). And didn't Jesus Himself swear under oath that He is the Christ, the Son of God? (cf. Mt. 26:63-64).

So Jesus is not saying that we should disobey the laws of our government by refusing to take oaths when we need to do so. He is rather talking about living and behaving with integrity and truth. We must not take oaths that are superficial, casual, and unnecessary to impress other people by trying to emphasize that our words are true. We must simply always do what we say we will.

How often we fail to keep our promises! Let us confess this and apologize to others for breaking our word. Let us not fall into the present world trend of saying one thing and doing another.

November

Useless salt

"Salt is good, but if it loses its saltiness, how can it be made salty again?"

LUKE 14:34

On a previous occasion Jesus had said that His disciples were to be like the salt of the earth. Salt gives flavor, preserves food, and so much more. But here He talks about salt that has lost its effectiveness and that cannot be used anymore.

Salt plays a big part in our lives. Eat food without salt just once, and you will realize how important it is for our lives. It is a wonderful flavoring. But salt can quickly lose its savor and become tasteless. Salt that is harvested from the morasses and lagoons or from the rocks around the Dead Sea very quickly loses its flavor and becomes alkaline and bland. And then it has little value. *"It is fit neither for the soil nor for the manure pile; it is thrown out"* (v. 35). The only thing that can be done with it is to throw it outside, for people to trample on.

The message is clear. Christians are the salt of the earth and they need to be good, strongly flavored salt. When they become like ineffective salt they are really good for nothing. Perhaps Jesus was referring to the religious people in Israel. There was a lot of religion but little power. The Scribes and the Pharisees were like people who gathered heaps of salt, but none of it had any taste.

We can only remain effective salt, salt that has a positive influence on the community around us, if we are filled with God's Holy Spirit and if the truth of God works through us in all we say and do. Ask the Lord to once again fill you with His Spirit so that you will be filled with new strength from above. Then you can make a difference everywhere you go and in the lives of every person you meet today.

November 2

Quickly forget

"But when you give to the needy, do not let your left hand know what your right hand is doing."

ᘓ MATTHEW 6:3 ᘐ

Jesus Christ taught us to give freely. He gave Himself to us as a gift from heaven so that our lives could be enriched and changed. What an indescribable gift He was!

He teaches us to give things away because it is more blessed to give than it is to receive. The attitude in which we give things to others is just as important as the fact that we give. If we give because we want everyone to know, then our giving is almost meaningless, says Jesus. And if we give in the hope that someone will give us something in return then that is also meaningless. If, for example, you help the poor, Jesus says that you must not announce what you are doing. Rather, when you give to the poor, your one hand shouldn't even know what the other is doing. You must do your good deeds in secret. The only one who needs to know is God and He will, in His own way and in His own time, reward you.

This principle also applies when we give things that are spiritual in nature. We do not put on a show. We do not show our commitment to God by, for example, going to church, or making financial contributions in such a way that everyone notices what we are doing and says how great we are. Our religion is supposed to be a love-relationship with God Himself and everything we do is out of our love for Him. No one else needs to see what we do as long as our service to Him is done in sincere love. The religious leaders in Jesus' day did all kinds of religious good deeds as publicly as they could so that other people would notice them and think that they were good. Their service was so empty, so false, so in vain!

Let us give freely and generously to God and to others. And then let us forget just as quickly what we have given.

Sharks or fish?

"Once again, the kingdom of heaven is like a net that was let down into the lake and caught all kinds of fish."

MATTHEW 13:47

In New Testament times most fishing was done by using nets. The boats went out onto the Sea of Galilee and the fishermen cast their nets into the water and then later hauled them in, bringing with them the fish that they had netted.

Jesus uses this image to explain what it will be like in the last days. The kingdom of heaven is a kingdom in which people are sorted out. When the world comes to an end and the Final Judgment takes place, the angels will go out and separate the good people from the bad.

It will be like a fishing net that has been cast into the sea and is filled with a great assortment of fish. When the net is full the fishermen drag it onto the shore and select all the good, edible fish and put them in a basket. But the sharks and everything that cannot be used are thrown away. And this is exactly what the net of the kingdom of heaven is like.

The good fish are not good in and of themselves but they have received the goodness of God because they have been made spiritually whole by the healing hand of God through Jesus Christ. These are the people who have become believers. They have been justified by the blood of Jesus. They are the children of God.

The bad people, those that have no place in the kingdom of God, are quite simply those who do not accept Jesus Christ as their Lord and Savior and who do not believe in God's plan for being reconciled with Him.

This parable is still to be fulfilled. We must make sure that we tell others of God's fishing net.

The precious kingdom!

"The kingdom of heaven is like treasure hidden in a field. When a man found it, he hid it again, and then in his joy went and sold all he had and bought that field."

Matthew 13:44

Oh, how precious is the kingdom of God. There is not enough money in the whole world to buy what God offers us in His kingdom. It is a treasure of immeasurable worth. Do we really understand how precious the riches of God's kingdom are for people who were lost?

Jesus says that the kingdom of God is like a treasure that has been buried under the ground in a field. One day, a man who was walking through the field discovered the precious treasure that was buried there. It was worth so much that it took his breath away. So he buried it again in the spot where he had found it. He was so excited that he could hardly speak properly. But he made a plan to put in an offer on the field. If he could buy the field he would get an unbelievably large treasure with it. And that's exactly what happened. He went and sold everything he had and used the money to buy the field. The treasure then belonged to him, and he became a very rich man. If you and I "sell" our lives and surrender to God, we will make a huge profit because we will receive the kingdom of God.

The Kingdom of God is also like a merchant who deals in pearls. He was always on the lookout for good pearls. One day he came across a very valuable pearl, the best he had ever laid eyes on. So he went and sold his house and everything he owned so that he could buy this pearl. What he gave up could not be compared with what he gained when he bought the pearl. It was worth far more than all he had sold.

We should rejoice and be glad because of the wonderful treasure we have received in the kingdom of God. It is worthwhile to give up everything to gain it.

Come!

"Come," he said. Then Peter got down out of the boat, walked on the water and came toward Jesus.

ꕤ MATTHEW 14:29 ꕤ

The disciples were preparing to travel to the other side of the lake while Jesus was sending off the crowds who had eaten the miraculous fish and bread. Once Jesus had sent the people away, He went alone into the mountains to pray. He had had a long day, but still He found time to pray. Jesus considered it a privilege to be able to spend time with His Father.

The disciples were a few miles off shore when suddenly, just as the dawn was breaking, they saw Jesus walking toward them on the water. Imagine how shocked they must have been! A man was walking on the water straight toward them. They were convinced they were seeing a ghost and they began to cry out in fear and horror. They couldn't even get away. They were trapped in the boat.

Immediately Jesus told them not to be afraid. It was Him they had seen. Peter could not believe his eyes or his ears, and, as always, he reacted impulsively when he called out, *"Lord, if it's you tell me to come to you on the water"* (v. 28). So Jesus invited him to come. And Peter climbed out of the boat and began to walk on the water toward Jesus.

Suddenly Peter became conscious of the waves and the strong wind, and he was scared. As his fear grew he began to sink and called out for the Lord to save him. Jesus reached out His hand and lifted Peter up out of the water. Then He spoke to him saying, *"You of little faith, why did you doubt?"* (v. 31).

Sometimes we are quick to judge Peter because he did not have enough faith, but at least he did try. The other disciples just stayed in the boat. And so Peter experienced something supernatural while they just looked on. His miraculous walk inspires us to live a life of faith. Respond to Jesus' call, and keep your eyes on Him.

November 6

Angels

"See that you do not look down on one of these little ones. For I tell you that their angels in heaven always see the face of my Father in heaven."

ꟿ Matthew 18:10 ꟿ

There is much talk about angels these days. You can buy images of angels in shops all over the place, but unfortunately most of these images are not scripturally accurate. Baby angels with wings do not actually exist in the kingdom of God. There are also people who believe that if babies die they become angels. This is just not true!

Angels are not little baby beings with wings. They are great and mighty. Read the book of Ezekiel to see how the prophet described angels! They are like storm winds, like flames of fire. And the most wonderful thing is that they are actually sent to minister to us. God sends them out on missions, commanding them to support and serve His children.

In this passage Jesus mentions that little children – who are an important example of people who want to enter the kingdom of Heaven – have angels who minister to them. These angels can often be found in heaven near the heavenly Father, seeking His instructions on behalf of the children.

Calvin believed that each one of us has an angel appointed to look after and protect us. Jesus mentions that children definitely have angels who watch over them and care for them. This does not mean that angels intercede for them before God. But they do stand ready to be sent by God to help these little children.

Only when we are in eternity will we really see how many times angels have come to our assistance. That is why we do not need to worry about our children or grandchildren. The angels of God are looking after them.

God's accounting

"Don't I have the right to do what I want with my own money? Or are you envious because I am generous?"

Matthew 20:15

A man hired some laborers to go and work in his vineyard. He told them that they would be paid the usual wages for a day's work. Around nine o'clock he went out again and found some more workers that he hired to help with the work. And he did the same thing again at noon and then again at three o'clock.

At five o'clock in the afternoon, just a short while before knocking-off time, he hired a few more men. When the day's work was over, he said that the men who had begun to work last should be paid first. Imagine how great their surprise was when they were given a full day's wages for only an hour or so of work. The men who had been hired first, and who had been working since early in the morning, began to rub their hands in anticipation. They thought that they were going to receive a fantastic salary that day. But their smiles disappeared when they also received a normal day's wages.

They asked how it was possible that they who had worked the whole day, born the brunt of the day's work, only received a day's wages while those who had done almost no work at all received the same amount. The answer was straightforward, *"Friend, I am not being unfair to you. Didn't you agree to work for a denarius? Take your pay and go. I want to give the man who was hired last the same as I gave you. Don't I have the right to do what I want with my own money?"* (vv. 13-15).

God's bookkeeping is different from ours. This parable seems unfair to us. But the key to understanding it is found in the words of Jesus – "I will". Jesus wants to set us free and He gives the same opportunity to all people. It does not depend on anything that we can earn. He saves us simply because of His grace.

November 8

The reason

Jesus replied, "You are in error because you do not know the Scriptures or the power of God."

ꟙ MATTHEW 22:29 ꟙ

Jesus often had disputes with the experts in the law, the Sadducees and the Pharisees. The Sadducees did not believe in the resurrection of the dead and yet they asked Jesus what would happen in eternity to a woman who had been married to five, six, or seven different men. Who would be her husband in heaven?

Jesus answered that they were mistaken because they did not really understand the Scriptures or the power of God. Then He went on to say that there would be no marriages in heaven. People would, in this regard, be like the angels. We will not become angels but we will live like them. We will recognize each other in heaven but we will enter into a new kind of relationship with our spouses if they are in heaven with us. We will no longer have a marriage relationship but we will have a wonderful, unsurpassed, glorious relationship with Jesus Christ. All our earthly needs will have fallen away. All we will want to do is praise and worship God and enjoy the abundance of His perfection.

The problem with the Sadducees was that they had lost sight of the truth because they did not really know the Scriptures. Let's take these words of Jesus to heart and remind ourselves that we need to study God's Word. There are many people who stray from the truth and then ask foolish questions and wrestle with all kinds of incorrect notions in their hearts, all because they do not really know what God says in His Word. It is not just the work of the preachers and pastors and ministers to learn to know the Scriptures. The Scriptures are available to every person who makes an effort to read the Bible. Let us make a concerted effort to read God's Word so that we do not make the same mistake that the Sadducees did. When God's Word lives in us richly it will shed much light on the many questions that we have.

Titles are out

"But you are not to be called 'Rabbi,' for you have only one Master and you are all brothers."

MATTHEW 23:8

The Scribes and the Pharisees were very conscious of the positions that they held, their appearance, and their status. They enjoyed the fact that people noticed them. They loved getting the most important seats in the synagogues and being addressed as Rabbi by people on the streets.

Jesus knew that many people want to be given titles and designations of honor because it makes them feel important. He did not object to the position of rabbi. In fact, on quite a few occasions people called Him Rabbi. What He did object to was the fact that people used such titles to elevate themselves above others. That is why He said that people should not be called *Rabbi*. He said that there is in fact only one Teacher, His Father and Himself. Every one of us is after all a student of the Great Teacher, and therefore no one has the right to think of themselves as important teachers. Jesus said that we have only one Father, and we are all equal as brothers in the Lord. That is why we should not call any man Father for we have only one Father, the One in heaven. Jesus was not referring to our biological fathers but to the custom of calling members of the Sanhedrin "father" (cf. Acts 7:2). People should also not be called Master, a reference, probably, to the highest level of teacher in the synagogue. This is, once again, all about the fact that those who want to be the greatest among men must be prepared to serve others and that those who are arrogant and self-important will be brought low. But those who humble themselves will be raised up by the Lord Himself.

November 10

Feeble flesh

"Watch and pray so that you will not fall into temptation. The spirit is willing, but the body is weak."

so Matthew 26:41 cs

When the Bible talks about our flesh, it refers to that part of our nature that has not yet been brought under the rulership of God. The flesh is our rebellious nature that resists the will and the word of God. The flesh is the "old person" where "I" sits on the throne and pride takes the upper hand.

When Jesus, in the Garden of Gethsemane, struggled with the anguish of the pain and suffering that He was to go through, He used the word flesh in a different way. He was referring here to the fragility of life with all its needs, both physical and psychological. It's very similar to what Isaiah said in Isaiah 40:6-7: *"All men are like grass, and all their glory is like the flowers of the field. The grass withers and the flowers fall, because the breath of the Lord blows on them."* And Paul talks about the treasure of God that has been poured into clay jars. He defined his own existence as a clay jar, with all kinds of chips and cracks, but within him there was a treasure without spot or blemish – the gospel message of Jesus Christ.

Our greatest struggle is often against the brokenness in our human nature. We desperately long to be stronger but all too often we find that the weakness of our flesh causes us to struggle. That is why it is so important for the Holy Spirit to be within us. The Spirit, in the fullness of His strength, helps us to ensure that the flesh and all its pressing needs does not get the upper hand.

When Jesus saw that His disciples were asleep after He had asked them to stay awake and pray with Him, He told them that they needed to keep watch and pray that they would not fall into temptation, because the spirit is willing but the flesh is weak.

Let us make an effort to pray more and to live with more purpose and strength so that our feeble flesh does not cause us to stumble.

Unity is strength

"That all of them may be one, Father, just as you are in me and I am in you. May they also be in us so that the world may believe that you have sent me."

ꕥ JOHN 17:21 ꕥ

One of the most beautiful prayers in the Bible is this prayer, the High Priestly Prayer that Jesus prayed for His disciples and for us. What a prayer! There is so much intensity, so much clarity, so much passion, so much wisdom in it.

A recurring theme in this prayer of Jesus, one that comes up quite a few times, is unity (vv. 21-23).

The devil knows only too well that if he can divide people, then he can rule over them. If he can cause disruption among Jesus' flock, and scatter His sheep, then he can break their strength. There is, after all, strength in unity. Jesus knew how important unity is for His children, and that is why He prayed four times, in this wonderful prayer, that the Father would bring about unity among believers so that they can work together in harmony.

We must do everything in our power to safeguard unity among Christians. The devil likes to sow discord in our thoughts, and he uses the words of others and various circumstances to try to convince us that we should not agree with one another. We must resist this divisive strategy of Satan that tries to get us to live at odds with people. Let's rather bend over backwards to forgive and to understand so that we can live in harmony with fellow believers.

If we do this, we deduce from Jesus' prayer that something wonderful will happen. The world will take note that God the Father truly did send Jesus into this world. Unity in the body of Christ is something so wonderful that it will convince other people that Jesus is alive. *"Let us therefore make every effort to do what leads to peace and to mutual edification"* (Rom. 14:19).

November 12

"Glory!"

"I have given them the glory that you gave me, that they may be one as we are one."

JOHN 17:22

When John thought back on everything that he could remember of Jesus' time on earth, he declared, *"That which was from the beginning, which we have heard, which we have seen with our eyes, which we have looked at and our hands have touched – this we proclaim concerning the Word of life"* (1 Jn 1:1). He also said, *"We have seen his glory, the glory of the One and Only, who came from the Father, full of grace and truth"* (Jn. 1:14). Later, when Jesus rose from the dead, the glory that was upon Him was awe-inspiring.

The glory of God is something beyond human experience, and yet ordinary people are given the chance to partake of it. When we enter into an intimate relationship with Jesus, then the Father reveals His Glory to ordinary, fallible people. This glory is not always visible to the natural eye because we are still confined to our earthly, broken, fleshly bodies. And yet He does reveal His glory to us. The more the Holy Spirit has control of our lives, the more of the glory of Jesus Christ is revealed in us. *"And we, who with unveiled faces all reflect the Lord's glory, are being transformed into his likeness with ever-increasing glory, which comes from the Lord, who is the Spirit"* (2 Cor. 3:18).

Jesus petitions the Father to show us His glory. And then He says something startling, *"I have given them the glory that you gave me, that they may be one as we are one"* (Jn. 17:22).

It doesn't matter where on earth we are, or which people we find ourselves with, we can quickly tell when the glory of the Lord is upon someone in our company. Even if you cannot understand that person's language, you will immediately sense a connection because of the glory of the Lord that radiates from their lives. There is an immediate sense of unity because you are both in a relationship with Christ.

What a prayer!

"Father, the time has come. Glorify your Son, that your Son may glorify you."

JOHN 17:1

The wonderful high priestly prayer of Jesus reveals a lot to us about His personality and about how we should pray.

If we just look at the ways in which Jesus addresses His Father God in this prayer, then we see His attitude of heart. In the first place He naturally and simply calls Him Father. This Father-Son relationship was of such a nature that Jesus could share everything with His Father. I trust that you too have such a relationship, through Jesus Christ, with your heavenly Father, the God of heaven and earth.

Jesus also calls Him Righteous Father (v. 25). Through this He points to the fact that the Father is righteous in all His judgments. That is why when we are in Christ we need not fear the Father. He does not condemn us because He knows all things, and when He does judge then His judgment is perfectly accurate.

Have you noticed that Jesus interceded specifically for you in this prayer? *"My prayer is not for them alone. I pray also for those who will believe in me through their message"* (v. 20). Jesus interceded for you all those centuries ago on the slopes of the Mount of Olives. Amazing!

Jesus also calls His Father Holy (v. 11). And the prayer of Jesus' heart is that His disciples will be made holy just as the Father is holy. They must live pure lives set apart for God and committed to Him. That is why He also prayed that they would be protected from evil. They will not be removed from the world, but they can be protected from the effects of evil while they are in the world.

These are just a few moments of this wonderful prayer. Perhaps we should set aside time to go and read through the whole chapter again and so hear the heartbeat of Jesus' love for the Father and for us.

November 14

Come and rest

"Come to me, all you who are weary and burdened, and I will give you rest."

℘ MATTHEW 11:28 ℘

Religion can tire you out. It can wear you out completely. If, for you, religion is a matter of all kinds of rules and regulations, then each day is a constant struggle to keep doing what is right, and this is exhausting.

Jesus makes this wonderful promise in the light of the criticism He leveled against the Pharisees in Matthew 23:4. There He accused them of placing heavy spiritual burdens on people's shoulders. Jesus wanted to put the situation right as quickly as possible. He emphasized that people do not need to come to Him carrying a heavy load. They do not need to sweat over rules and regulations. They simply have to enter a relationship with Him. Jesus would remove the heavy burden of rules and regulations that had been placed on their shoulders by the Pharisees and they would find rest for their souls. If they submitted to Jesus they would find that religion is really about love and forgiveness and an invitation to follow Him. Then they would not need to feel afraid of the Father but would find joy in His presence.

He gives us a new yoke, a new command, and it is based on love. In Jewish literature the term *yoke* was often used to refer to the sum total of all the regulations that the Jews had to keep in accordance with the teachings of the rabbis. But Jesus now presents a new and different yoke. This yoke is not heavy but light. The One who places the yoke on our shoulders is gentle and humble of heart. He does not want to deal harshly with sinners but reaches out a hand of love and care to us. He wants to give us rest and peace deep within our hearts. We will find rest for our souls. This yoke is not heavy and we will not double over under its load. It is not a burden at all. In fact, it brings us joy.

Beloved enemy

"But I tell you: Love your enemies and pray for those who persecute you."

Matthew 5:44

Each day God causes the sun to rise on the good as well as the evil people and His rain falls not only on the fields of the Christians but also on the fields of the atheists and of those who do wrong. In this we can see that God's goodness is visible to all people, and will be until the Day of Judgment.

And Jesus, in the light of this fact, urges us to be good toward others and love not only those who are good and loveable but those who are not so good or not so easy to love. Jesus is saying that we need to follow God's example. Like God, we must want His sun to shine on all people and His rain to fall on all who need it. If we only love those who love us, it doesn't really mean very much! Even sinners do that. If we only greet our own family and the members of our own congregation warmly then we actually do nothing more than what the world does.

We must be prepared to go further than that. We must even love people who are our enemies and those who oppose us and hurt us. This starts hitting home quite hard, doesn't it? And suddenly it doesn't seem so easy any more. It's good and proper to be friendly and amiable toward the people we meet in the streets or in a store, people we don't actually know, but to love our enemies and treat them well is quite a bit harder. And yet that is what Jesus expects of us. A popular saying in New Testament times was that you could love your nearest and dearest, but that you should hate your enemy. This was derived from twisting the words in Leviticus 19, and it certainly isn't stated anywhere in Scripture. And so Jesus set the matter right by saying that we should love our enemies.

If we do this then we will demonstrate that we really are children of God, who Himself loves and cares for all people. So today let's make a point of loving our enemies.

November 16

Four resurrection words

"Peace be with you! As the Father has sent me, I am sending you."

JOHN 20:21

What a wonderful surprise it must have been for the disciples when Jesus, after His death and burial, suddenly stood before them again. Supernaturally, Jesus came into the room and stood in their midst. And He spoke these words to them, "Peace be with you!"

Now, for the first time, He could speak these words with the fullness of their meaning. That which He had come to earth to do – to establish peace – had been done. He had died for their sins and He had risen again from the dead. The first gift a person who has been reconciled to God through the death of Jesus receives, is peace. Peace because you know that all your debt has been paid and you are no longer guilty in the eyes of God.

The second thing He said to them was, *"As the Father has sent me, I am sending you"* (v. 21). Once they had received the peace of God that passes all understanding, they received an instruction from God. They were commissioned to be the "sent ones" of God. He was going to return to His Father but the work that He had begun had to be carried on. There was a whole world waiting to hear what He had done for them. Were they ready to go and do what He wanted them to do?

The third thing that Jesus said to them was, *"Receive the Holy Spirit"* (v. 22). He said this and then He blew on them. It is impossible to do the work of one who has been commissioned and sent without the Holy Spirit.

The last thing Jesus mentioned was, *"If you forgive anyone his sins, they are forgiven; if you do not forgive them, they are not forgiven"* (v. 23). When they had been filled with the Holy Spirit then they would also have the authority to proclaim that people's sins had been forgiven, if they through faith began to follow Jesus.

Restored

"Simon son of John, do you truly love me more than these?" "Yes, Lord," he said, "you know that I love you." Jesus said, "Feed my lambs."

ꕥ John 21:15 ꕥ

After Jesus had died the disciples once again went out fishing one night. Suddenly they saw Jesus about 100 yards away from the boat, standing on the shore of the sea. As soon as Peter realized that it was Jesus, he took off his outer garments and jumped into the water and went to Jesus. His heart was filled with excitement and joy, but there was also very likely a great deal of embarrassment and shame in his heart because the last time he had looked into Jesus' eyes was just after he had betrayed Him.

The Lord longs to restore people. He knows our weaknesses and He knows how often we fall into sin. If we repent of our sins, as Peter did when he wept bitterly, then God is ready and willing to forgive us. This was, after all, why Jesus came into this world – so that we could be forgiven.

Peter denied Jesus three times. Three times he pretended that he did not know Jesus. And three times Jesus asked him, *"Simon son of John, do you truly love me?"* (v. 15). And each time Peter answered that he truly loved Him. As he said these words he must have realized how hollow they actually sounded. After all, hadn't he allowed his fear to overshadow his love? And yet now he really wanted to let Jesus know how much he did love Him. Each time that Peter said that he loved Jesus, Jesus commanded him to feed His sheep and His lambs.

Jesus restored Peter. His past sins and mistakes were dealt with and forgotten. His guilt and heartache over his denial of Jesus were replaced with a new boldness.

The Lord wants to forgive you for whatever mistakes you made yesterday or the day before. Tell Him you're sorry, and then move on.

November 18

Sheep that graze

The third time he said to him, "Simon son of John, do you love me?" Peter was hurt because Jesus asked him the third time, "Do you love me?" He said, "Lord, you know all things; you know that I love you." Jesus said, "Feed my sheep."

JOHN 21:17

Jesus wanted to forgive Peter. Peter had denied that he knew Him, but that was in the past and so He drew Peter into a conversation in which He did not talk about rules and regulations, but about love. Did Peter really love Him? Peter answered with an emphatic *yes* and so his love-relationship with Jesus was restored.

In response to Peter's declaration of love, Jesus told Peter that he should feed His sheep and His lambs. If Peter truly did love Jesus, then he would be compelled by that love to show love to others. This love would help him to reach out to other people in need. He would now be able to accept the responsibility for caring for others. Jesus' little flock. People with needs, people who needed to be taught, people who needed to be helped, people who needed to be supported and encouraged, people who needed prayer and who needed to be plucked out of the grip of the evil one.

If Peter did all these things then his love for Jesus would be evident to all who knew him. Jesus mentions two kinds of sheep: sheep and lambs. Perhaps Jesus was thinking about small children, grownups, and perhaps young people. Each one of them needs to be ministered to.

Peter was given a very specific commission. But you and I are also able to show our love for the Lord by caring for the Lord's people. We have also been called to serve His flock. He asks you today if you love Him, and if your answer is *yes* then He asks you too to, "Feed my sheep."

How does it affect you?

Jesus answered, "If I want him to remain alive until I return, what is that to you? You must follow me."

JOHN 21:22

After Jesus had risen from the dead He restored Peter, who had denied Him. After that He said to him, *"Follow me!"* He also mentioned that when he was old he would stretch out his hands and then someone else would bind him and lead him where he did not want to go. Through these words Jesus prophesied that Peter would be martyred for his faith in Jesus.

When Jesus said this to him, Peter turned around and saw John walking behind them. Immediately he was concerned for his friend, and so he asked Jesus what would happen to John. But Jesus said to him, *"If I want him to remain alive until I return, what is that to you? You must follow me"* (v. 22). What Jesus was saying to Peter here was that he did not need to be worried about John and neither did he need to take spiritual responsibility for him because Jesus Himself knew what He had planned for John's life. The most important thing for Peter to do was to be obedient to the specific call of Jesus in his own life.

We are often concerned about other people, people like husbands, or wives, or children. And this concern could hold you back from following Jesus. Your concern for their well-being could cause you to begin treading water spiritually. Do not allow other people to hold you back from the commission God has given you. Love those people, support them, and help them, but do not keep turning round to see what is happening to them and so put off doing what Jesus has asked you to do. Follow Him with all your heart. He will care for those you love.

A personal encouragement

One night the Lord spoke to Paul in a vision: "Do not be afraid; keep on speaking, do not be silent. For I am with you, and no one is going to attack and harm you, because I have many people in this city."

ꕥ Acts 18:9-10 ꕥ

Paul changed completely when God intervened in his life. The Saul of Tarsus who had persecuted Christians suddenly became the Paul who served passionately in God's kingdom. And now his life was in danger because the Jews did not understand the complete turn-around in him, and they did not approve of it. After a while Paul arrived in the city of Corinth. When he was there he began to preach in the synagogue, and Crispus, the leader of the synagogue, and his whole family were saved. Many other people in Corinth who heard the gospel message also believed and were baptized.

One night the Lord spoke to Paul in a vision. He heard the words of Jesus very clearly. It was an encouraging word for Paul. The Lord told him not to be afraid. He was to continue preaching the truth and not to keep silent. Jesus assured him, *"For I am with you, and no one is going to attack and harm you, because I have many people in this city"* (v. 10). Perhaps Paul had been concerned that he would run into trouble in Corinth, but Jesus comforted him by saying that He knows everything that happens, that He was with Paul and that no one would attack him or harm him, because many people in Corinth belonged to the Lord. What a word of comfort!

The Lord speaks specifically and directly into our situations too and He assures us of His encouragement, care, and support. When we do what the Lord has called us to do and are committed to serving His kingdom, then the Lord will be our continual support and comfort because He knows all the details of our specific situation. What a comfort that is!

He knows everything

"Quick!" he said to me. "Leave Jerusalem immediately, because they will not accept your testimony about me."

ꟈ ACTS 22:18 ꟈ

The Lord God knows everything about us. He understands all about the circumstances we find ourselves in. And He also knows the plans He has for us. All He asks is that we obey Him and remain pliable in His hands so that He can carry out His plan.

A short while after Paul was converted to Christianity, he returned to Jerusalem. While he was praying in the temple, he had an extraordinary spiritual experience. He fell into a trance and was taken in spirit into the kingdom of heaven where he saw the Lord, who began to speak to him. Jesus told him that he needed to leave Jerusalem as quickly as he could. The Lord knew that the people of Jerusalem would not accept the fact that Paul was now preaching about Jesus. They all remembered that he was there when Stephen was stoned and lay bleeding to death. He approved of what had happened and even looked after the cloaks of those who murdered Stephen.

Have you ever found that just before you enter a dangerous situation or something difficult happens in your life that the Lord warns you in your spirit? God knows all things and He shares His plans with His beloved children. If you are sensitive to the guidance of the Holy Spirit then you will know that the Lord prepares you for certain things that will happen in your life. I can testify of the many times that, before something happened in my life, I was already prepared in my spirit for what would happen. Romans 8:14 reminds us that the children of God are led by the Holy Spirit. Our God is never caught unawares by circumstances. Long before things happen, He knows what events will cross our paths through life. When we are faithful and obedient then He leads us and prepares us for what is coming. He gives us His instructions and His wisdom so that we can deal with the situation effectively.

November 22

I will send you

"Then the Lord said to me, 'Go; I will send you far away to the Gentiles.'"

ꟹ Acts 22:21 ꟹ

One of the most wonderful things that could ever happen to you is to realize that God has a specific plan for your life. Not the generic, broad-based will in His Word that is for everyone, but something specific, a very definite plan for your life. There can be no greater adventure than hearing the voice of Jesus regarding your life and then obediently responding to His call.

Paul's life changed completely. He had persecuted believers, but God had a plan for his life. In this verse Jesus said, *"I will send you far away."* And in Acts 9:5, He told Ananias what He planned to do with Paul. *"This man is my chosen instrument to carry my name before the Gentiles and their kings and before the people of Israel."* There was a specific commission for Paul, because that was what Jesus wanted for his life.

The mistake that we often make is to think that there are only some exceptional people that God wants to use in His service. That is just not true! Even though God commissions different people to do different things, each one of us has a specific task that Jesus wants to give us to do. Some have been called to turn the world upside down by going on missionary journeys, as Paul did. For one season of your life you might be an ordinary stay-at-home mother looking after your children and bringing them up in the fear of the Lord. Whatever God has planned for you will bring meaning to your life.

Never make the mistake of thinking that Paul's commission was romantic and exciting. Remember that he was often imprisoned, and that five times he received thirty-nine lashes on his back, not to mention the number of times he was rejected. Stick to what God has called you to do. And discover what His will for your life is.

Open eyes

"I am sending you to them to open their eyes and turn them from darkness to light, and from the power of Satan to God, so that they may receive forgiveness of sins and a place among those who are sanctified by faith in me."

ꕤ ACTS 26:17-18 ꕤ

The commission that the Lord gave to Paul is recorded in the Bible with such freshness and clarity that it not only causes us to take notice of it, but also to want to go and do likewise. The Lord sent Paul to the heathen nations. Paul was to go and help open the eyes of the heathen.

Of course Paul could not do this in his own strength. He was completely dependent on the Holy Spirit. Only He can open the spiritual eyes of people and lead them out of their spiritual darkness. And you and I have been given a similar task.

When people's spiritual eyes are opened, they will move from the darkness into the light, from the bonds of Satan into the power of God. There are many people around us who live in spiritual darkness. If their spiritual eyes could be opened through the witness that you and I give and the work of the Holy Spirit in their hearts, then a light will go on for them. The darkness will change into glorious light and they will be able to see clearly. Our task is to let people hear the message of salvation so that they can be loosed from the shackles that Satan used to bind them. People today are very reluctant to talk about Satan, but the Bible tells us that he is very real.

Faith in Jesus is repenting and turning to God, making a decision of the heart to turn away from Satan to the light of the Lord. When people believe in Jesus their sins will be forgiven and they will become members of the family of God. Our most important task is therefore to help people to come to the place where their eyes are opened, to bring them to the light, to set them free from the power of Satan, to help them to turn around and to follow God.

November 24

Stars and lamps

"The mystery of the seven stars that you saw in my right hand and of the seven golden lampstands is this: The seven stars are the angels of the seven churches, and the seven lampstands are the seven churches."

꙳ Revelation 1:20 ꙳

Jesus had a message that He wanted to convey, messages for specific congregations in the province of Asia. The lamps symbolized the congregations that Jesus was addressing. Here Jesus talks about the seven churches as the seven lamps upon a lamp stand. Like a city built on a hill, they must shine for all to see. In Matthew 5:15 the same words are used for the lamp stand on which a person places a lamp that he has lit, rather than hiding it under a bushel or under a bed. The lamp is placed on top of the lamp stand so that everyone can see what is in the house. And we, in the same way, need to let our light so shine before people so that they will see our good works and glorify our Father in heaven.

Is your church like a lamp that has been placed on a lamp stand? Does it bring light to the whole community within which it is placed? Is the light in your congregation the reflection of the glory of Christ in your midst?

Jesus held seven stars in His other hand. These seven stars represent the seven preachers or pastors or spiritual leaders. They are the leaders of the seven congregations and are expected to shine as brightly as the stars. Leaders are to be filled with the light of God, and when they live in the light of the Son of Righteousness they reflect His light and shine brightly in the dark skies of life. Pray for your pastor! Pray for the leaders of your church so that they will be filled with the Holy Spirit, faithful to God's Word, and that they will shine like bright stars.

The living One

"I am the Living One; I was dead, and behold I am alive for ever and ever! And I hold the keys of death and Hades."

ꝏ Revelation 1:18 ꝏ

When John saw Christ in all His glory, he fell to his face before Him. But then Jesus touched him with His right hand and told him that he had no need to fear. It was Jesus that stood before him, the first and the last, the Living One. And then Jesus said, *"I was dead, and behold I am alive for ever and ever! And I hold the keys of death and Hades"* (v. 18).

Through this statement He proclaimed the majesty that had been given to Him because He had conquered death. Christians can rejoice every day because Jesus is alive and will live for all eternity. Because we live in Him we too have eternal life that will never end. We serve a Living God! That is why Christians in the early days of the faith used to greet one another with the words, "The Lord has truly risen! He is alive!"

What is more, He holds the keys to the kingdom of the dead. He Himself died, but He rose again to life. And the key He refers to here is the absolute and mighty power He demonstrated over death through His resurrection. Death could not hold Him, and nor it could destroy Him. The moment that we die and leave this earthly body behind, we will be with Jesus and we will live with Him forever. Not only does He have the keys of death, but also those of Hades. Hades is the realm of the dead and the place where those who die without God will live forever without Him. It is the place where death reigns and all life ceases.

The grave was not a prison for Jesus, but the runway to heaven, and each time Jesus receives a believer into heaven He demonstrates that He does indeed have the keys of Hades.

November 26

Cold fire

"Yet I hold this against you: You have forsaken your first love."

Revelation 2:4

When Jesus spoke to John on the Isle of Patmos, He asked him to write down the exact words He spoke. He wanted to send a very specific message to the church at Ephesus. And it wasn't all that flattering.

Jesus said that He knew everything that they were doing. He was aware of their tireless work and also of their perseverance. They were a congregation that hung on till the end, and they took a strong stand against wicked people. They tried to live according to the truth. They persevered, even when they faced opposition. They endured much for the sake of Jesus. And they did not easily tire of doing good.

And yet Jesus had one major problem with them. And this problem was so big that it overshadowed all the good things they were and did. He said to them, *"You have forsaken your first love."* The fire of their love for Jesus had cooled off and become lukewarm. A cold fire is not really good for anything. Jesus had told His disciples that they were to love God with their whole heart, their whole spirit, and all their strength. The life of the Christian should be characterized not by what is done, not by how well he or she perseveres, not by the ability to stand up against the people who mock the truth, but by how much he or she loves the Lord.

How can it be possible for someone to be committed to the work of the Lord and yet to lose his love for Jesus in the process? That is what happened to the church at Ephesus. At first they were excited about Jesus and loved Him so much that their passion for Him ruled their lives. But then that love had cooled off. He was no longer the most important Person in their lives.

We must realize that the important factor in our lives is our love for the Lord Jesus.

The lamp has been removed

"Remember the height from which you have fallen! Repent and do the things you did at first. If you do not repent, I will come to you and remove your lampstand from its place."

℘ Revelation 2:5 ℘

Jesus said some hard things to the Ephesians. He rebuked them because they no longer loved Him as they had at first. They were still busy with all their religious activities and all kinds of community projects, but their relationship with Him was not one of fiery passion.

Jesus said that they should go and think carefully about what He had said, about how far they had moved away from their love for Him. And then He urged them to return to the passion they had at first. He said that they should repent and begin doing those things that they had previously done. They should relive their early experiences with Jesus. If they did not do so, then He would come and remove their lamp from its place. Let's remind ourselves of what the lamp represents. It is the congregation and the witness they bore within the great city of Ephesus among all those heathens.

These words of Jesus unfortunately came to pass. If you were to wander through the ruins of the city of Ephesus in Turkey today then you would realize that there is no longer a church there. And even more upsetting is that there is almost no trace of Christianity in Turkey at all. In fact it is one of the places in the world where Christians are persecuted. Jesus did remove their lamp from the lamp stand. They did not turn back to Him. They simply continued doing the work in the community that they had been doing. And then, finally, one day the city of Ephesus was destroyed, and the church at Ephesus fell with it.

November 28

The Spirit speaks

"He who has an ear, let him hear what the Spirit says to the churches."

༄ Revelation 2:7 ༄

Jesus was very direct when He spoke to the seven churches in the province of Asia. He listed their positive attributes, but He also mentioned the things that He was not happy with. At the end of almost all the letters He sent to them, He says that those who have ears to hear must listen to what the Spirit of the Lord is saying to them. That is the crux of the matter. We need to listen to and obey the voice of the Holy Spirit whom Jesus sent to lead and guide us and keep us on the path of truth.

The biggest problem with some of the congregations in Asia was that they had not listened to the voice of the Holy Spirit. They simply ignored His guidance. They became insensitive to what the Spirit wanted to say to them. That is why Jesus felt that it was so necessary to have these things written down for them. They were clearly not hearing what the Spirit had been wanting to say to them. He urged them to be open to the things that He wanted them to hear, to open their ears so that they could be led by the Holy Spirit in these matters.

It is a sorry state of affairs when the body of Christ becomes insensitive to the voice of the Holy Spirit. The ears that should be open to hearing His whisper are blocked by insensitivity and a lack of faith. How many times have congregations gone off on the wrong track because they have followed their own desires and listened to human opinions? Let us ensure that we are always sensitive to what the Spirit is saying to us.

The Spirit still has things to say to you and to me today. Do we hear His voice? Do we hear the whisper of God's heart in our souls? Are we focused on listening to what He says to us? He does not speak to us in an audible voice, but His sheep do hear His voice.

The Author

"These are the words of the Amen, the faithful and true witness, the ruler of God's creation."

☙ Revelation 3:14 ❧

Jesus has many names, each of which reveals something of His nature and personality. They refer to His might, His majesty, and His authority.

- The Amen: This name assures us that Jesus confirms and substantiates the things He says. The word amen literally means "let it be so." So when Jesus says these things to the churches, there should be no doubt that what He has said will come to pass.
- The Faithful and True witness: This designation continues the thought of the previous one. It reminds us that the witness and testimony of Jesus is always true, sincere, and righteous. He sees all that happens. Therefore, what He says to the churches is the truth. They can depend on everything He says.
- The ruler of God's Creation: Jesus is the Creator, who, before the creation of the world, already knew us. And He also makes those who believe in Him new creations because of His death on the cross.
- The Alpha and the Omega: This title refers to the fact that Jesus is the first and the last. He holds the full span of eternity in His hands. He existed before anything was made, and when everything that has been made has come to an end, He will still be there.
- The Holy One: Jesus, the Author, is holy. And He calls all those who follow Him to be holy.

This Author has also written a letter to you and me. Let us listen to what He says.

November 30

The Author (part 2)

"These are the words of him who holds the seven stars in his right hand and walks among the seven golden lampstands. These are the words of him who has the sharp, double-edged sword."

Revelation 2:1, 12

Jesus is the author of the messages that were sent to the churches in Asia. He signs these letters with the authority of His name. Jesus further identifies Himself in these letters as:

- The true God: There are many false gods in many cultures around the world that try to pass themselves off as the true God. But Jesus said that there is only one true God, and that is Him.
- He who has the sharp double-edged sword: This is very definitely a reference to His Word (cf. Heb. 4:12). The words Jesus speaks cut like a sword between our souls and spirits, revealing the deepest secrets hidden in our hearts. His Word also cuts through to the heart of the churches and the situations they face.
- The One who died and came to life again: The One who speaks to them and who sent this letter is indeed the Living Christ Jesus Himself. Through His words and His Spirit He is alive in their midst.
- He holds the seven stars in His right hand and walks around among the seven golden lamp stands: Jesus is the one who walks through the churches and who holds the elders and the pastors and the members of the congregations in His hands. They are His and He is theirs. He knows everything there is to know about them.

Jesus, the Author, has something to say about our lives today. He has a right to speak. Let us listen to Him today.

December

December 1

Slanderers

"I know your afflictions and your poverty – yet you are rich! I know the slander of those who say they are Jews and are not, but are a synagogue of Satan."

Revelation 2:9

Jesus sent a letter to the church at Smyrna. He mentioned that He was aware of their afflictions and their poverty. They might not have had much money, but they were spiritually very rich.

Jesus was also aware of the wickedness of the people who lived near them and who persecuted them. The devil was at work stirring up people to slander and harm the church. These people were Jews and they tried to make other people believe that they were actually righteous and practiced their religion with integrity. But Jesus knew that they were really being used by Satan.

One of the devil's strategies is to stir up trouble between people. He brings discord and misunderstanding so that Christians within a community find it hard to live in harmony with one another. The devil is a master strategist at getting people to rise up against one another.

And yet Jesus assured the church at Smyrna that they did not need to be afraid of the suffering that they would endure. The devil would manage to have some of them arrested and thrown in prison and it would be a difficult time for all of them. But Jesus encouraged them to remain faithful, even to death. And then they would receive the crown of life. And He ends off by saying that when they overcome they will definitely not be harmed by the second death. They would live forever.

Perhaps you find yourself in a difficult spiritual situation today. Perhaps you are experiencing opposition from people. Possibly the devil is working behind the scenes trying to discourage you. Do not give up. Persevere on the right road. Do what the Lord expects of you and hold fast to what you have in Him.

Satan in the community

"I know where you live – where Satan has his throne. Yet you remain true to my name. You did not renounce your faith in me, even in the days of Antipas, my faithful witness, who was put to death in your city – where Satan lives."

℘ REVELATION 2:13 ℘

Jesus' message to the leader of the church in Pergamum was that He was pleased with them because they had remained faithful to His name and they would not renounce their faith in Him even though Antipas had been martyred for his faith.

Jesus said that He knew the place where they lived. Satan's throne was there. Jesus probably meant that the devil had a secure stronghold in Pergamum. He had many instruments and channels that he could use and his influence in the city was enormous.

The problem with the church at Pergamum was that they had allowed themselves to be influenced by the doctrine of the Nicolaitans. They had deviated from the pure doctrine of the Bible and had begun to incorporate heathen practices into their worship. They began to eat meat that had been sacrificed to idols and indulged in all kinds of sexually immoral acts. The devil's influence had begun to affect their lives negatively. But Jesus called them to repentance and urged them to stop sinning.

Beloved, we do not want to chase after phantoms, yet we must ask ourselves what influence the devil has in our community. What strongholds and channels has the devil set up for himself in your town, suburb or city? We must not be ignorant or foolish about these matters. Resist the devil in your community and he will flee from you.

December 3

The living dead

"These are the words of him who holds the seven spirits of God and the seven stars. I know your deeds; you have a reputation of being alive, but you are dead."

℘ REVELATION 3:1 ℘

When Jesus sent a letter to the church at Sardis He did not have very pleasant things to say to them. He said that they were fast asleep. They had a reputation for being alive, but they were in fact dead.

What a dreadful thing it is when Jesus addresses people who think they are vibrant and alive Christians, but who are really spiritually dead. Jesus says that they must think back to when they first heard the gospel and remember how they had initially received it with open hearts. But somewhere along the way they lost sight of the truth and they stopped listening to what Jesus had to say to them. Now He encourages them to hold fast to the good news and to turn away from their sinful ways. He says that they are asleep and must, *"Wake up! Strengthen what remains and is about to die, for I have not found your deeds complete in the sight of my God"* (Rev. 3:20).

Beloved, these words are not intended to discourage us or to cause us to be fearful regarding our relationship with Jesus. Rather, they are intended to encourage us to examine our own hearts and to ensure that we are not asleep when it comes to spiritual matters. We must not be like the living dead who have a reputation for being Christians who are alive and yet we are dead inside. Let us examine our hearts and put things right with God.

White clothes

"Yet you have a few people in Sardis who have not soiled their clothes. They will walk with me, dressed in white, for they are worthy."

ꕤ Revelation 3:4 ꕤ

There were some members of the church in Sardis who had remained faithful to God and who were committed to keeping themselves holy before the Lord. Jesus used symbolic language when He described them, saying, *"Yet you have a few people in Sardis who have not soiled their clothes. They will walk with me, dressed in white, for they are worthy."*

White is always used symbolically to reflect purity, cleanliness, holiness, perfection, and also of celebration. Whenever angels appeared to people they were touched with glory, and people often testify that the angels are dressed in white. Opposed to this, it is interesting to note that people involved with things like Satanism and who serve the dark, unholy kingdom of Satan, often choose to wear black clothes. Of course that does not mean that children of the Lord cannot wear black clothes. It is just that when the Bible uses colors symbolically, white is usually associated with the kingdom of God.

In Revelation 19 we read the description of the Wedding Feast of the Lamb that will take place in heaven, and which only those who have been made holy can attend. It says, *"Let us rejoice and be glad and give him glory! For the wedding of the Lamb has come, and his bride has made herself ready. Fine linen, bright and clean, was given her to wear. (Fine linen stands for the righteous acts of the saints)"* (vv. 7-8).

When we sin our clothes become dirty in the eyes of God. Let's therefore make sure that each day we dress in clean, white spiritual garments.

December 5

When Jesus unlocks the door

"These are the words of him who is holy and true, who holds the key of David. What he opens no one can shut, and what he shuts no one can open."

Revelation 3:7

Jesus knew that the Christians in Philadelphia did not have very much strength. They were a fairly small church and were not very wealthy and yet they remained faithful to the gospel and never brought any dishonor to the name of the Lord. And so He gives them a wonderful promise.

The phrase *"the key of David"* referred to the position of highest authority and power in the Kingdom of God. Jesus holds the keys of the Kingdom of David and will lock and unlock doors. If He opens a door no one in heaven or on earth or under the earth will be able to shut it. And if He locks a door, no one will be able to open it. Jesus was referring to the wonderful opportunities to share the gospel in the areas surrounding them.

What a great source of comfort it is for children of the Lord to know that the success of Christian work does not essentially lie with them. Our task is simply to preach the Word. We must sow the seed. God will cause it to bring forth fruit. On bended knees, we pray that God would prepare hearts and open doors. One big mistake we Christians can make is to force doors open or try to kick them down. Rather spend more time on your knees in prayer so that He Himself will open the doors when and where He sees fit.

Those who live their lives in complete trust and dependence on God, will begin to realize that God opens many doors, and shuts doors when He knows it is for the best. Paul himself in his ministry for the Lord saw many doors slam shut – doors that he longed to see open before him. And then, much to his surprise, other doors opened for him. We can trust the Lord to open and shut the doors in our lives as He considers best.

Rabboni

Jesus said to her, "Mary." She turned toward him and cried out in Aramaic, "Rabboni!" (which means Teacher).

ᘓ John 20:16 ᘐ

Many people thought that Mary was a wicked woman, but she had been manipulated and controlled by forces that were too strong for her. But Jesus changed it all! He stilled the storms in her life. Instead of the dark forces that had thrown her life into turmoil, she now had a deep and quiet peace.

That is why she loved Jesus with all her heart. How could she ever show Him how grateful she was for all He had done? But now He was dead. What a dreadful thing to have happened! Her Jesus dead on the cross! She had felt so helpless and hopeless when she had seen Him hanging on the cross.

She simply had to get up early that morning, even though it was still dark. She wanted to be near Him – even though He had died. She clung to the memory of His presence – the way He laughed, the way He walked, the words He spoke. But when she came to the tomb the stone had been rolled away. She was horrified! Quickly she ran to Simon Peter and John and told them that someone had stolen His body. They ran to the tomb together, and found it empty.

Later on, when the disciples had returned home, she stayed in the garden weeping bitterly. Suddenly she saw two angels in the tomb where the body of Jesus had been laid. They asked her, *"Woman, why are you crying?"* (v. 13). The only answer she had was, *"They have taken my Lord away, and I don't know where they have put him."* (v. 13). Then suddenly she turned around and saw another man in front of her. He spoke to her. "Mary!" She realized it was Jesus, and fell to her knees uttering the single word, "Rabboni!"

Waves of pure joy and relief washed over her. Jesus was alive!

December 7

A radical intervention

"Saul, Saul, why do you persecute me?"

ꟈ Acts 9:4 ꟈ

Saul had been a brilliant student at the University of Jerusalem. His future seemed bright because not only was he a good student, but he was also diligently committed to the Jewish religion and culture. That was why he reacted so vehemently when this new sect arose around the teachings of Jesus Christ of Nazareth. This man, whose ideas seemed so at odds with what he believed, had been killed, but His disciples continued to live according to His teachings – and to teach others these things too. And so he felt compelled to persecute them.

One day he was on his way to Damascus, bound on another mission to find and arrest followers of Jesus. Suddenly a bright light streamed down on him and blinded him. It was so intense that he fell to the ground, and then he heard a voice say, *"Saul, Saul, why do you persecute me?"* Without having time to gather his thoughts, he answered, *"Who are you, Lord?"* (v. 5). What he experienced was so overwhelming in its power and majesty that he realized that it could only be a work of God. And then the answer came. *"I am Jesus, whom you are persecuting"* (v. 5).

Everything in him and around him came to a standstill. He prayed as he never had before. He realized that he had been in the presence of the living God.

What a radical intervention this was in a man's life. He had been born again from above, through a mighty work of God. His conversion experience was unique and few people experience such a dramatic calling. The way in which you come to understand that Jesus is Lord, is not important. What is important is that we, like Paul, can testify that everything was made new for us.

Lukewarm

"I know your deeds, that you are neither cold nor hot. I wish you were either one or the other!"

Revelation 3:15

God had taken the spiritual temperature of the church in Laodicea and He was disappointed. They lived in a city well known for its hot springs, and they knew all about hot water. Jesus therefore used this image to show them that although their relationship with Him had initially been hot, they had since become lukewarm. They knew all about lukewarm springwater that was often used as a medicine but had a horrid, unpleasant taste.

Jesus said that they had become like that lukewarm water and He wanted to spit them out of His mouth, just as people spat out the lukewarm waters of Laodicea. Lukewarm, fleshly Christians usually rely too much on their own riches, their own position in society, and their own abilities.

Lukewarm Christians are not really enthusiastic about God. They remain involved in all kinds of religious activities but the temperature of their love is sadly very low. The people of Laodicea were proud and arrogant. There was a famous medical school in the city and a large and successful wool industry. All this prosperity made the Christians in Laodicea dissatisfied. They were so caught up with earthly matters and riches that their relationship with God had cooled off.

From this letter we can learn that the Lord wants us to be on fire in our relationship with Him. We must be careful that our spiritual temperature is not cooled by our passion for the things of the world. How hot is your passion for Jesus today?

December 9

Come and buy!

"I counsel you to buy from me gold refined in the fire, so you can become rich; and white clothes to wear, so you can cover your shameful nakedness; and salve to put on your eyes, so you can see."

࿐ REVELATION 3:18 ࿐

The words that Jesus addressed to the church in Laodicea focused on their lukewarm spiritual condition. They were a prominent congregation in a rich and affluent environment, but their spiritual relationship with God was tepid. They were like the lukewarm waters of Laodicea that tasted awful and made you want to spit it out.

They said that they were rich, extremely rich, and had everything they could possibly want. But the Lord said that they were in fact poor, blind, and naked. They measured their riches on a false scale.

That is why Jesus urged them to come to Him and buy what they really needed. In the first place He wanted to give them gold that had been refined through fire, and would make them truly rich. Jesus was talking about spiritual riches that give real meaning to life. "Come and be rich in faith," urged Jesus.

In the second place He offered them white clothes to cover their shame and nakedness. But Jesus was not offering them garments from the renowned textile manufacturers in Laodicea. He offered them pure white spiritual clothes to cover their shame and sinfulness with glory.

In the third place, Jesus urged them to buy eye salve. Apparently there were doctors in the well-known medical schools of Laodicea that were able to help people with eye problems in wonderful ways. But Jesus invites them to buy the genuine eye salve that He sells, a salve that would open their spiritual eyes.

Let us ask the Lord to cover our spiritual nakedness, to let us receive the true riches of salvation, and to open our spiritual eyes.

He stands outside

"Here I am! I stand at the door and knock. If anyone hears my voice and opens the door, I will come in and eat with him, and he with me."

Revelation 3:20

When Jesus sent a letter to the church in Laodicea, He mentioned that they had many earthly riches but were poor in spiritual matters. He said that they dressed in beautiful clothes but that they were spiritually naked. He mentioned that the city was full of famous doctors who helped people with eye problems but they were in fact spiritually blind.

Jesus urged them to repent and to turn back to Him. They needed to once again realize that their true spiritual needs could only be met by God. And then He used an image that is actually quite tragic.

Jesus said that He was standing at the door of the church in Laodicea, knocking. He wanted to go inside. Is it possible that Jesus, the head of His church, was not in the church? How could this have happened? Perhaps they programmed Him out of their church programs. Perhaps they were so busy with their own congregation's decisions, functions, and religious rituals that they did not even realize that Jesus was no longer with them. Perhaps their church board meetings sounded more like political rallies. Perhaps the preachers used fancy words devoid of spiritual power.. Whatever the reason, Jesus was no longer there. He had left. And He was standing outside.

Yet He wanted to be inside. He knocked. Would they perhaps realize that He was standing outside? Perhaps they would open the door for Him and He would come in and share a meal with them.

Oh, let us never get so busy with spiritual things that we lose Jesus' presence in our midst.

December 11

Seekers of light

"But whoever lives by the truth comes into the light, so that it may be seen plainly that what he has done has been done through God."

☙ JOHN 3:21 ❧

There is a close connection between truth and light in the Bible. People of the light are people who walk in truth. The truth is sometimes referred to as the light. In Psalm 36:9, David explains, *"In your light we see light."* In the light of God, a light goes on for us and we discover the truth. Jesus came to us as the Light and the Truth so that we could begin to know the true meaning and purpose of life. This knowledge can only be found in God Himself.

When Jesus came to earth He brought division. He was the Light that came into the world and yet many people preferred the darkness to the light. People who do wicked things and choose not to walk in the truth have an aversion to the light. They hate the light. Why? Because their actions are evil and they cannot handle the exposure that the light brings. If you do something wrong then you really don't want everyone to know about it. Most people, including those who are wicked, try to hide the things in their lives that are bad. They do not like everything to be laid bare. They do not like it when the light shines on their bad deeds and sins. All those who do wicked things hate the light and will not come to the light to have the spotlight shine on their actions (cf. v. 20).

But the opposite is also true. Those who walk in the truth come to the light so that it is clear that what they do is done in obedience to God. It means that you are not ashamed of your life and you do not try to hide your actions because they are, after all, done in the light. Therefore you are not anxious when the light of God falls on your life. In fact, you welcome the light of God because it reveals the evidence that you walk in the truth.

Let us live today in such a way that we are not afraid or ashamed of being seen in the light.

Reward time

"Behold, I am coming soon! My reward is with me, and I will give to everyone according to what he has done."

℘ REVELATION 22:12 ℘

When John, in Revelation, refers to the Second Coming of Jesus Christ, he quotes Jesus Himself who promised that He will indeed return. He said, *"Behold, I am coming soon!"* Sometimes it feels as though the return of the Lord is not as quick as these words seem to suggest it would be. And yet when we think in terms of eternity our life here on earth is just a fleeting moment. Jesus promised that He will come, and He will.

We are called to live lives that are holy, pure, and right before God. And if we do so then Jesus gives a wonderful promise. He says that when He does come again He will bring His reward with Him so that each of us will be rewarded for what we have done.

A sinful life will reap its rewards, but there is a reward in store for God's children who continue to walk in the path of truth.

Of course we do not serve God because of the reward that we will receive. We are eternally grateful to Jesus for what He did for us on the cross to set us free through the wounds He bore in His body. We commit our whole life to Him because of our gratitude. And yet He has promised that we will receive a reward if we commit our lives to Him and if we hold fast in faith.

Are you looking forward to the coming heavenly payday? I know we will feel embarrassed to receive anything on that day, but out of the great goodness of His heart, God will give each of us a reward. Now that's something to look forward to!

December 13

A final invitation

He who testifies to these things says, "Yes, I am coming soon." Amen. Come, Lord Jesus.

℘ REVELATION 22:20 ℘

In this wonderful book of Revelation the words that Jesus spoke to John on the island of Patmos are recorded just as He dictated them. At the end of the book, once again an urgent invitation is issued. Jesus says, *"I, Jesus, have sent my angel to give you this testimony for the churches. I am the Root and the Offspring of David, and the bright Morning Star"* (v. 10). The morning star heralds the dawning of the new day that Jesus came to bring. And that day will come in all its fullness the moment that eternity dawns for you.

The Holy Spirit, together with the Bride, echoes the heartbeat of Jesus. This is the final invitation. *"Come!"* and *"Whoever is thirsty, let him come; and whoever wishes, let him take the free gift of the water of life"* (v. 17). It is as if Jesus, through the Holy Spirit, wants to make one last plea to invite people to come and drink the living water and to enjoy all its benefits. All those who hear this invitation should not hesitate to come and receive what is offered. And then Jesus, the One who testifies to all these things, promises that He will come soon. Don't lose hope, but answer together with all the saints, *"Amen. Come, Lord Jesus"* (v. 20).

Before Jesus finally does come back we should take every opportunity to pass His invitation to drink of His Living Water on to everyone we meet.

Crowns

"I am coming soon. Hold on to what you have, so that no one will take your crown."

℘ REVELATION 3:11 ℘

There is a wonderful chorus, almost like a gospel-minstrel song from the southern tip of Africa that talks about the crowns that we will one day wear. *We will wear crowns, we will wear crowns ...* This song is a celebration of the wonderful fact that ordinary, everyday people, even those who live in slums and hovels and who come from the wrong side of the tracks, will wear crowns of gold on their heads.

Jesus promises this in Revelation 3 when He says that when He returns we will be given crowns to wear. That is why we should persevere in spiritual things and hold fast until the end. We know that Revelation uses symbolic language and we cannot know for certain if these will be actual crowns, but I like to think Jesus will place a real crown on the heads of those of us who never wore a crown in our life on earth. *"Surrounding the throne were twenty-four other thrones, and seated on them were twenty-four elders. They were dressed in white and had crowns of gold on their heads"* (Rev. 4:4). *"Be faithful, even to the point of death, and I will give you the crown of life"* (Rev. 2:10). Yes, the children of God will reign and we will receive crowns.

The first thing that people who are given crowns in heaven will do is to lay them down again at the feet of Jesus, the only one who actually deserves a crown. They will lay their crowns before the throne and say, *"You are worthy, our Lord and God, to receive glory and honor and power"* (Rev. 4:11).

December 15

Angling for position

"You don't know what you are asking," Jesus said to them. "Can you drink the cup I am going to drink?"

✠ MATTHEW 20:22 ✠

It is remarkable to note how many times in the gospels the disciples were concerned about positions of honor. Jesus often talked about the human tendency to want to be noticed by other people. On occasion He spoke out sharply, particularly against spiritual leaders who did things just so that people would notice them. Even the disciples were sometimes shameful enough to fight among themselves about who was the most important in the kingdom.

In spite of the fact that the disciples knew how Jesus felt about this striving for positions of honor, and the desire to regard themselves as more important than others, we read here about how the mother of James and John, the wife of Zebedee, came to Jesus with a very special request. The fact that they went with her shows that they agreed with what she wanted to ask Jesus. She asked Him, *"Grant that one of these two sons of mine may sit at your right and the other at your left in your kingdom"* (v. 21). What happened here was a blatant attempt at self-promotion, an angling for position. As if some people are elevated above others in Jesus' kingdom!

Jesus turned down their request. He said that they did not understand what they were actually asking for. They would not be able to endure the kind of suffering that He was about to experience. Who will sit where in the kingdom is something that our Father in heaven will Himself determine.

Let's not angle for positions. Let's rather serve one another and take the lowest places. The one who wants to be foremost in the choir might very well have to stand in the back row in heaven.

Do you look away?

Jesus said to her, "You are right when you say you have no husband."
JOHN 4:17

When Jesus spoke to the Samaritan woman at the well at Sychar He did something that was unheard of in His society. It was considered a dreadful scandal for a Jewish man to enter into a conversation with a Samaritan woman. It was just not done! But of course Jesus was not the run-of-the-mill religious leader. He is the Son of God who came to earth to address the needs of humankind. His desire was to bring her into contact with the true life He offered. He wanted her to turn away from her sinful life and to find eternal life in Him. He did not beat about the bush, but went straight to the heart of the matter.

He asked her to go and call her husband and then come back to the well where He was waiting. But she answered that she had no husband, and with that she was at the point where Jesus could begin to minister to her. He began to talk to her about all the men in her life. The sixth man, with whom she was now living, was not her husband. As Jesus put His finger on the sore spot in her life, she tried to divert His attention with religious arguments.

Isn't it interesting how many people begin discussing extraneous religious issues as soon as you begin to talk to them about Jesus? The more you emphasize the importance of a relationship with God, the more they discuss church. Like this woman. She began to talk about the way her forefathers had practiced religion. But each time Jesus brought her back to her own life, her own need for water that would really quench the dryness within her, and the fact that this water was available for her.

Don't be put off by people who divert you from the gospel of Jesus Christ by introducing all kinds of discussions about religion. Like Jesus, in love concentrate on their needs, respect their pain, and offer them the Living Water.

December 17

Keys

"I tell you the truth, whatever you bind on earth will be bound in heaven, and whatever you loose on earth will be loosed in heaven."

ᘓ MATTHEW 18:18 ᘐ

Jesus empowered us to be His ambassadors on earth. He puts the keys that unlock His kingdom into our hands. This is an awesome privilege, but also an overwhelming responsibility.

Of course Jesus does not intend for us to become petty, arrogant despots on earth as we serve in His kingdom. We should develop a sensitivity to the will of God, and within our congregations and communities we should be guarded by the Spirit of Jesus so that we can make the right decisions. The Holy Spirit helps us to apply the truth of God and His will to our lives day by day.

We need to develop self-discipline that equips us to live according to the words of Jesus. We must resist everything that opposes itself against the knowledge of God. We might even have to disassociate from congregation members who continously and deliberately disobey the Word of God. But we also have the key to set people who repent of their sin and are forgiven free. Then we do not bind, but loosen. If what we do on earth is in line with God's will, what we bind on earth will be bound in heaven.

Spiritual authority from the Lord carries with it a great responsibility. We should continuously pray for the wisdom to know how to respond in different situations so that we do not abuse our spiritual authority. When we bind or loosen we must always do so within our congregation. Others need to agree that God is leading you in this matter. If a situation does arise in which someone needs to be bound or set loose, it is safest to have the confirmation of all the Christians involved with the matter. We are ourselves too broken to judge others and we too easily make mistakes.

May the Lord help us to handle the keys of His kingdom correctly.

Agreement

"Again, I tell you that if two of you on earth agree about anything you ask for, it will be done for you by my Father in heaven."

℘ MATTHEW 18:19 ℘

The way to ensure that we get the guidance we need concerning specific issues is to kneel with other Christians before God and together hear what He says about the situation. Something wonderful happens when Christians bow before the Lord in the right attitude. It is sometimes hard for one person alone to discern the will of God and the guidance of the Holy Spirit. It is easier for a group of Christians to pray together and to be led in the right direction. That is why Jesus said that we should pray together with one or two other believers.

The kind of prayer that God delights to answer, is a prayer that is prayed with humility and with childlike faith. This kind of prayer is also a sincere prayer prayed in the right attitude. This kind of prayer is prayed with love for all those concerned. It bows in dependence on and commitment to the will of God. It doesn't selfishly concentrate on only asking for its own needs to be met, but asks that God's will be done in every situation. This kind of prayer is prayed with perseverence, and it is always prayed in the name of Jesus Christ.

Where people pray in this way Jesus promised that our Father who is in heaven will give them what they pray for, because they are praying in God's will. Their prayers echo the things that are on God's heart and therefore what they pray for come to pass.

Finally Jesus mentions that when two or three are together in His name then He is with them. The implication is not just that God is with them – after all, He is always with us – but His strength, His wisdom and His guidance and His loving presence are with us in an exceptional way.

December 19

The yes-man

"Then the father went to the other son and said the same thing. He answered, 'I will, sir,' but he did not go."

MATTHEW 21:30

We are disappointed when someone doesn't follow through on his promises. There are many yes-men who promise the earth, moon, and stars to people but it is nothing more than fancy words. It is better not to promise anything than to say all kinds of grand things that remain empty words.

Jesus told a parable about two brothers. Their father asked one of the sons to work in the vineyard that day. The son was immediately defensive and rebellious. In fact he was somewhat rude because he said to his father, *"I will not!"* (v. 29). After a while he reconsidered what his father had asked and was sorry about what he has said and about his attitude. And so he decided to go and work in the vineyard after all.

In the meantime the father went to the other son and asked if he would work in the vineyard. This son answered with an eager, "Sure, Dad!" But he did not go into the vineyard that day.

The question Jesus asked was which of the two sons did what the father wanted him to do. Of course the answer is the first one. It wasn't about who *said* what, but who *did* what.

The kingdom of God is a kingdom of action. It is not primarily about what we say, but about what we do. Words should simply be a preface to the things that we do. Jesus pointed out that tax collectors and prostitutes who repented would be accepted into the kingdom of God more readily than supposedly religious people who did nothing but stand around and talk all day long. The Pharisees and the Sadducees talked about living righteously, but never really committed themselves to God. James reminds us that faith without works is dead.

Let's be slow to talk, but quick to take action.

Keep your lamp full

"The foolish ones said to the wise, 'Give us some of your oil; our lamps are going out.'"

⸙ MATTHEW 25:8 ⸙

Very few people strike it lucky just by chance. Most successful people prepare themselves to take advantage of opportunites that present themselves. Joseph's amazing success as a leader of a nation came because he had prepared the Egyptians for the years of famine. For seven years he gathered food and provision into storehouses in response to the warning of coming disaster. When the famine came he was ready to achieve his greatest success.

Jesus told the story of ten girls, each of whom had a lamp. They were bridesmaids at a Jewish wedding. Jewish weddings were celebrated over a long period of time, unlike our wedding receptions today. Guests needed to be prepared to wait for the groom to arrive, and he could do so any time of the day or night. Five of the girls had enough oil and some to spare, but the other five did not have enough. Suddenly they heard that the bridegroom was on his way, and the five empty lamps were beginning to go out. These five girls tried to borrow some oil from the girls who had enough oil, but that's not how things worked. Each of them was responsible for caring for her own lamp. So the five girls who had too little oil went to try to buy some more, and when they came back the wedding had started and the doors were closed.

Jesus told this parable to let us know that we should always be ready for the arrival of the Bridegroom. Everything that you do for the kingdom of God increases your supply of oil, ready for the return of Jesus. Every bit of knowledge or wisdom that you gain from the Word is stored up to ensure that when the time is right you will have enough to keep your lamp burning brightly. Plan properly and be prepared to make the most of every opportunity that comes your way.

December 21

"I was thirsty"

"For I was hungry and you gave me something to eat, I was thirsty and you gave me something to drink, I was a stranger and you invited me in."

ꟸ MATTHEW 25:35 ꟹ

Over and over in the gospels Jesus emphasized that the most important aspect of each of our lives is not what we say, but what we do. A tree is known by the fruit it bears, and the good that comes forth in our lives is evidence that our roots are healthy.

That is why Jesus was so outspoken about the fact that we need to do things from a heart of love to bless other people. We have been called to be servants. The eternal judgment will be based not only on what we have believed, but on what we have done. Our actions confirm what we believe.

On the Day of Judgment the goats and the sheep will be separated from one another. Jesus says that the sheep are those who, when He was hungry, gave Him something to eat. When He was thirsty they gave Him something to drink. When He arrived as a stranger in their town, they welcomed Him with open arms. When He had no clothes they gave Him something to wear. The sheep of the kingdom of God are the people who help other people, and do good.

Of course the question is, when was Jesus sick or hungry or thirsty or in prison or naked or a stranger? And Jesus Himself answers, *"I tell you the truth, whatever you did for one of the least of these brothers of mine, you did for me"* (v. 40). Every glass of cold water that you give to someone in the name of Jesus is as good as giving it to Jesus Himself. And that is why, on the Judgment Day, Jesus will say, *"Come, you who are blessed by my Father; take your inheritance, the kingdom prepared for you since the creation of the world"* (v. 34).

No set pattern

After he took him aside, away from the crowd, Jesus put his fingers into the man's ears. Then he spit and touched the man's tongue.

Mark 7:33

The ministry of Jesus on earth was fascinating and unique. One of the most interesting things about Jesus was the way in which He related to people. He was never predictable. In every situation His actions were fresh and new.

For example, if we look at the healings of Jesus we see that there was no specific pattern in the way He ministered to different people. In Mark 7:33 we read about how He healed the man who was deaf and mute. Jesus took him to one side, pressed His fingers into his ears and spat on his tongue. Then He called out loud, *"Ephphatha!"* (which means, "Be opened!") and the man was healed.

On another occasion when a leper came to Jesus and fell on his knees before Him begging to be healed, Jesus reached out His hand and touched him and said, "I will" and the man was made well. And then when He healed Peter's mother-in-law who was feverish and ill, He simply took hold of her hand and she was healed immediately.

One day Jesus was in the synagogue and there He saw a man with a paralyzed hand. To him, Jesus said, *"Stretch out your hand."* As the man stretched out his hand he was healed instantaneously (cf. Mk. 3:5).

There was also the woman who had been bound by an evil spirit for eighteen years. She was a permanent invalid. Jesus laid His hands on her and she was instantly made well (cf. Lk. 13:13).

From these examples it is clear that there is no single method for ministry. The Holy Spirit will show us what to do in different circumstances. We can never predict the way God will do something. We cannot know what He will do, but we can always be assured of His faithfulness and love.

December 23

To pray is to believe

"Therefore I tell you, whatever you ask for in prayer, believe that you have received it, and it will be yours."

Mark 11:24

Jesus emphasized faith. He often talked about faith to His disciples and He also taught them to believe in Him.

Without faith it is impossible to please God. The whole of Hebrews 11 discusses faith and shows us how important it is. In this chapter the illustrious members of the Faith Hall of Fame are listed. They were fallen, ordinary people like you and me, but they knew how to trust God. *"And without faith it is impossible to please God, because anyone who comes to him must believe that he exists and that he rewards those who earnestly seek him"* (Heb. 11:6).

Jesus said that whenever we bring anything to God in prayer, we must do so believing that we have already received it, and we will receive it. Faith should be so strong in your spirit that you can actually see the answer before it really comes to pass. Jesus is not talking about wishful thinking but of the kind of prayer that places so much trust in God that even as you pray the Holy Spirit confirms the answer to your heart. Strength and power flow from God to the one who is praying and then flows from the one praying back to God. In the conviction you sense in your spirit because the Holy Spirit of God agrees with you about the issues with which you are struggling in prayer, the answer is truly and fully realized.

James tells us that if we pray, but do not believe what we are praying for then it doesn't help us at all. Someone who prays with such an attitude cannot expect to receive an answer. Therefore we should pray with greater boldness and believe the things we ask God for. As we pray the Spirit will also confirm if something is not God's will for our lives or not.

A thwarted spirit

"Be careful, or your hearts will be weighed down with dissipation, drunkenness and the anxieties of life, and that day will close on you unexpectedly like a trap."

LUKE 21:34

We have a very descriptive word for Christians who have turned off the road of commitment to God. The word is *backslider*. This word refers to someone who has started along the road with Jesus Christ but somewhere along the road decides that it is no longer worthwhile to continue. Or sin becomes like a rope twisting around his legs so that little by little he stumbles and falls. Then he begins to stagnate. He stops moving forward, becomes discouraged, and is no longer enthusiastic about Jesus. The process that follows is unavoidable. That person slides backwards in his relationship with the Lord. There is no place to stand still in the spiritual life. Either we are moving forward with God or we are slipping back from Him. The moment you stand still you begin to slip backwards. That is why you must always keep moving forward.

In this passage Jesus mentions some of the things that cause us to become disillusioned and unenthusiastic about the things of the Lord. He said we must guard against excessive eating and drinking and of being weighed down by the cares of this world. Living it up or succumbing to stress. These things tend to stunt our spiritual growth. When people place too much emphasis on these things, they loose their spiritual sensitivity and are suddenly caught in a bird net. Someone said, "Don't be like a bird that sees the bait and ignores the trap."

We must be alert and keep watch and pray regularly so that we will be strengthened spiritually. Then we will be able to come boldly before God.

December 25

Christmas time

"For the Son of Man came to seek and to save what was lost."

LUKE 19:10

On Christmas Day we rejoice and thank and praise God because Jesus Christ was prepared to lay aside His heavenly glory and humble Himself to become a Man (cf. Phil. 2:7-8). On Christmas Day we remember that the Child who was laid in the manger was sent to us because of God's love for us (Jn. 3:16). But those who gaze only at the baby in the crib and sing about the angels who rejoiced and the shepherds who came to see this miracle and the wise men who came from afar to honor Jesus, do not understand the fullness of the message of that first Christmas.

Of course, we do celebrate the fact that Jesus came to live among us, that He became Immanuel, God with us. But what was the purpose of His coming? Jesus described it as a great search. It was an expedition to hunt for those who were lost. To find people who had lost their way in the storm of sin, and who needed a strong rescuer. Only Jesus can save us from our sin. Jesus, the Son of God, was sent by the Father to save people out of the jaws of death. He found us and rescued us and brought us to safety.

The rescue mission was the death of Jesus on the cross and His glorious resurrection. Those who believe Him and who accept Him in their hearts pass from death to life. They are taken from a situation in which they were lost and helpless and reconciled with the Father for all eternity. This is the message of Christmas: sought, found, and saved for all eternity. *"For God so loved the world that he gave his one and only Son, that whoever believes in him shall not peirsh but have everlasting life."* (John 3:16).

They murdered His Son

"So they took him and threw him out of the vineyard and killed him."

ꕥ Matthew 21:39 ꕥ

Jesus told a story about a landowner who planted a vineyard and built a stone wall around it. Then he dug a winepress in the vineyard and erected a watchtower. After that he rented the farm to tenants and went away on a long journey. The contract that he drew up with the tenants stated that he would receive a percentage of the harvest as payment for the rent.

When the time for harvesting the grapes came he sent some of his servants to collect the rent that was due. When his servants arrived there, though, the tenants beat one, killed another, and stoned the third. So the owner once again sent some servants to the farm, but the same things happened to them.

Finally the landowner decided that he would send his son. He thought that the tenants would at least treat him with a little more respect. But unfortunately they decided that because he stood to inherit the farm they would in fact kill him.

Jesus told this parable to explain that God had sent prophets through the years with a message from Him to His people. But the people killed the prophets and would not listen to them. After a while God sent His own Son, Jesus Christ, but still the people would not listen. Jesus was referring to the Jews and their leaders who did not accept Jesus as the Messiah. The same people who had, through the years, rejected the prophets God had sent to them.

But there was a remnant in Israel who had remained faithful to God and who believed in Jesus.

Let us thank Him because He was prepared to die so that we could receive His holiness and salvation.

Crumbs

"First let the children eat all they want," he told her, "for it is not right to take the children's bread and toss it to their dogs."

Mark 7:27

It was clear that Jesus' ministry was initially focused on the Jews. He was sent to the lost sheep of Israel. His mission was to care for them and to teach them the wonderful news of the kingdom of God.

But often, while He was busy with His primary purpose of ministering to the Jews, He became aware of the plight of people around Him who were not Jewish, and then He reached out to them too. Of course from the beginning Jesus knew that God wanted to bless all the nations of the world. His task was to establish the kingdom of God through the people of Israel.

When a Greek woman came to Jesus because she was so worried about her child that she didn' care whether He was a Jew or a Greek, He reminded her that He had not been sent to work among the heathen nations. Jesus was so impressed with her boldness that He left a tiny gap for her to take. *"First let the children eat all they want," he told her, "for it is not right to take the children's bread and toss it to their dogs."*

Jesus was not speaking down to her as if she were a dog. He was simply using an illustration to make His point. Immediately she scraped together her hope and courage and said, *"Yes, Lord, but even the dogs under the table eat the children's crumbs."* What she was actually saying to Jesus was that just a few crumbs from Him would be sufficient for her daughter. And based on what she said Jesus healed her daughter.

Just crumbs from the hand of Jesus can change your life and mine. And He gives us far more than just the crumbs. He gave to us the Living Bread.

What a gift!

"They all gave out of their wealth; but she, out of her poverty, put in everything – all she had to live on."

℘ MARK 12:44 ℘

We are probably all familiar with the incident in which the poor widow gave everything she owned to God because her heart was so full of love and gratitude for Him. Even Jesus was amazed at what He saw happening right before His eyes.

They were outside the temple. Jesus enjoyed going to the temple where people gathered to worship God. That was, after all, the essence of Jesus' existence. Jesus sat directly opposite the place where people gave their offerings to the temple. And He watched as people put their money into the chest.

Lots of rich people arrived, dressed in elegant and expensive outfits and elaborate headdresses. Some made a grand show of throwing their contribution into the offering basket. Then ordinary people who were not as wealthy brought what they wanted to give to the Lord. One by one people came to place their offerings into the treasury.

Then suddenly He noticed an old woman coming that way. Her sandals were worn, her dress ragged, and her head covering was full of holes. Jesus watched her carefully. When she came to the treasury chest she took out a little scrap of material that had been fastened inside her dress. Carefully she untied the knot and took out two coins. The coins were not worth very much at all. But she put them into the treasury.

Jesus was amazed when He realized that she had actually put everything she had into the treasury. Then He said, *"They all gave out of their wealth; but she, out of her poverty, put in everything – all she had to live on"* (v. 44).

If you and I do not give Him everything that we have then we have not really brought Him an offering.

December 29

False Christians

"For false Christs and false prophets will appear and perform signs and miracles to deceive the elect – if that were possible."

MARK 13:22

When Jesus spoke about the end times He was quite explicit about all the things people would have to go through. Among other things, He talked about the tribulation that will come upon the earth. In the last days there will be famine, wars and rumors of wars, earthquakes, and all kinds of other such disasters.

But He also specifically referred to the fact that there will be false Christians in those days. These will be spiritual leaders who come with what they will call great spiritual revelations and truths, but that will actually mislead people. These people will even be able to do all kinds of signs and wonders and miracles.

There are so many so-called leaders in the world today who present themselves as the saviors of the modern world. They are the antichrists who lure people away from the truths of God's Word through their teachings. Some of them even claim to be able to do miracles. The devil is a master of disguise and, with his power and might, is also able to perform some signs and wonders. Remember the things the Egyptian priests did in Moses' day.

Jesus wants us to be on our guard against such people. There is more and more pressure these days to compromise with other religions. Beware that you do not get trapped in sinking sand. Keep to the truth that you have been taught. Hold fast to the Word of God as the only source of spiritual truth that can bring us into contact with the only true God. Turn away from all false gods and false priests.

Tyrants

Jesus said to them, "The kings of the Gentiles lord it over them; and those who exercise authority over them call themselves Benefactors."

ꙮ Luke 22:25 ꙮ

Nations suffer under corrupt rulers. While you are reading this passage there are dozens of places in the world that are governed by corrupt governments that manipulate people and abuse them as a result of the corrupt laws that they have implemented.

There are little children who are suffering, communities who live with constant hunger, large-scale poverty, the spread of disease and sickness, abuse of women, and all kinds of other crimes against humanity that are perpetrated by tyrannical leaders.

How many countries there are in the world where so much potential has simply gone to waste. Think of Angola, Iraq, or Afghanistan, or Zimbabwe and many other countries that are suffering as the result of war, tyranny, and general havoc.

A person who is given power and does not know how to use it meaningfully and in a way that will bless others, is a dangerous person. The abuse of power always leads to heartache – think of King David who misused his power to have Uriah killed.

In this verse Jesus tells us that we must not be like kings who dominate others. We should rather humble ourselves completely and serve people to the best of our abilities.

December 31

The manipulator

"Nevertheless, I have this against you: You tolerate that woman Jezebel, who calls herself a prophetess. By her teaching she misleads my servants into sexual immorality and the eating of food sacrificed to idols."

℘ REVELATION 2:20 ℘

Jesus' letter to the congregation of Thyatira once again revealed that He knew everything that they did. He knew their love, faith, their good deeds, and their perseverance. But there was one big problem in their congregation. A woman.

Her name was Jezebel. She was a prophetess and she had a lot of influence on the congregation. Unfortunately her teachings were based on false assumptions about the devil and his demons. She taught the people that in order to defeat the devil, Christians should be intimately knowledgeable about his ways and means of exploiting people. She urged people to learn about his way of doing things by experiencing them for themselves. Only then would they be able to oppose him properly. She taught that Christians should learn the deep dark secrets of the devil by attending all the heathen festivals, where orgies took place.

It is astounding to consider the amazing greatness of the grace of Jesus Christ. In verse 21 He says that He has given her a chance to repent. But she would not. And that is why He allowed an illness to come upon her and some of her followers.

Often there are very serious, negative and manipulative powers at work among Christians. These powers come to the fore through certain personalities. Some people have very manipulative personalities and can even cause congregations to be torn apart. They can cause the servants of God to fall into sin. Beware of Jezebel; beware of the spirit of manipulation!